The Laws of Physics
Are On My Side

WALTER HAUGEN

This book is dedicated to Toni Lyons –

crack editor, fellow weeder and best companion.

Every day she gets up and does something positive.

When that is done she does something else that is positive.

CONTENTS

PREFACE

I graduated from high school in 1968. It was the year of the Tet Offensive, the My Lai massacre, the Pueblo Incident, the assassinations of Martin Luther King and Bobby Kennedy, the decision by President Johnson not to seek re-election, and the police riots and brutality in Chicago. I got involved in the antiwar movement that fall. Over the next few years, it became increasingly obvious the American empire was in deep trouble. The draft was the flashpoint, but the endemic racism, inequality and downright nastiness of the American political and economic system insinuated its bloody fingers into every corner of a person's life.

In May 1970, the killings at Kent State made it obvious the federal government had no compunctions about killing people in the streets during demonstrations. Nixon called us traitors and did his best to stomp us into bloody little hippie radical meatballs. It became obvious we were NOT going to be able to reform the system. We had to do for ourselves. In that year, my little group opened up a community headshop in order to try and make some money to buy land. We had already been kicked off two farms we rented because of the length of our hair and the cut of our jib, so we had to buy a place to grow food.

That fall, my roommates and I turned vegetarian and I started volunteering with a buying club. After the head shop failed to make a profit, I closed it down and decided to make some quick bucks in the business world to buy land. The idea was to get the slimiest job I could find, so I would appreciate it more when I left the city in the spring. I got a short hair wig, borrowed some ties, dress shirts and a couple of suits and bought some wingtips. Then I got a job at a brokerage firm in the market room. Back then everything was done on the phone, stock certificates were delivered to brokerage houses every day, and NASDAQ was just coming out. I worked there for several months until they had me apply for a brokerage license with the SEC. I was turned down because I had been arrested in the past. [Not convicted, just arrested. So much for innocent until proven guilty.]

In the spring of 1971, I also got involved in the first food co-op in Minneapolis – North Country Co-op. Even then, I hated meetings, so I tended to go for the grunt work – filling bins, working the cash register, helping put in a new floor, etc. Over the next few years, I was quite involved in the co-op movement and I saw it change for the worse in 1975. The signal event was a takeover of North Country Co-op and the People's Warehouse by the communists, leaving us anarchist types out in the cold. What was truly amazing about this experience was the anarchists and liberals just started more co-ops and a new warehouse. Soon the commies ran North Country and the People's Warehouse into the ground and walked away. The anarchists and liberals just took the stores back and paid off the debts of the commie mismanagers. By this time there were quite a few "business majors from Oberlin" getting involved in the co-op movement, so it was inevitable the liberals would win. Not to put too fine a point on it, but the communists fought the anarchists and the liberals won. This was an important lesson.

Also in 1971, I moved out of the city and bought some land. I sold some to friends and even put my land in their name. Owning land was a difficult concept at the time and I only paid money for it because there was no other way to get land. There was a bunch of us with land scattered around the township and we built several cabins and grew our own food. Some people had bees and goats and did maple syrup. I was back and forth from city to country and on the road for several years and I built my own cabin in 1976. I dropped the trees on the site and used vertical logs. I had the cost well under Thoreau's 1845 cabin cost of $28.12½ until I had to put on a roof.[1] I used plywood and roll roofing rather than attempt a more difficult roof with poles or planks, so the total cost came to a little under $150. As an interesting exercise, I recently looked up the value of Thoreau's 1845 dollar on the Web and it was worth approximately $6.089 in 1976, so my cabin was actually cheaper to build than Thoreau's. Although the cabin was small, it had windows on three sides and was cozy when the weather was below zero (which happens a lot in Minnesota).

I had first gone on the road in 1969, but during the mid-1970's, I started going on the road more and more. After a short stint with a traveling circus as a roustabout and ringmaster, I became a migrant worker and soon settled on a year-round route. In June I started cherries in Washington, and then moved on to Hood River (Oregon) and then Flathead Lake (Montana) cherries. Then back to Hood River or Tonasket (Washington) for peaches and pears, then Omak (Washington) or Tonasket for apples. By that time it was the end of October and I took a few days up in the Pasayten Wilderness before I settled in to prune in Tonasket for the winter. Then I started all over in the spring. After a few years, I started ski-bumming in Vail for the winter and then returned to the tramp in the spring. When I started having good luck playing poker in Vail, I also went to Europe in the summers to bicycle the coast of Norway and other adventures.

In the fall of 1981, I found myself looking at pistols in a hardware store in Tonasket, so I decided it was time to leave the tramp. It was more dangerous than adventurous and I was sick of the greedy farmers exploiting both me and the Mexicans. I went back to Minnesota and got my fingers back into the soil and worked at a local orchard in the fall of 1982. Then I went back to the ski bum life and eventually drifted into college. Anthropology soon became my discipline of choice and it is an academic field I follow to this day. Culture and evolution by natural selection are still my dominant paradigms. Over the last twenty years I have done contract archaeology, factory work and office work, did a year in law school, finished a master's in biological anthropology and even taught a couple of anthropology courses at the community college level. However, the political will did not die – it was just simmering on the back burner.

Now, those of us active in the 1960's and 1970's need to rekindle our logic and desire. Back when we first left the city, we used to say, "We need to be ready when the shit hits the fan." That is why we built cabins, dug our own wells, killed our own meat, and grew our own food. Even though we got stomped back down into mainstream American lifeways, we were not wrong; we were just forty years ahead of our time. It is time to get active again. It is time to take care of those we care about. It is time to be competent and cosmic again. This time I think we are on the cusp of new opportunities. Just as in the 1960's, what works best is when each person can take care of himself or herself. Then when they come together, they get more done.

This is a book for the future. It is unlikely Americans will adopt enough of the solutions herein to forestall their fate. Consequently, the empire has to fall before we can begin remaking the world. From a desire for justice in the 1960's to simple observations of the breakdown in 2012, the solutions are the same. Since I am over 60 now, I will probably not see the new world come to fruition. You might.

INTRODUCTION

Culture is what makes us human. We are cultural primates - cultural mammals - cultural animals. Culture gives us an edge because it provides a filter, or *buffer*, between our bodies and the physical environment. Most people do not grow food or chop down trees or dig ore out of the ground to make a living. Instead they deal with other humans. Culture is the real environment.

Culture is simply *sets of behavior passed between generations*. This definition includes behavior passed between members of each generation, as humans learn from their age peers as well as older humans. Culture is transmitted both ways between generations – older humans also learn from the young. Culture allows us to adapt behaviorally to our environment instead of the slower processes of genetic change or physiological adaptation. This buffer of culture provides us with the ability to ride out the volatility of the physical environment by accumulating more energy in the form of material goods. We can store food against the lean times, wear warm clothing when it is cold, and construct shelter to keep out the heat and the cold and the rain and the snow. This buffer of culture distances us from the environment – it gives us social space.

Humans have done a lot with this social space – the buffer provided by culture. We invented some worthwhile things, like art and agriculture. We also invented some ridiculous and dangerous things, like kingship and organized warfare. The ability to gather resources from the physical environment, without being immediately subject to its stresses and strains, gives us an edge on the rest of the earth's species. The result has been our spread over the entire globe and the development of civilization.

Even though civilization provides us with more and more resources, the resources are unevenly distributed and slaves are a necessary component of civilizations, past and present. In the last 150 years, we were able to get rid of human slaves only because we substituted the energy slave of liquid petroleum. Oil now provides us with the energy formerly provided by human labor. Not only did we trade human energy for cheap oil energy, but we greatly increased the amount of energy we use daily. Now most of us in the US live as luxuriously as medieval princes.

We have been able to do this because oil energy was cheap in price. The rise of the United States as a global power coincided with this rise of cheap petroleum energy. Our infrastructure, food production, and virtually every aspect of daily life now depend on copious amounts of cheap petroleum in the form of gasoline, diesel fuel and natural gas. This ability to throw more and more energy at any and all problems has its downside, however. As we used cheap energy instead of behavioral culture change to solve problems, we replaced our buffer with petroleum energy. In other words, we replaced culture with cheap oil.

Now, the era of cheap oil is over. New wells are being drilled every year but they are not replacing all the wells that are played out. We have improved technology to recover marginal oil reserves, but it takes more energy to get the oil than ever before. The actual net energy of petroleum, or energy return on investment (EROI), is going down every year. Once we got about 100 barrels of oil energy for every barrel used to produce the oil, for an EROI of 100:1. Now it is down to 20:1 or even lower.[1] Since oil is the principle driver of modern civilization, petroleum availability and lower EROI impacts the economies of all countries. As the price of oil goes up, it accounts for a greater percentage of the cost of doing business. If the price is too high, business is stifled and the economy stalls. As the economy stops growing or even contracts, demand for oil goes down and so does the price. Then the lower price for oil allows business to grow again so demand increases and the price rises. As the price of oil again reaches a higher percentage of business costs, the economy stalls again and the cycle repeats.

This price/demand cycle causes its own strain as speculators exacerbate price swings. Even though supply is a structural component, market speculators create a "whipsaw" effect.

The volatility of crude oil pricing and the whipsaw effect on the economy does not necessarily indicate the death knell of civilization. However, the pollutants and waste from an excess of cheap energy do. This is where climate change interacts with peak oil. At a time when we are changing the climate to a more unstable system, we are running out of necessary energy to deal with new challenges. As an example, consider the prodigious amounts of oil energy required to develop wind and solar power. The turbines and photovoltaic panels are made in factories run on oil energy. Transportation to factories for workers is powered by oil. Transport of materials and setup for wind turbines or solar panels is provided by oil. The grid to distribute power was built on oil energy. Even the capital needed to invest in building renewable energy comes from a system powered by oil. Oil energy is high-quality energy and absolutely essential to building renewable energy for the future. If we tried to develop renewable energy resources using only power from the wind and the sun, they would have already stalled out.

The old tried and true ability of culture to adapt to environmental changes is no longer as readily available to us either. Because we have decimated our cultural buffer, we are losing our protection from the physical environment. Soon enough, we will be subject to the laws of physics – without the buffer of culture. This is not a promising future.

In the last 150 years the world's population has increased dramatically. Now we have over 7 billion humans on a planet that would normally be unable to support so many. We have been able to exceed the carrying capacity of the earth only because we had cheap energy to squander and the ecosystem could absorb much of the pollutants and wasted energy. Using more oil energy to produce more food allowed the human population of the planet to grow, which required more food and more energy, which then allowed more people to reproduce, and so on. Previous natural environmental constraints on human fertility were overcome by applying huge amounts of cheap energy. Now, we are reaching limits on how much oil energy we can use through price and supply constraints. We are also reaching limits on how much waste the ecosystem can absorb. Not only have we created significant amounts of pollution on land and sea and in the air, we are also changing the very climate of the earth.

Because of the interactive variables of peak oil and climate change, we are in a dangerous situation. If we continue to burn as much oil as we can get out of the ground, we foul the environment to an even greater degree than we have in the past and quality of life suffers even more. Meanwhile climate stability degrades to the point of endangering the staple crops on which we all depend. If we stop using oil energy altogether, people starve on a scale unknown in the past. Either way, dieoff is a certainty. In either of these two scenarios, the laws of physics will affect us directly. This is new. For the last two million years we have depended on culture to buffer us from the environment. Soon we will have to interact directly with the environment. Despair and decline would seem to be our destiny.

However, if we reduce fossil fuel use and do more work by hand, we can apply the positive feedback loop of human labor growing crops to feed human labor. We can also put many of the unemployed back to work. Dealing directly with the laws of physics, we can embrace our destiny, channel our energy use and get the laws of physics on our side.

My work during the last several years embraces destiny and changes it. I have developed a flexible, sustainable model that uses small amounts of fossil fuels and mostly human labor to grow more food energy than the energy I use. Input/output analysis is used to calculate how much energy goes into the model and how much comes out as usable food energy. I can also build soil and fertility. It is a model based on the credo, "Many hands make light work," and is specifically adapted to small-scale gardening. It is adaptable to both urban and rural settings and can be scaled up for market gardeners with various levels of production. This book provides a solution based on doing what works using low energy inputs. It also focuses on low capital needs. It provides YOU – the person who will have to grow your own food – with a template you can customize to your own needs. It already works; you just have to use it.

PART 1: THE PROBLEM

1 CULTURE

If you want to solve a problem, start at the beginning. You may find a solution readily available, but even if you do not, you will be on a path of understanding the history of the problem and the roots of our current dilemma. Since we are caught in a human dilemma, what we need is a discipline that looks at humans in the widest possible sense and starts with the very beginning of the human species. Fortunately we already have such a discipline – anthropology.

Anthropology is the generalized study of humans and encompasses the whole range of human behavior and physiology. As with any academic discipline, there are subfields and specializations within subfields. Paleoanthropology is one such specialization that looks at human origins and our evolutionary history. It provides us with the earliest evidence for culture as the defining trait of humankind. Paleoanthropology can be a rather romantic field, with researchers roaming the wilds of exotic places like Ethiopia and Tanzania, looking for odd bits of bone or worked stone sticking out of very old geologic formations. Very often what researchers find is due to sheer dumb luck. Let me give you an example of dumb luck from my own experience doing contract archaeology in the western US.

Many years ago, I was working on a contract job in North Dakota. We were doing site survey on a proposed pipeline route and digging the occasional test pit. The ground was so hard we were using a motor-driven auger to drill test holes. In one hole we got bits of Knife River Flint, a chocolate-colored translucent flint that is easy to work and makes very nice tools. After seeing bits of this very distinctive stone and clear markings of human work, we dug a one-meter test pit and came down on the source of the artifacts. What we found was an example of Upper Paleolithic technology using the blade core technique. In this technique, a core is first prepared and blades are then struck from the core. This technique represents a quantum leap from older stone techniques because of increased efficiency. More blades can be manufactured from a given amount of stone using this technique, as well as reducing wasted material, or debitage.

We had come down right on top of this blade scatter with our machine and unfortunately broke some of the beautiful blades. However, this was still quite a find and so we widened out our pits to encompass a larger area. Although we hoped to find more artifacts, careful digging produced nothing more. We marked the area as a site and it was later mapped and included in the environmental impact statement. The artifacts ended up at the state historical society and I do not know if the pipeline took a dogleg around the site or if it was mitigated (salvaged). The point of this story is that it was just dumb luck that we came down right on top of a blade scatter.

In looking at human origins, we have been lucky to find tantalizing bits of evidence suggesting we have been humans (in the genus *Homo*) for about two million years. The earliest member of our species was *Homo habilis* ("handy man") and discovered by the famous husband and wife team of Louis and Mary Leakey in 1960. The whole Leakey family, including son Richard, daughter-in-law Meave, and granddaughter Louise, have made many contributions to our knowledge of early humans as well as other species, such as the Australopithecines. The date range for *Homo habilis* is about 2.4 million to 1.7 million years ago.[1]

The most important finds associated with *Homo habilis* are the tools found in the same geologic context as the bones. These are called Oldowan tools after the Olduvai Gorge in Tanzania where they were first found. The tools are crude but effective. They were made by striking one rock against another to chip off flakes and fashion choppers. The flakes could be used to remove meat from bones and open up carcasses. The cores and choppers could be used to break bones for marrow. Using these tools allowed humans to add more meat to their diet, especially the energy-rich marrow. Unlike the Australopithecines, *Homo habilis* was not limited to what could be torn from scavenged carcasses with the hands and teeth.

With Oldowan tools we have the first clear evidence of human tool-making behavior. Even though other materials could have been used as rudimentary tools by *Australopithecus* or other pre-*Homo* ancestors, they are not preserved. We know modern chimpanzees are adept at modifying branches to capture ants to eat. It is likely Australopithecines were already scavenging meat from carcasses left by predators 4 million years ago. Since Australopithecines were bipedal, they had the capability to both carry and throw rocks to scare away predators or other scavengers. However, the use of manufactured Oldowan tools allowed a greater energy capture. Of course, the first tool made by humans or Australopithecines could have been a sling to carry a baby on its mother's back while she was foraging, but we have no evidence in the fossil record – thus the Oldowan pebble tools are usually noted as the marker for true human culture based not just on using, but making tools that can be used again and again (repeated use is the key here).

Tool-making represents the triumph of an idea and a vision transposed onto the physical environment. Not only did a person have to look at the stone and see what was possible, but he/she had to translate that abstract idea into a real product through hand/eye coordination. And make no mistake; hand/eye coordination is critical. I have cut my hand open more than once demonstrating flintknapping (the modern term for chipping out stone tools) to students. Most modern flintknappers resort to the use of gloves or a piece of leather over the palm while making tools. Tool-making is evidence of **culture**, or *sets of behavior transmitted between generations* (my own definition).

After *Homo habilis*, other human species broadened and deepened how culture benefits us. *Homo ergaster* and *Homo erectus* were able to migrate out of Africa and settle in Asia. *Homo neandertalensis* was able to survive and thrive in the periglacial environments of Ice Age Europe. Modern *Homo sapiens* eventually came to dominate the world by 40,000 years ago. All of these humans used culture as their primary behavioral tool. Culture allowed them to pass down toolmaking traditions, develop trade and keep their social groups intact. Culture is the *sine qua non* (Latin for "without which nothing is done") of the human species.

Every anthropologist has his/her own definition of culture and some are quite lengthy. There is even a book by Alfred Kroeber and Clyde Kluckhohn entitled *Culture: A Critical Review of Concepts and Definitions* (1963, 1952), which treats the topic in depth.[2] Some anthropologists regard culture as a *thing* and I usually capitalize the word as Culture when discussing these views. For instance, Alfred Kroeber wrote an essay on "The Superorganic" in 1917. In this essay he developed the idea of Culture as something greater than the individual. The individual was merely the agent of cultural forces.[3] For those acquainted with the medieval mindset of humans as icons in the battle between good and evil, this should sound familiar. However, the real problem of Culture as a thing existing outside individual humans is that it falls prey to reification and determinism.

Reification is treating a concept as if it is a material entity. Reifying culture is problematic because you cannot put your hands on it. Culture is a notoriously slippery concept. You can touch the human being standing in front of you and even detect something going on behind the speech and the actions. You can even quantify cultural interactions and elements. For instance, primatologists report cultural interactions among macaques who teach each other to wash sweet potatoes. Chimpanzees exhibit cultural behaviors they teach to one other, such as trimming branches to extract ants.[4] The quantitative measurement consists of defining a cultural behavior, or element, and totaling them up for each species. In these examples, macaques may have fewer than 10, chimpanzees fewer than 100 and humans over 1000 cultural behaviors. On the continuum of cultural behavior the macaques and chimpanzees aggregate close together on the low end and there is a large gap between them and the human animal. This quantitative approach is not new and Julian Steward used this idea to make a very simple comparison back in 1955. In his discussion of Shoshonean cultures in the Great Basin of the US, he remarked one could total up over 3,000 cultural items, like basket weaves, religious beliefs, etc. A more complex culture has an exponentially higher list of items and he speculated modern American culture would probably have over a million cultural elements.[5] However, quantification is more of an academic exercise and the province of graduate students arguing over pints in the pub.

Reification is different from mere quantification. Reification is useful in literature or interpretation of dreams, where the simplification of complex concepts into a word or phrase "unlocks" the mind of the reader or subject. For instance, if I have a dream about Japanese construction workers and one of them has the name "Mr. Regee" on his hardhat, that might be a clue from my unconscious to pay attention to a "mystery."

Not all reifications are so fanciful, however, and some are harmful. As an example, Stephen Jay Gould, in *The Mismeasure of Man* (1981), pointed out Charles Spearman's attempts to quantify general intelligence using the "g factor." By postulating g (or *Spearman's g*) as the essence of intelligence (i.e. a "thing"), Spearman could devise tests to measure it and therefore measure the intelligence quotient (IQ) in human subjects.[6] Of course this is antithetical to the original IQ tests devised by Alfred Binet, which measured multiple factors and used subjective measures to include differences among the children tested who grew up in different environments.[7] Nevertheless, IQ testing based on a general quantity of intelligence that can be measured is still used and continues to condemn both children and adults to being labeled "stupid" or worse. Intelligence testing does this without even addressing the basic assumption of reifying intelligence as a *thing* rather than an amorphous complex of behaviors. Reifying culture as a thing (i.e. Culture) that exists above and beyond the human organism falls into the same trap as intelligence testing.

Culture, with a capital C, is also prone to *determinism* and this has been the main criticism leveled at Kroeber's "superorganic." When individuals are mere actors in a play written by a larger entity, there is precious little free will and, as is often the case, this concept is used by the unscrupulous to justify domination of indigenous cultures by industrialized nation states. In fact, Kroeber cribbed the idea of the superorganic from Herbert Spencer, who is famous for social Darwinism and the view that evolution is "survival of the fittest."[8]

It should also be noted that in 1916, three years after his first wife had died, Alfred Kroeber did some traveling in Germany and Austria while the First World War was raging. While in Vienna, he became intrigued with psychoanalysis. When he settled in New York in 1917 to work at the Natural History Museum, he underwent Freudian psychoanalysis. After a year of analysis and study, he returned to the University of California at Berkeley and established the first psychoanalytic practice in San Francisco. Kroeber was 42 by this time and he was going through his own version of a mid-life crisis – questioning both his personal and professional life.[9] He had already written his magnum opus, the *Handbook of the Indians of California* (written 1915-1917, published 1925), which ran to 995 pages and cemented his reputation as a modern day Renaissance Man.[10] Kroeber could do it all in the social sciences, but he was restless and gave up his clinical practice after only two years.

Over the next few years, Alfred Kroeber became more and more critical of psychoanalysis and of Freud's concepts, but he was able to compartmentalize and differentiate his studies of anthropology and psychoanalysis. This is perhaps the key to Culture as a *thing*. It has definable limits and is no longer slippery and amorphous. Culture is like a fish you pull into a boat. You have it hooked, but it flops around and is difficult to grip. Once it stops moving it is easier to handle. Of course the fish is now dead, but it is easier to filet and debone it. If you assume culture is a thing or is deterministic, it is easier to handle.

Many people cherish determinism. There are plenty of high-profile researchers and authors who insist human behavior is determined by genes or organic compounds in the bloodstream. In a world of nincompoop bureaucrats, nasty drivers and incompetent salespeople, it is quite seductive to just imagine people cannot help themselves. Restraint is so much more difficult than just giving in to gratification of desire. In the first part of the twentieth century, when Kroeber was writing and doing research, nationalist myths were in the ascendant. Even the concept of culturally-determined decline was popular and Oswald Spengler's *Decline of the West* (1918, revised 1922) was much discussed on both sides of the Atlantic. This two-volume examination of history asserted a recognizable pattern in cultural florescence culminating in civilization and followed by decline. According to Spengler, cultures pass through recognizable cycles of rise and fall that last about a thousand years. Unlike the economic determinism of Marx, Spengler's notion was that cultures are life-forms themselves and so must be born, develop and inevitably die.[11] There is more than a little similarity to Kroeber here.

Even in the second half of the twentieth-century, cultural determinism was still hanging onto life. At the University of Colorado, where I did my undergraduate work, the anthropology department had a strong bias towards *cultural materialism*, a paradigm developed by Marvin Harris in his 1968 book, *The Rise of Anthropological Theory*.[12] Where cultural materialism differed from earlier cultural determinism was in its emphasis on material realities and structure. In this sense, it was similar to Marxism. Where cultural materialism differed from Marxism was in its ability to see power traveling up and down classes in society, instead of only one-way from the poor to the rich (like Marxism). Cultural materialism was sort of a "kindler, gentler" Marxism, the same as modern evolutionary psychology is a "kinder, gentler" sociobiology. They are both deterministic.

The problem with determinism is that it is too slow. *Genes* can determine structure and behavior in an organism, but the process of fixing traits can take thousands of years in humans. [This is why fruit flies are so popular for genetic experiments, as you can get a new generation in a week.] Meanwhile the climate may change or the humans may move someplace else. *Developmental adaptation* to the environment, such as greater lung capacity for living at altitude is much faster and some adaptation to cold and high altitude, for instance, can be accomplished in just a few lifetimes. *Acclimatization* can be accomplished in a week or two, as I learned when I moved to Vail, Colorado, which is at 8,000 feet. [After two weeks at altitude your red blood cell count dramatically increases in order to utilize the thinner air more efficiently. You can then return to normal activities, like climbing stairs without gasping for breath.] *Cultural adaptation* to a new environment is faster still. If I want to climb a high mountain, I can put warm clothes on and breathe bottled oxygen rather than adapt physiologically. However, once we adapt with behavior rather than physiology, we may still be too slow for a changing environment.

Cultures become set in their ways and for good reason. Over time, behaviors which enhance group fitness survive and are reinforced. This works well over time and within a relatively stable environment. However, if the environment changes quickly, the culture may be too slow to react. In other words, there is a push and pull between the cultural behaviors and the environment. The culture adapts to the environment and protects the individuals within the culture – at least most of the time. New experimental adaptations are usually carried out by the young, who can push the cultural envelope without leaving a whole mess of children behind to starve to death. We see this all around us, as teenagers grapple with a society that looks quite stupid from the standpoint of their raging hormones and newfound muscle strength. What usually happens is young people do the heavy lifting by experimenting with new lifeways and the adults reap the benefits. We can see this all around us even now, as young people seek to reshape the world by putting massive amounts of energy into social change for little or no recompense. However, at the end of the month they still have to pay rent to their middle-aged landlords.

As I said, the process of culture change is too slow for a rapidly changing environment and this is the ultimate argument against determinism. Going along with the rest of the group while making small changes is progressive and safe. However, if the group is rushing headlong to catastrophe, going along with the group is not only difficult, but suicidal. This is the real lesson of the 1960's. The world was changing fast. While the US government pursued a war in Vietnam, decimating the social fabric and ruining the national economy, many of us could see the cliff we were approaching. If some of us had not stood up and said "NO!" it is likely we would have fallen prey to nuclear annihilation well before 1975, when the Vietnam War finally ended and the world breathed a little easier. This time, "going along to get along" and incorporating nominal cultural changes while accepting one's place in the group (as modern "progressives" still do) was suicidal. This is where the primacy of the individual became critical in developing a political and cultural philosophy. Mainstream culture could not adapt. The group failed. The individuals survived.

What really happens in cultural conflict, such as the upheavals of the 1960's, is the conflict between culture carried by the individual and culture exploited by the group. Groups come into contact with other groups and even engage in catastrophic conflicts with each other. However, the culture will continue as long as there are *individuals* left to carry on the culture. We can see this in remnant languages that survive as long as there is at least one native speaker. Many anthropologists and linguists are involved in preserving some record of these declining cultures via multi-media recordings and they do this precisely because a culture does not exist without individual members. The individual is the base unit of culture.

We often speak of indigenous cultures and label groups with the label "culture." There is a definable Mexican culture, plus smaller units like Oaxacan culture and Sinaloan culture. There are hundreds and even thousands of localized cultures around the world. These are all referred to in the aggregate, but they are still labeled and measured and defined by their behavior. Material goods merely reflect behavioral adaptation to the environment – ever since *Homo habilis* started making stone tools to access more food energy. What we really have in these "cultures" are groups of individuals who have similar cultural behaviors. The culture will no longer exist once these individuals are gone. All we will have are memories and records. Kroeber's original idea of something that exists beyond the individual, i.e. the "superorganic," does not hold up.

So what does hold up when we look at culture? As I said, it is a slippery concept. We can observe that we are cultural beings with behaviors that allow us to adapt to our environment. We can see the tension between the cultural group and the individual. We can see that without the individual the group ceases to exist. We can also see that our behaviors allow us to get more energy from the physical environment. This is the key to culture – capturing more energy.

2 ENERGY

Energy capture is the *raison d'être* of culture – its reason for being. With the first pebble tools, humans were able to capture <u>more</u> energy from the environment by changing behavior than adapting physiologically. Making new technology was part of the change, but the visions behind the tools were more important than the tools. We developed an ability to adapt to changing times and fill in with technology as needed. In the time of *Homo habilis*, it took little time to make technology. One can still chip out a serviceable stone tool in less than half an hour and the knowledge gained by doing it once can be remembered AND passed on so others do not have to reinvent the wheel (a mixed metaphor that is actually quite apt here).

Culture, then, is a low-energy, high-impact evolutionary adaptation. To put it in modern terms, it has a high energy return on investment (EROI). Even though our large hominid brains require energy to maintain, we can do a lot of thinking and a lot of talking with little effort. With our efficient bipedal locomotion we can do a lot of walking with little effort. We can do a lot of grasping and manipulating material objects using our opposable thumbs and nimble fingers – again with little effort. The energy expenditure of a human is minimal for its size and very efficient. For example, a fit human can outwalk a horse. Two of us did so in 1978 up in the Pasayten Wilderness of Washington over a distance of twenty-one miles. We started from Tungsten Mine at the same time as a pack string and reached Iron Gate trailhead well ahead of the horse packers. We were carrying our own gear and the pack horses were carrying humans plus the human's gear and food for both horse and human. Our energy requirements were about 2500 kilocalories per day, while a 1000-pound horse needs a minimum of 15,000 kilocalories per day – 25,000 if it is doing moderate work (like carrying a human) and 33,000 for heavy work (like plowing).[1]

The horse became useful to humans because of its speed, its use in war, its ability to carry a cumbersome load or pull a heavy plow, and the sheer luxury of riding instead of walking. Most of the time, the horse is a luxury. In the above example, I walked through the wilderness carrying everything I needed for an energy expenditure of about 2500 kilocalories a day, while the human using a horse had to provide about 25,000 kilocalories a day for his horse plus the 2500 for himself – eleven times more energy. And was the load carried eleven times higher? Probably not, because pack strings have a horse for each rider and several more for gear and feed - more like 50,000 kilocalories per day per rider. Even against the old standby – the horse – humans have a much smaller energy footprint and greater efficiency. In our modern world, an even greater disparity exists between the human and the machines that do most of our work. We are many times more efficient than an engine using fossil fuels, or an electric motor, or any other machine we can name. This is because of the laws of thermodynamics.

Thermodynamics is the relation of heat to other forms of energy. There are four laws which govern these relationships. The first law is actually the "Zeroth Law of Thermodynamics," because it was formulated nearly a hundred years after the "First Law of Thermodynamics" was stated by Rudolf Clausius in 1850.[2] The Zeroth Law says, "If two systems are in thermal equilibrium with a third, they are in equilibrium with each other." This seems obvious to us now, but prior to this formulation, temperature was defined in terms of entropy (from the Second Law) and so a bit circular. Actually stating the Zeroth Law in this way allowed a more precise definition of temperature and cleaned things up.

The First Law of Thermodynamics states, "The change in internal energy in a system is equal to the work done minus the heat produced." Implicit in this is the law of conservation of energy, which states, "Energy in a system can be neither created nor destroyed, but only changed to a different form." Also implicit is that both heat and work are forms of energy transfer. This law is useful because it codifies transfer of energy, but it does not allow for the observation that energy flows in a certain direction. For example, heat flows from a higher temperature to a lower temperature - unless more energy is applied to increase the temperature.

This directional aspect was addressed in the Second Law of Thermodynamics, which states, "Heat cannot spontaneously flow from a colder to a hotter location." What is implicit here is that differences in kinetic and potential energy dissipate over time in an isolated system. In other words, the temperature or pressure or other forms of energy even out over time and the system reaches equilibrium. Entropy is a measure of how far along the system has progressed towards equilibrium. As entropy increases, energy flows downhill towards equilibrium. This is very important in understanding the real costs of wasting or conserving energy in our world.

The Third Law of Thermodynamics simply states, "The entropy of a system approaches zero as the temperature approaches absolute zero." This is the state where the system has the minimum energy possible and entropy is defined as zero. The importance of this law is to set a bottom limit for entropy. Since we cannot easily get to absolute zero, it rarely concerns us.

What does concern us in our daily lives are the First and Second Laws of Thermodynamics. Succinctly put, energy can be neither created nor destroyed but only changed to a different form. As we change energy from one form to another, we cannot capture all of it, but lose some to the surrounding environment. A classic example is the engine in your car. When you drive your car, the engine uses energy from gasoline to power itself and do the work of moving the car and its passengers from one point to another. The internal chemical energy of the gasoline is changed to motion. But not all the energy is turned into the work of motion. In fact, most of it is dissipated as gases and heat, which are absorbed by the environment. Most automobiles are about 20% efficient, so 80% of the energy in gasoline is dissipated into the environment. [It varies from about 14% - 26%, depending on vehicle weight and other factors.][3]

Here is an experiment which should drive this point home. Next time you go out for a drink at your local brewpub or bar, ask the bartender for five beers. This should cost you about $20, depending on where you are drinking. After the bartender pours out five beers, pour four of them down the nearest sink and drink the one left. When you are ready for another beer, pull out another $20 and order another five beers in order to drink one. This is what you do each time you drive your standard American automobile (and most foreign cars too!). Not only is it wasteful, but it is extremely costly. In the case of the beer you waste, you are picking up the tab, but in the case of the energy wasted using a car, the tab is dissipated throughout the physical and cultural environments. Someone else (or something else) picks up the tab.

The laws of physics frame the boundaries of our world. Gravity limits the way we stand, sit, or lie down. The laws of motion describe the ways we can move and the forces that limit our motion. The conservation of mass, energy and momentum remind us we exist in a limited environment where total energy is constant, even though it changes form. The laws of thermodynamics describe the effects of changing thermal energy from one form to another. The speed of light reminds us of the upper boundary on speed in the universe. In all these relationships, the laws of physics remind us we have limits. It was no coincidence Isaac Newton was the father of physics AND the co-inventor of calculus, which is all about limits.

We would expect culture to have limits, too, since culture is an adaptation by humans to life in the real world. Even though culture is not a thing (i.e. not Culture), it is a description of relationships between people. We transmit culture both within and between generations and so we should expect the energy transfers to exhibit entropy. In other words, the more relationships we have, the more energy we expend as we reach out. However, since other humans are also reaching out to us, we are gaining energy too, albeit less than was extended by the other person's behavior. So as humans deal culturally (or behaviorally) with each other all day long, some sort of energy is passing back and forth, with some of it being dissipated into the environment at large. It is understandable that some anthropologists would default to *Culture* as existing outside the human – a sort of ball of invisible energy that surrounds us. It is a very seductive idea.

However, this seductive idea of something existing outside of us that we cannot really put our hands on is the realm of *metaphysics* (above and beyond physics) and religion. Before there were anthropologists, there were priests and philosophers. This realm of the subjective and personal is their domain. We do not need to go beyond the laws of physics in our discussion because we have plenty of evidence of how culture impacts the world we touch everyday. As mentioned in the last chapter, we have been using behavior to modify items in our environment for two million years or more. In all that time, we have not changed the fact that we capture more energy because of cultural behavior than we could by changing our physiology or genetics. What we have changed is how we capture it. Now, instead of making tools directly, we trade to get what we need and want. With the invention of *trade*, we were able to specialize and distinguish ourselves as individuals. If everyone is a hunter or farmer, we have a commonality in everything we do. Once we start to specialize, we trade the commonality for individuality. Then it becomes exciting and unique to become a comedian or a scientist or even a computer programmer.

Trade and specialization go hand in hand. Trade and specialization reinforce culture because they allow a group to ride out the vicissitudes of the environment. If there is a drought or flood, trade allows people to exchange their unique product or skill for the food to keep going in a harsh environment. Once again, the ability to adapt behaviorally to the environment confers an edge over other species – an edge that derives from the primary adaptation of culture.

So if we are exchanging goods and services amongst ourselves within our own culture (the group) but also between cultures (groups) with which we have contact, the exchange is favorable to each side (in principle at least – exploitation is another matter which I will address in the next chapter). But then what about the entropy? Surely each exchange has a loss of energy as we travel to the marketplace. The key here is that the energy is not monitored or measured – only the price. In other words, traveling by foot or by bullock or even by automobile to the marketplace is not factored into the benefits of the trade in terms of energy. The physical energy in kilocalories burned to attend the market or to wait for buyers is not assessed. The trade is not calculated in energy terms at all. And in addition to the disconnect between energy and price, the exchange is measured by each partner separately.

As an example, let us suppose you are a farmer who lives 150 miles away from Seattle and you vend at a Seattle farmers market because you can get more money in the metro market than in your local town. To get there you have to drive 300 miles roundtrip and it costs money to sell your produce – gas, capital costs for the truck and equipment, maintenance, market fees, etc. You carefully calculate how much it costs you to sell your produce plus how much your time is worth. You then calculate how much you have to sell to make it worthwhile. If it is not worthwhile, you do not go. However, this emphasis on price does not measure the actual energy you are using. In this example, the vendor traveling 300 miles roundtrip in a small truck to sell in Seattle has the same energy load (or carbon footprint if you like) per pound as the produce in a supermarket that travels 1500 miles on a semi to the supermarket. [I will go through the calculations shortly.]

In the modern marketplace, there is a disconnect between price and energy use. Just like the vendor, each customer at the market calculates whether the produce is worth his/her time and money to purchase. There is a difference between how each person calculates the exchange but a shared disconnect between both the vendor and the customer. The energy value is not calculated since it is outside customary price calculations. As the economists like to say, energy value is an "external."

This disconnect (energy as an external) is an intrinsic aspect of culture and it is based on the efficiency of human physiology. Because the human is efficient and can get a lot done for little effort, human energy use is essentially insignificant. Chipping out an Oldowan chopper requires some energy and there is energy loss as the hand guides one stone to chip another stone, but for all practical purposes, it is irrelevant. The safety concerns of not getting cut from a mistimed blow dwarf the energy concerns. In the larger scheme of things, being able to use the tool over and over again dwarfs the amount of energy used to make the tool. In fact most of us go through life unconscious of the small amounts of energy we use in daily life until we are injured or ill. Then we understand all too well how much energy it takes to raise a hand or drink from a glass.

As in the modern marketplace where price does not take energy use into account, humans have been treating energy use as insignificant for two million years. The human uses some physiological energy, but gains the ability to capture much more energy than is used. As mentioned before, culture has a high EROI. By adapting behaviorally to our environment we have been able to capture many thousands more kilocalories from the environment than we put out physiologically.

Other social scientists have looked closely at this question of energy capture over the last forty years. In 1971, Earl Cook published an essay in *Scientific American* entitled "The Flow of Energy in an Industrial Society."[4] Cook was a geologist who used empirical modeling to look at resource supply systems and how they pertained to broader social issues associated with energy. His estimates of energy capture from the time of *Homo habilis* to 1970's America have stood the test of time and are still used today. In Cook's formulation the measurements were in kilocalories captured per capita per day and started with early humans before the use of fire. By the way, BCE stands for Before Christian Era and BE for Christian Era, the more politically correct version of Before Christ and *Anno Domini.*

Early humans (pre-fire *Homo habilis*)	2,000
Hunter/gatherers (all other *Homo* species used fire)	5,000
Early agriculturalists in SW Asia 5000 BCE	12,000
Advanced agriculturalists in NW Europe 1400 CE	26,000
Industrial societies in Western Europe 1875	77,000
Modern 20th century developed countries (US in 1970)	230,000

Homo habilis did not control fire, but there is plentiful evidence later humans did, starting with *Homo erectus/ergaster*. The calculation for *Homo habilis* is based on capturing only as much energy as he/she needed to eat each day and establishes a baseline for measurement of later humans. *Homo habilis* was a smaller human than we are today (70 pounds for females and 114 pounds for males), so the estimate of 2,000 kilocalories per day squares well with modern dietary assumptions, such as the Percentage Daily Values listed on the back of your breakfast cereal box.[5] As humans captured more energy from the environment, they captured more energy for non-dietary purposes – to make fire, build structures, travel without relying on walking, making products to trade, etc. This eventually led to our current extreme energy use.

The use of kilocalories for measuring thermal energy is not without controversy. There are many ways to measure the physical universe and the standardized terms are called SI units. In this system - called SI for the abbreviation of its French name - *Système International d'Unités* – there are seven base units which are mutually independent.[6] The seven are:

Meters for length

Kilograms for mass

Seconds for time

Amperes for electrical current

Kelvin for thermodynamic temperature

Mole for substance amounts (as in chemistry)

Candelas for luminous intensity

Beyond these base units are derived units, defined by equations using the base units. One example of these derived units is the *newton* (N), which is the SI measurement for force and is the movement of one kilogram over one meter for one second squared (or per second per second in some quarters) so $N = m*kg/s^2$. Another example is the joule (J), which is a newton meter, or $J = m^2*kg/s^2$. The joule is the preferred SI unit for measurement of energy, work and heat. However, the term "newton meter" is also used to measure the moment of force, which indicates how closely linked force and work are to heat. In a very real sense, the development of our modern industrial age is the discovery of relationships that already existed in the real world. We do work by changing energy from one form to another and our standardized units measure the energy in various ways.

The kilocalorie is not an SI unit, even though it is convertible to SI units and vice versa. Before the International System of Units was fully adopted in 1960, other measurements of heat and force were popular, so a conversion from the SI units to these earlier units is both necessary and convenient. For example, thermal energy can be measured in British thermal units (BTU) and the power of a machine can be compared to the power of horses and expressed in horsepower (hp). There are even various definitions of horsepower, such as imperial horsepower - hp (I), metric horsepower – hp (M), and electrical horsepower – hp (E).[7] The key here is to not get caught up in the terminology but look for conversions from one unit to another. So, for example, if we want to use kilocalories because we are familiar with this measurement, we can do so because we know 1 joule = .000239 kilocalories and 1 kilocalorie = 4184 joules.

The kilocalorie is the modern term for the amount of heat needed to raise one kilogram of water one degree Celsius with a temperature range from 14.5 to 15.5 degrees Celsius. It is often called the Calorie (capital C), the large calorie or the nutritionist's calorie. Most Americans are familiar with this term because nutritional information is on the package for most foods sold in the United States and Canada. The precise usage of "calorie" (lower-case c) is the amount of heat needed to raise one gram of water one degree Celsius, thus the "kilo" prefix for the amount needed to heat one kilogram of water one degree. However, the nutritional calorie (or Calorie) actually hews closer to the original derivation of the term.

The term "calorie" was coined by Nicolas Clément for an industrial chemistry course he was teaching in Paris and was first published in a Parisian scientific journal in 1825.[8] He specified that the term applied to the heat needed to raise one kilogram of water from 0 to 1 degree Celsius and the original 1825 report in French uses the lower-case "calorie." He developed the term for calculating mechanical power obtained from steam engines, so the term started out as an energy measure in industry. Wilbur Atwater introduced the Calorie (capital C) to Americans in 1887 as an energy unit for food. He used the kilogram of water measure so the calculations would be less cumbersome (e.g. 2500 Calories per day vs. 2.5 million calories per day to measure the food energy needs of a human).

European chemists had been using "calorie" (lower-case c) for the heat needed to raise only one gram of water since 1852, so there was some confusion. For some time the terms "g-calorie" and "kg-calorie" were used, while nutritionists still used the Calorie until 1964. Even today, popular writers use both "Calorie" and "calorie" for the amount of energy needed to raise a kilogram of water one degree Celsius. In my earlier writings I followed the popular convention but now I use the term kilocalorie, rather than Calorie or calorie. The standardization to SI units threw out the term in favor of the joule, but since we still see it every day on our food labels, it is a convenient term. The key is to use standard conversions and a metric that crosses all platforms. The kilocalorie (kcal) serves us well because we can measure the energy in a gallon of gasoline, the amount of feed needed by a horse to plow or carry loads, AND the energy both produced and consumed by a human being with the use of a single term. Joules would work as well, but few people are conversant with the term. Here are some conversions.[9]

1 joule = .000239 kcal (2.39×10^{-4}) = 0.000000278 kilowatt-hours (2.78×10^{-7})

1 joule = 0.000948 BTU (9.48×10^{-4}) = 0.000000373 horsepower hr (3.73×10^{-7})

1 kilocalorie = 4184 joules = 0.001162 kilowatt-hours (1.162×10^{-3})

1 kilocalorie = 3.968 BTU = 0.001558 horsepower hours (1.558×10^{3})

1 kilowatt-hour (kwh) = 3,600,000 joules (3.60×10^{6}) = 860.4 kcal (8.604×10^{2})

1 kilowatt-hour (kwh) = 3414 BTU (3.414×10^{3}) = 1.34 horsepower hours

1 BTU = 1054 joules = 0.252 kcal = 0.000293 kilowatt-hours (2.93×10^{-4})

1 BTU = 0.000393 horsepower hours (3.93×10^{-4})

1 horsepower hour = 2,684,520 joules (2.6845×10^{6}) = 641.62 kilocalories

1 horsepower hour = 0.7457 kilowatt-hours = 2546 BTU's

Note: You often see energy units in older literature that do not have a time element. For example, 1 horsepower = 745.7 watts. In this case you simply multiply both sides of the equation by the new relationship, so 1 horsepower hour = 745.7 watt hours = .7457 kilowatt-hours.

As I stated earlier, if we have a metric that crosses all platforms, we can measure and compare how much energy we use to grow food whether using fossil fuels or human labor. We can also compare the energy needed to transport the food as well as that needed to grow it. We can calculate the energy load per pound whether we are driving to the store to sell food or buy food. We can compare the energy footprint of growing our own food and walking the short distance to the house to cook it versus the energy footprint of driving to the farmers market, plus the energy footprint of the farmer growing and transporting the food to the centralized market. This is a very powerful tool for assessing the impact of our activities on the world at large and other metrics have been proposed for the same reason.

One country ahead of the curve on this idea is Sweden, where food labels now list carbon emission equivalents and some restaurants are following suit. For example, oatmeal is listed as having carbon emissions of .87 CO_2 kilograms per kilogram of product. Another example is chicken purchased in a store, which has 1.76 kilograms of CO_2 per kilogram of chicken and the carbon emissions are broken out into categories of breeding, feeding, processing, packaging, marketing and transportation.[10] The striking aspect of these numbers is how high they are. Even purchasing something as simple as oatmeal puts nearly the same mass of carbon dioxide into the atmosphere as the mass of the oatmeal (.87 vs. 1.00). Retail chicken is worse, with 76% more carbon dioxide put into the atmosphere than the mass of the chicken meat. If these numbers are valid indicators, we are releasing a huge amount of heat and gases into the environment. There are large entropy footprints implicit in these large carbon footprints. The two go hand in hand.

But are these numbers correct? We do not really know because of the problem of scale. The carbon emissions on the food labels in Sweden are calculated from a "gross" or "macro" perspective, using industry-wide standards for agriculture and food processing. In other words, the modern industrial agriculture in Sweden clearly has a large carbon footprint, but does the oatmeal and chicken grown by a small-scale farmer in Sweden and consumed locally have the same footprint? It is not likely, so amounts calculated may not be valid for non-industrial agriculture - a rather pernicious and pervasive leveling effect that skews the narrative. Also, the level of industrialization may vary in different parts of Sweden and transportation may have a higher carbon footprint in the north, with fewer people than the more populous south. There may also be problems of corruption in calculating the numbers. Although Sweden has a very "clean" reputation in international politics, there may still be the same "massaging" of data discussed in the daily newspapers in the US, Canada and Britain. Can we really trust calculations from any governmental entity from any county? The most parsimonious position is to assume these "macro" measures are questionable.

A better approach is to compare energy on an intimate, *microscopic level* and make our own assessments of how much energy we are using. By using kilocalories and measuring our own inputs, we can do this quickly and easily, in a framework understood by all. By collecting our own data, we know how accurate the data collection is. By using our own methodology, we can check and recheck anytime we want. By doing our own calculations, we are forced to "own" our unique energy footprint – the conclusions will strike home. This psychological aspect is nothing to sneeze at. If someone else is doing the numbers they are just numbers. If we are doing the numbers ourselves, they are "our" numbers and mean something in our day-to-day lives.

Let us look at my earlier example of a farmer who lives in Whatcom County, three counties north of Seattle, and vends at several Seattle farmers market because he gets more money in the metro market than in the nearest town with a farmers market. In this case the mileage includes stops at several markets within the city, so the total is 150 one-way or 300 miles roundtrip. This is a real-world example by the way, based on information from a particular farmer. The mileage on the truck used is 15 miles per gallon and the poundage taken to market is 3,000 pounds. We have all the data we need to make our calculations, but we need a conversion factor, i.e. how many kilocalories there are in a gallon of gasoline to power this truck. You may notice we are not making any distinction between the work the truck actually does versus the energy lost to the environment. We are simply calculating how much energy the truck uses when it consumes the gas. In this case the gas used is 20 gallons for 300 miles at 15 miles per gallon.

A gallon of gasoline has an energy content of 1.3176×10^8 joules.[11] From our conversion table we know there are 4184 joules in a kilocalorie, so we can calculate 31,500 kilocalories in a gallon of gasoline ($1.3176 \times 10^8 / 4184 = 31,491$ and rounded to 31,500). The comparable figure for diesel is 35,000 kilocalories per gallon ($1.4651 \times 10^8 / 4184 = 35,017$ and rounded to 35,000).[12] It should be noted there are differing grades of gasoline and diesel that have more or less energy potential, so the figures used are based on the best compromise. There are 6.1 gigajoules in a barrel of crude oil, or 6.1179×10^9 joules in a 42-gallon barrel (bbl) of crude oil for a kilocalorie equivalent of 35,000 kilocalories per gallon of crude (6.1179 x 109/42/4184 = 34,815 rounded to 35,000 kilocalories).[13] The similarity in energy potential between diesel and crude oil is actually an indirect reflection of the difference between gasoline and the other two because of additives and a more complicated refining process for gas.

So back to our calculation of the energy cost of selling at a farmers market in Seattle where the roundtrip is 300 miles, the load of produce is 3000 pounds and the mileage is 15 miles per gallon. As noted, the farmer uses 20 gallons of gas for this trip, or 630,000 kilocalories. Since the farmer carries 3000 pounds of produce, the resulting energy load is 210 kilocalories per pound to sell at a farmers market in Seattle when the food is grown several counties away. This number may not seem high until we consider tomatoes have about 80 kilocalories per pound in food energy and lettuce has about 90 kilocalories per pound.[14] Adding another 210 kilocalories to a pound of tomatoes or lettuce - just for transportation - is wasting about 2 ½ times more energy than the food contains. Compare this to a kilogram of chicken in Sweden which releases 1 ¾ kilograms of carbon in its total production, marketing, and transportation. (No comparable figures are available for the US so the Swedish example is used here.) Even if we accept that the US farmer's vehicle is 20% efficient and only releases 80% of its gasoline energy to the environment as waste gases (including CO_2) and heat, transport to the farmers market – all by itself - is still wasting twice as much energy as the food energy in the tomatoes or lettuce it carries. This is astounding, especially when you factor in the public perception that farmers markets are an alternative to industrial agriculture. They certainly can be, but not in this case.

Some economists have had great fun poking holes in the ideas of "food miles" and mocking farmers markets, pointing out that semi-trailers hauling large loads have economies of scale not available to a small-scale farmer. This is certainly true in this case. The number bandied about for how far our food travels from farm to plate is 1500 miles on average. The origin of this number was from a study done by the Leopold Center for Sustainable

Agriculture at Iowa State University in 2001.[15] The source of the data was the origin of fruits and vegetables sold at produce terminals in Chicago and their state of origin, as recorded over 30 years. No actual mileage was recorded, so tomatoes from Miami were listed with the same mileage as tomatoes from Tampa. Although this study had lots of data, the coarseness of the data only provided rough estimates. Nevertheless, the media have been using this study ever since and you can find references to it all over the Web. With tongues firmly in cheek, let us use this number.

If a diesel-powered semi-trailer hauls produce 1500 miles on average and gets 5 miles per gallon (based on personal trucker comments over the years), then a load of produce uses 300 gallons of diesel to get to its destination. Note that we only have to account for a one-way trip, as trucks routinely travel loaded both ways or make triangulated trips to get back to base. We know that a regular load on the average semi is 40,000 pounds but we also know they can get special permits to carry 50,000 pounds (more common than you might think). Therefore, we should make a calculation for both load figures. If we are using 300 gallons of diesel, we are burning through 10.5 million kilocalories of diesel (300 gallons*35,000 kilocalories/gallon). If our semi is carrying 40,000 pounds, the energy load is 262.5 kilocalories per pound for transport. If our semi is carrying 50,000 pounds, the energy load is 210 kilocalories per pound – exactly the same energy load as the farmer from Whatcom County selling at a farmers market in Seattle! In these examples, it really does not matter, from an energy standpoint, if the Seattle consumer gets tomatoes grown by a "local" vendor in Whatcom County or shipped from Arizona and sold in a supermarket! It is no wonder the mainstream economists had a field day with the concept of food miles. It was an easy target. It would actually be more beneficial to the environment to improve diesel engines to get better mileage.

The concept of food miles has flaws because it has no theoretical basis. It links mileage with the value of a social "good," for lack of a better term. Somehow, driving less becomes a "thing" of great value, rather than a means to an end. It is similar to reification. Focusing on one facet and elevating its importance simplifies the dialogue to sound bites that are as vapid as the TV personalities who spout them. Real problems of energy waste and structural economic problems devolve into simplistic solutions, thus cheapening the conversation and any real alternatives presented. Why spend the time to develop local markets when you can buy cheap gas and sell at fancy markets for high prices in a metro area? Focusing on food miles alone gives a false sense of accomplishment and does not solve the problem of energy waste in transport. A real alternative is to vend at a local market. Here is an example from Whatcom County.

There are three local markets near me: three miles away in Ferndale, twelve miles away in Bellingham, and sixteen miles away in Lynden, so the roundtrips are 6, 24 and 32 miles. When I sold at these markets I usually brought 300 pounds of produce. At the closest market (Ferndale) and using a truck that gets 20 miles to the gallon, I used .3 gallons of gas, so my energy load was 32 kilocalories per pound. At the next closest market (Bellingham), I used 1.2 gallons of gas in the same truck, so my energy load was 126 kilocalories per pound. At the market in Lynden, with a 32 miles roundtrip, I used a car with 26 miles per gallon, so I again used 1.23 gallons for an energy load of 129 kilocalories per pound.

Notice how quickly the energy cost, just for transportation, rises once you get beyond a few miles from the farm. The key here is not just distance but the load factor. The farmer carrying 3000 pounds of produce to Seattle markets benefits from the economies of scale, just like the semi driver. The crux of the matter is the interaction of three variables: 1) distance traveled, 2) load carried and 3) amount of fuel used. If you have only a small load, the distance accelerates the energy cost, even with a more efficient vehicle. If you can carry a huge load like a semi-trailer, the efficiency of the vehicle diminishes in importance and long-distance transport becomes viable. This is why trains and ships are such efficient means of transport for bulk goods.

Energy waste is a complex problem and short-sighted "feel good" panaceas do little to solve the problem. To take a cue from the scientific method, we can start with a theory, set up a hypothesis to test the theory and then use the result to modify our theory or reject it entirely. In the case of food miles, the theory is the further food travels from farm to plate, the more greenhouse gas emissions are produced. The term was coined by Tim

Lang in 1990 as a way to highlight the hidden ecological, social and economic costs in food transport.[16] In setting up my hypothesis, I first developed an energy metric that crosses all platforms and then used the metric to test the question, "Do food miles correspond to actual greenhouse gas emissions, as measured by amounts of energy consumed in transport?" Based on simple math and available data, I rejected the hypothesis that food miles correspond to actual greenhouse gas emissions, because a tomato can have the same energy footprint whether it is transported from Arizona to Seattle (1500 miles) or from Whatcom County to Seattle (150 miles). Since my hypothesis is very similar to the theory, we can reject the whole notion of food miles. This frees our mind to look at the problem in a different light. But first, let us look at problems with our methodology.

I can envision quibbles with my hypothesis-testing, one of which is comparing the diesel engine to a gasoline engine. Diesels are generally more efficient and a good compromise measure is 30-35% greater efficiency than a gasoline engine.[17] In other words, a diesel engine operates at 26-27% efficiency if a gasoline engine is operating at 20% efficiency. This can be significant on a large scale, which is why most long-haul trucks are diesel-powered, but the increase in efficiency means our conclusion comes down even more on the side of the tomato transported in a diesel-powered semi from Arizona rather than a gas-powered truck from Whatcom County. Our conclusion still holds.

Another quibble may be that energy consumption may not adequately represent greenhouse gas emissions. However, since every internal combustion engine produces carbon dioxide (a greenhouse gas) as part of burning a carbon-based fuel in the presence of oxygen, the question is not IF there are greenhouse gases, but rather how much each engine produces. There are certainly other engines that could be used for overland fuel transport, but they all have problems not found in the current gas and diesel engines. Electric cars are only beginning to be available and are not in widespread use. Gas turbines are inefficient at low power outputs, such as city driving. Rail transport has only limited application for food transport because the infrastructure of the US is biased towards highways. For point-to-point delivery, the question is really between gas and diesel engines. If a small-scale grower has a diesel-powered truck for food transport, he/she could calculate their energy footprint and see how they stack up against long-haul transport. However, then the question would be diesel versus diesel and the deciding factor would still be the interaction of load and distance, not just distance, or "food miles." It should be noted here that some readers may jump to the conclusion better infrastructure would solve some problems in our profligate energy use. That sounds good, but as I hope to show later, it is too late for smart improvements within the current business model and policy structure.

We need energy for everything we do. The energy we use originates from the sun, which floods the earth every day with copious amounts of radiation across a broad electromagnetic spectrum. About 30% is reflected back out into space right away and 70% is absorbed by the atmosphere, land and water.[18] This energy is transformed into heat and powers the planetary system. A little over 30% of this absorbed energy is radiated back out into space (about 22% of the total) as energy passes back and forth between air and land and sea, so about 48% of the energy flooding the earth every day stays in the system.[19] This energy is changed back and forth into motion and heat and light and so forth. Some of the energy is stored, for example in fossil fuels like coal and oil. Some is stored in biomass, like the forests around the world. As we capture more and more of this stored energy for things like cars and electric lights, we liberate energy which has to go someplace, so most of it goes into the atmosphere, often as greenhouse gases (GHG) like carbon dioxide, methane and ozone. This creates global warming.

The problem with greenhouse gases in the atmosphere is they reflect heat back down to the earth instead of letting it pass through the atmosphere out into space – like a greenhouse. More greenhouse gases in the atmosphere means more heat kept in the planetary system rather than being released into space. As the heat retained in the planetary system increases, the system changes, or adapts. Since our human species has come to depend on a relatively narrow range of temperatures to feed ourselves, the adaptation of the planetary system could mean a harsher environment for growing food and a resulting reduction in our population levels. However, since the development of culture, we have been tricky enough to transform non-human sources of energy into motion and heat that we use to expand the number of humans on the planet. Now we essentially "eat" oil, since the food we eat uses increasing amounts of fossil fuels for production, transport and processing. This is a good trick, but not necessarily smart nor creative.

The first example of our human "trickiness" is the use of stone tools to increase our access to animal protein. Another good trick was fire – controlling heat energy to cook food to make it more palatable. By the European medieval period, we could control hydraulic energy for watermills to grind grain. By the 18th century, we were able to use coal energy to power machines and in the latter half of the 19th century, we were also using oil energy to power industrial society. In all that time, our ability to tap into more sources of energy because of culture gave us the edge to outcompete and dominate other species. We have become even "trickier" than we could imagine even a hundred years ago. I hesitate to use "creative" here because the complex of behaviors we call *culture* is truly a creative response, but other clever uses of energy may not be. If we just throw more energy at a problem, is that creative?

Perhaps we should look at invention and adaptation in light of another term – *elegance*. Domesticating wolves into dogs not only reduces competition for animal protein in a particular eco-niche, but also uses their domesticated cousins to keep the wolves away. This is an elegant solution. Encouraging cats to hang around to eat the rats and mice that get into your grain stores is an elegant solution. Developing a violent video game to indulge criminal fantasies without risk or danger is not elegant. Nor is it elegant to use so much energy the ecosystem is hard-pressed to absorb it all. It is just banal energy capture. The development of human societies over the last two million years can be simplified into how much energy was captured and made available, but this is a rather sad metric. Nevertheless, let us look at the situation through this lens.

3 ORGANIZATION OF HUMAN SOCIETIES

There are distinctive morphological characteristics which separate us from our nearest primate cousins - like bipedalism, opposable thumbs and grotescuely enlarged brains - but what really gives us the edge is *culture*. At the risk of sounding simplistic, *morphology* is what we <u>are</u> - our physical form and structure. *Culture* is what we <u>do</u>. Since culture is tied so closely to energy capture, some anthropologists have fallen into the trap of equating more energy capture with the "evolution" of culture. In other words, as we organized ourselves into more complex societies over time, we "advanced." This is a value judgment closely allied to racism.

Racism is as old as recorded history and probably older. The definition of the *savage*, the *barbarian* or the *primitive* has been modified over time, but is still based on the "other," someone outside your group. Our word savage comes from the Latin *silvaticus* or "of the forest," i.e. someone other than the urbanized Roman. Barbarian comes from the Greek *barbaros*, or someone who speaks a strange language, i.e. strange to Greek ears. Primitive comes from the Latin *primitivus*, or "first," as in the first stage of being. On the surface, it would seem we could carefully use primitive if we were rigorous, but even in academic circles, the term is so loaded with cultural baggage it is useless. For example, Elman Service wrote an important ethnological text called *A Profile of Primitive Culture* in 1958, which organized human cultures into bands, tribes, chiefdoms and states. This was a monumental work and his system is still used today as a cornerstone of cultural anthropology, but he was forced to rename the text *Profiles in*

Ethnology in 1963 because "the term *primitive* has become so pejorative in ordinary usage."[1]

Some of you may recognize this system, as Jared Diamond uses it in a very nice table in *Guns, Germs and Steel* (1999).[2] William Haviland also uses the same classification as Service and the same table as Diamond in his textbook *Anthropology* (2003).[3] I suspect there are other visuals that explain it as well. Curiously, neither Diamond nor Haviland credit Service as author of the original classification scheme. I suppose it is as superfluous as crediting the first person to come up with a definition of *culture* in its scientific meaning (which was E. B. Tylor in 1871, by the way).[4] Let us look at this organizational scheme from the standpoint of energy capture.

Consider what happens when we capture energy from another human. The "other" human has already captured energy from the environment with a large EROI – just a few kilocalories input for a large kilocalorie output. By re-capturing this large EROI from the other human, with only a small energy investment on our part, we "leverage" our energy capture, just like a bank leverages its deposits by holding on to only a small percentage as reserves and lending out the rest at a higher interest rate than it gives its depositors. In fact, we can view banking as a refinement of energy capture by culture; a *tertiary* economy built up from the *secondary* economy of trade in goods and services, as well as the *primary* economy of farming and extractive industries (timber, mining, oil drilling). The energy capture we get from other humans can be far in excess of what we could get ourselves, or indeed far in excess of the exchange (or trade) itself. From an energy standpoint, the preferred trade is between humans rather than getting energy directly from the environment. Why bother to go out and hunt or grow food if we can get it from someone who does, at a much more favorable EROI?

We see this all around us in the marketplace. Someone with the ability to get money easily can use price to leverage their time. An office worker, for instance, gets a beneficial energy capture from a farmer for a pound of potatoes at $1.00 a pound. The office worker may work only 3 minutes to get the $1.00 (at $20 per hour), but the farmer has likely already spent 12 minutes to grow and sell that pound of potatoes. This 12 minute figure is based on my direct experience with production rates of 15,000 pounds of food grown for 3,000 hours of labor in a year, or 10,000 for 2,000 hours, equal to 5 pounds of food grown per hour of work. Substantially more than this requires huge fossil fuel inputs. The "time" EROI in this example is 4:1 for the office worker but only 1:4 for the farmer. If we put the exchange in terms of kilocalories, we might expect an even higher EROI for the consumer, plus an advantageous EROI for the farmer. This would explain why the farmer is willing to grow food even though it remains underpriced.

Our supposition is confirmed. If the farmer is getting 5 pounds of potatoes for every hour of labor and potatoes have 350 kilocalories of energy per pound, the farmer is getting 1750 output kilocalories for his labor. But what about the farmer's labor input? I calculate the input kilocalories in human labor at 125 kilocalories expended per hour, so the farmer's EROI would be 14:1. Note that the disadvantageous "time" EROI of 1:4 for the farmer becomes an advantageous EROI of 3.5:1 when measured in strict energy terms $(14/4 = 3.5)$. In other words, the farmer generates such an advantage he/she can afford to sell cheap. This helps explain why farming can provide surplus to build civilizations, even when the farmer's time is undervalued.

My claim of 125 kilocalories per hour for labor over the whole year in farming is based on simple calculations of actual body mechanics in the world of work. Certainly there are labor-intensive tasks (like weeding), as well as minimal-energy tasks (like doing spreadsheets), but over a whole year, the ups and downs even out. Here is how I arrived at this number. The consensus view of sleep is that dreaming, body maintenance and cell repair consumes about 500 kilocalories in 8 hours of slumber. If we assume we need 2500 kilocalories in a 24-hour period to thrive, not just survive (survival requires only 1600-1800 kilocalories), then we have 2000 kilocalories left over for a 16-hour period. Having done a variety of jobs in my life, I know that very few people work hard all day long. Most people do tasks rather than sweat and strain. Going to work every day is not like playing soccer for 90 minutes. People who work long days, like farmers, do a variety of tasks and take breaks (even naps if you are lucky!).

I routinely work 16-hour days in the summer and I hardly crack a sweat most of the time. The 16 hours also takes into account my time doing spreadsheets, making lunch and dinner, and naps. It is all about getting things done efficiently and moving from task to task. The same is true for office workers. The strain of working in an office, from my experience in several office jobs, is due to disruptions and poor management, rather than actual physical labor. So if our office worker is putting in the same 125 kilocalories per hour as the farmer but gets 20 pounds of potatotes AND gets an EROI from the farmer of 4:1, the office worker gets a total EROI of 56:1 (14:1 in food calories to the farmer x 4:1 in time EROI from the farmer). You could also calculate it directly as the office worker getting 20 pounds of potatoes (7000 kilocalories) for one hour of labor (125 kilocalories) for an EROI of 56:1. This is a very good deal and belies the idea food is expensive. In our modern technological society, food is cheap.

Some may quibble with my number of 125 kilocalories per hour as invalid for women, who need only about 2000 kilocalories per day. However, if we use a single number in our calculations that is conservative in estimating energy capture, we err on the side of caution. Also, experience shows women work as hard as men, either on the farm or in the office, so I feel the single number is warranted because of the tasks done. As for comparing work done at the office or on the farm as equal to leisure hours or making dinner or watching TV for example, consider what happens on weekends. Most people spend as much energy on leisure as they do at work. Work really is about doing tasks and in this context, we are doing work (or activities) all day long. The essence of a job is getting someone to pay you money to do something, a much different question than the amount of energy actually involved in work over a year's time.

In this discussion leveraging is used in its colloquial, rather than strict financial sense, and is similar to the multiplier effect. For instance, your Chamber of Commerce may tout a new industry moving to town which will provide 100 jobs. The Chamber of Commerce may also say those 100 jobs will add another 50 more jobs because the new jobs bring money into the community, which is spent on goods and services – the multiplier effect. In this case trade is multiplying energy capture (EROI = 1.5:1), but at a lower rate than trading with primary producers. As in our previous examples, the best trade is to capture energy indirectly from farmers, rather than directly from the physical environment. This is the basis for all civilizations.

Elman Service's concept of bands, tribes, chiefdoms and states is a powerful starting point for investigating how energy capture increased over time for human societies. But first a note of caution is in order. I an NOT talking about *social evolution*. This is another term loaded with cultural baggage. Evolution is more properly restricted to biology and even then, the proper term is *evolution by natural selection*. Increases in social complexity are not necessarily improvements, as shown by the negative effect farming had on human physiology versus hunting and gathering. Examples are reduction in stature, vitamin-deficiency diseases, and other pathologies.[5] Indeed, over the last 10,000 years, we have traded quality of life for greater reproductive success and greater energy consumption. Some say this was a fool's bargain and Marshall Sahlins made the point in 1968 that hunter/gatherers were the original "affluent society."[6] Back in my first anthropology classes we often heard that hunter/gatherers spend only 4-5 hours a day in active work to procure their daily necessities, or 2.5 days labor per week in Sahlins' estimate. In other words, living as a hunter/gatherer is only a part-time job. So what were the other hours filled with? Singing, dancing, hanging about – sort of like carefree teenagers today. This sort of "original affluence" is only possible in a band or tribe, however.

A *band* is the smallest unit of human social organization. This structure is individualistic and familial. Settlements are usually mobile and population densities are low, measured in the dozens. The usual number is 20-60 people. Food is gathered by hunting and gathering and shared somewhat equally, but also by kinship. There are no luxury goods for the elite because there are no elites. Decision-making is usually by consensus or influence. Leaders arise, but usually for specific temporary functions. This is a very adaptable organization because it is rudimentary and close to the environment. Some modern examples are the Ju/'hoansi (often called the Kung) in South Africa and the Inuit in the Arctic.[7]

A *tribe* is larger and more complex than a band. Social organization can be egalitarian, status-driven, or based on a clan. Settlements can be mobile or semi-permanent and population densities are measured in the hundreds. Bands can coalesce into tribes as necessary. Food is procured by horticulture (small-scale, non-intensive gardening) and pastoralism, but hunting and gathering is still useful. Decision-making is still non-centralized but powered more by skills and knowledge. In this type of organization, you sometimes see the rise of a "Big Man" who gathers followers and comes to rule because of his ability to exploit tactical situations. Examples are loans to build relationships, fees for settling disputes and training apprentices to carry on the "Big Man's" influence.[8] This term is an unfortunate choice of words and a better term might be "godfather," but that may not be such a good term either (!). Examples of tribes range from Native Americans before the campaigns of genocide in the 17th-19th centuries, to modern-day tribal structures still existing for Berbers across North Africa.

At the next level are *chiefdoms*, which are regionally organized and allow thousands of people to gather in permanent communities. This level of organization requires centralized decision-making by a chief who can rule for life and pass down power to his descendants. Unlike bands or tribes, people in chiefdoms are ranked by their kinship group. Food production ranges from horticulture and pastoralism to intensive agriculture. Hunting and gathering cease to be a viable way to gather enough food energy once the size of a society reaches into the thousands, although these activities are practiced as adjunct procurement strategies. Along with intensive agriculture comes labor specialization and in a chiefdom, the capability for intensive warfare arises, as well as greater production of trade goods. Towns are formed, rather than just villages, but chiefdoms are more unstable than tribes or states (the next level) because of the constant jockeying for power among chiefs in neighboring chiefdoms. Bureaucracy also appears in chiefdoms, but it may contribute to instability because of its formation under a strong chief, rather than settled into place through a legal process. A change in chiefs means a change in bureaucrats, unlike in a state.[9] Examples of chiefdoms were native groups like the Nootka in the Pacific Northwest of the US and Canada, as well as medieval Iceland, with priest-chieftains constantly jockeying for power in a harsh environment.

Beyond the chiefdom is the *state*. Service cites the main difference between chiefdom and state as the legalized monopoly of force.[10] There is some disagreement on this aspect of a state however, and both Haviland and Diamond consider a chiefdom to have a monopoly of force too. However, the state constitutes itself *legally* and uses this legal basis to institutionalize force and reserve it for the state alone. In a chiefdom, the monopoly of force rests with the ruler, even though he may refer to the law. This difference is crucial, since a law can have a much longer life than a ruler or even a dynasty. One need only look at the constant tumult engendered by interpretations of the US Constitution, over 200 years old and spanning 44 presidents.

The state can be as large as the territory it can control and we can see how large the US (300 million) and China (1.35 billion) have grown in the present day. The organizational structure of a state is stratified by class and has a single capital. The settlement pattern is fixed with many villages, towns and cities. A state depends on intensive agriculture and there are plentiful luxury goods for members of the elite classes. Decision-making is centralized and disputes are settled by law.

A state can become more complex, such as moving from a republic to an empire, like ancient Rome, or even break down and decline, again like ancient Rome. In fact the degree of complexity of a society is the key to understanding the organization of society and its energy capture. As more energy is captured, more complexity can be achieved and this allows more energy to be captured, and so on. This is more like a continuum of organization than four typological categories, especially as the categories blend into each other. A simpler typology may even be clustering bands and tribes together on one end of a continuum and chiefdoms and states on the other end, or even a tri-partite clustering, with bands and tribes together, chiefdoms in the middle, and states of varying sizes clustered on the other end. We should also consider that bands and tribes are limited by the informality of their structure, which enhances adaptability. We might even postulate informality and adaptability as important when dealing directly with the physical environment, while informality and adaptability are less important when dealing with other organizations.

Chiefdoms and states are more centralized and formal, thus enabling them to capture more energy from the environment, but they also have limits of their own. The most notable limit is their increasing dependence on *intensive agriculture* to feed larger numbers of people.

Service's organizational structure is built up from one level to the next. Complexity increases as horticulture arises out of hunting/gathering and as agriculture arises out of horticulture. As agriculture becomes increasingly more intensive over time, moving from human and animal-powered to machine-powered, the need for more complexity, greater integration, and more energy capture become interactive variables. It is taken for granted that centralization is needed to manage greater complexity and is natural and valuable. But is it?

Joseph Tainter looked at the nature of complex societies in *The Collapse of Complex Societies* (1988). Tainter is an anthropologist uncomfortable with the concept of chiefdoms and favors a continuum of complexity, even though there seems to be a divide between states and other forms. Within the province of complexity, he identifies two main theories of what drives increasing complexity – the conflict theory and the integration theory.[11]

The *conflict theory* views states arising out of the needs and desires of individuals or subgroups that use the state to enrich themselves. The leading proponent of this idea is Marxism, with producers being exploited by the propertied classes. In this view, society is organized by the relationships based on production, with the owners always having the edge on producers. Surplus production is necessary to have something to exploit. But the flaw here is how the surplus got there in the first place, so Marxism's argument is a bit circular, or prone to "pyschological reductionism" in Tainter's view.[12] My own analysis of Marx and Engels is their ideas were "time-stamped" by conditions in the early 19th century that led to the Revolutions of 1848. Industrialism was well-established and rural populations were expanding, while food production was not keeping pace. The flight to the cities and factories was a change in social relations unique to their time. Marxism is a 19th-century doctrine and also suffers from the prerequisite of signing onto the whole system instead of picking and choosing elements. I have been dismissing it as invalid since 1968.

However, even without Marxism, conflict theory has some validity. We are surrounded by greedy, lazy people who use the group to enrich themselves individually. This is often celebrated as "Greed is good." We can see greed in the earliest writing, as well as in the archaeological record, where elite burials contrast with the sad remains of common folk. Tainter himself reckons there is some validity to conflict theory, but integration theory forms the basis for his study.

Integration theory simply states greater benefits go to those who fulfill administrative roles because they create surpluses in society.[13] In other words, as more energy is captured by bureaucrats organizing societal functions, they amplify the energy available to create greater EROI. Administrative control of irrigation, for example, allows more food to be grown and the administrators who facilitate this get more resources themselves – still leaving a massive net gain for society. Again, this is a case of a high EROI accruing to the administrators who deal directly with the primary producers (farmers), but the farmers gain in EROI too, because they capture hydraulic energy to transform into food energy. This is a simplistic view of complexity of course, and Tainter admits there are elements of both theories in his analysis.

The idea of administrative bureaucracies being either value-positive or value-neutral is problematic, whether in ancient or modern societies. In my earlier discussion of recapturing EROI from the "other" human, there was a hint of exploitation in my example. For instance, the first response to an office worker spending only one-fourth as much time as a farmer to get a pound of potatoes may well be indignation. The next response is to think about paying the farmer more for that pound of potatoes (and his time), but this usually sinks the analysis. Supporting fair trade in public speech is one thing. Actually reaching into your pocket and paying more for your groceries is quite another. After many years in American agriculture, I can state conclusively that consumers will not pay more for food unless they are forced to do so, or are tricked by a marketing scheme like Certified Organic. In the same way, when it comes to running society at the day-to-day level, individual benefits to the administrators drive the system. People compete with each other every day. Bureaucracy is just another way to do it.

Nature may be "red in tooth and claw," as Tennyson said, but human society has more of a black ink color.[14]

Tainter bases his analysis on *marginal returns*. Marginal return is defined by Tainter as the increase in output from adding one more unit of input.[15] A population derives benefits from increasing complexity, i.e. one more unit of input yields more than one unit of output. This can be visualized as a rising curve, such as we see on a left side of a bell curve. As the curve rises it increases in acceleration until it hits an inflection point. The line then changes from being concave upwards to being concave downwards. In other words, even though the curvature is still rising, (we have not yet reached the top of the bell curve) it has changed sign. A little bit of calculus helps here and Tainter never mentions *inflection point* in his analysis, but that is what it is.[16] At this inflection point, the energy inputs are diminishing in their returns and the yield decreases. It is not necessary to actually get a negative marginal return, merely that marginal return is approaching 1:1. As this process of diminishing returns accelerates, it costs more and more energy just to keep the society going and society becomes vulnerable. If more energy cannot be found or a catastrophe occurs, the society can collapse. As Tainter points out in his case studies, the centralized state breaks down into smaller regional polities. His examples are the Western Roman Empire, the Classic Maya and Chaco Canyon.

Tainter's analysis is profound and relevant to our own concerns. However, he is locked into the integration theory of complex societies because he bases collapse on reduction in marginal returns. In other words, bureaucracies arise because they provide increasing marginal returns in the first place, which presupposes the integration theory. If bureaucracies are simply <u>unable</u> to leverage more energy, no one is at fault. This is a much safer position than actually dealing with graft and greed as being <u>integral</u> to formal administrative structures (as in conflict theory). No one is at fault in integration theory – things just happen. As noted earlier, there is plenty of greed and graft to go around in bureaucracies and we can see it all around us. Tainter touches somewhat on administrative deficiencies that lead to collapse, one example being Diocletian's rigid tax system. However, his main drivers of collapse center on debasement of currencies, falling agricultural output, long frontiers to defend, and other phenomena which led to the inability of Roman society to amass sufficient reserves to deal with crises.[17] Nevertheless, his analysis is brilliant, even with my quibbles about predisposed outcomes.

In EROI terms using my previous examples, marginal return can start out at some low number, like 1.5:1 (the jobs multiplier effect example), then increase exponentially to 4:1 (the office worker and farmer example) and even 100:1 (EROI for US oil in 1930[18]). Then at the inflection point, the energy inputs yield diminishing returns. As the EROI of US oil production went down to 30:1 (as in 1970) we started to import more oil from countries like Saudi Arabia. In addition to oil from the Middle East, we now get oil from the Canadian tar sands, which have an EROI of 5:1. We also produce significant quantities of ethanol as an oil substitute, but the ethanol EROI is only 1.3:1.[19] The upshot here is we are still getting an advantageous EROI, but the diminishing returns mean we are on an energy treadmill. As we use more and more energy, we are spending more and more just to maintain our system, without improving our lives. In terms of marginal returns, we should have predicted collapse in the 1970's. Guess what? I have been doing so since that time, but for other reasons, such as overpopulation, costs of wars of empire, disenfranchisement of the population and low real wages. Other scientists, like Earl Cook, specifically sounded the alarm in relation to energy in 1971.[20]

Using Tainter's formulation of diminishing marginal returns, we are already in the first stages of collapse, simply because we are struggling to get enough energy just to keep the system going. But the perspicacious reader may already be asking him/herself, "Wait a minute, is that all this is about – energy? What about social development? What about the subjective measures of quality of life?" Fortunately, someone has indeed addressed these questions.

Ian Morris is a historian and archaeologist who looked at social development in his book *Why the West Rules -For Now* (2010).[21] He starts with Cook's 1971 formulation using *energy capture* over time and measured in kilocalories, but expands on it with three more categories. In order to measure organizational capacity, he chose *urbanism*, which fits in well with the modern world and the growth in cities. He also chose *information processing* as a way to accommodate cultural participation in society, for example in literacy rates. This is more or less an arbitrary category, the precedent being the United Nations Human Development Index, which measures life expectancy, adult literacy rates and standard of living based on GDP per capita.[22] For his fourth measure, Morris chose *war-making*, since it provides data over the whole span of human history/prehistory, as well as being a primary driver for societal expansion. I might add here that since soldiers are the ultimate consumers, war-making is a valid category. Morris' development index is similar to Cook's energy consumption figures, with a quantum leap in the West during the 19th century during the second half of the Industrial Revolution (or Second Industrial Revolution), dwarfing previous energy capture. For example, his index for the West jumps from 50.63 in 1800 CE to 906.37 in 2000 CE.[23]

Although Morris chose four categories that seem arbitrary, they do measure some subjective factors. Unlike Tainter, he acknowledges greed and graft in bureaucracies and sees the driver in social development as "sloth, fear and greed."[24] This is refreshing and enables him to address sticky issues. Morris also takes a novel statistical approach of testing error as a way to check the efficacy of his categories. For example, since the point of his book is to look at the differential rise of the East (mostly China) versus the West (mostly SW Asia and Europe), he calculates how a 10% or 20% error in his calculations correlate with actual events in history.[25] This is a brilliant strategy because it integrates events that may seem arbitrary and subjective, but fit together well and reinforce the objective measure of energy capture – his primary category.

Morris starts his social development index at 14,000 BCE, when the world warmed significantly after the last Ice Age (and before the reversion to colder conditions in the Younger Dryas - 10,800-9,600 BCE). Before then, everyone was a hunter/gatherer. Although social development changed significantly from *Homo habilis* to modern humans (*Homo sapiens*), social development (in Morris' view) only achieves major importance when farming becomes possible. This becomes a built-in bias against hunting/gathering – a far cry from Sahlins' view of the "original affluent society." In other words, social development based on greater energy capture is assumed to be a greater good than working part-time and spending a lot of time dancing and singing. This may sound a bit hyperbolic on my part, but an analysis based on energy capture alone is more parsimonious (something Morris admits[26]) and more value neutral than dismissing the march from Oldowan pebble tools to blade core technology (itself a quantum leap).

It has been apparent to me for over 40 years that we need to question the whole idea of farming, as well as the value of more complexity. Even though we are stuck with agriculture now because we have too many humans to rely on hunting and gathering, an investigation into the roots of farming is likely to serve us well in devising strategies for the future. As the old saying goes, "If you have a problem, go to the source and the solution will be self-evident." The most parsimonious argument I have discovered for the origin of agriculture is rooted in both biology and culture – *random mutations amplified by human agency.*

We know random genetic mutations occur on a regular basis. We also know accidents in cell division occur on a regular basis and this can result in extra sets of chromosomes. In this case the new species will be *polyploid*, meaning it has more than two sets of chromosomes. If self-fertilization occurs, which is common in the plant world, the result will be a tetraploid rather than a diploid. It is estimated up to 70% of flowering plants are polyploids, including mainstays like potatoes, apples, barley, coffee, sugarcane, cotton and wheat.[27]

The evolution of wheat is an example of random mutations setting the stage for human intervention - pre-domestication if you will. There are plenty of wild wheats in existence now and the same was true in the past, especially in the Fertile Crescent, the area now covered by Israel, Lebanon, most of Jordan, Iraq and Syria, and parts of Iran and Turkey. 10,000 years ago this area featured variable topography, seasonal changes including cold, wet winters and hot dry summers, varying amounts of rainfall, and a diversity of plant species.[28]

Diploid wheats, like *Triticum monococcum*, or einkorn, have 14 chromosomes, or 2n=14 in biological parlance. Einkorn was developed from *Triticum boeoticum*, a wild diploid variety, around 10,500-9,500 BP (before the present) in the Fertile Crescent, probably southeastern Turkey. The two wheats are similar enough they can both be called einkorn. As is usual in archaeology (and other subfields in anthropology too) there are disagreements on dates and places, but about 10,000 years ago, humans in the Fertile Crescent were growing and selecting wild wheats.[29] This is the human agency aspect. The differences between domesticated and wild varieties of einkorn are larger seeds, a tougher rachis (main stem) that holds the seeds together, and glumes (leaf-like structures) that release the seed more easily. Humans grew these einkorns and saved the best for re-seeding, just like we do today.

The next development was a cross between *T. monococcum* (domesticated einkorn) and wild *Triticum*, probably on the edges of the farmers' fields. We can label the *T. monococcum* AA and the wild *Triticum* BB. A cross would not be able to pair at meiosis and so would be a sterile hybrid AB. However, a failure of meiosis in this sterile hybrid and self-fertilization would produce a fertile hybrid AABB, or 4n=28. This is now a tetraploid and an example is emmer wheat, *Triticum dicoccum*. Once a tetraploid wheat goes through the same process of crossing with a wild einkorn (DD, 2n=14), the resulting cross is *Triticum aestivum*, our bread wheat (AABBDD, 6n=42 and a hexaploid). Wheat has seven chromosomes, so the *n* is equal to 7. Humans, by comparison, have 13 chromosomes and a diploid number of 2n=26.

Emmer wheat (tetraploid) was the most important wheat in the Fertile Crescent until the Bronze Age, probably because of its easy threshing. By 8,000 BP, free-threshing wheats had arrived in Mediterranean Europe and by 6,000 BP were being grown north of the Alps. The ancient wheat in Egypt that fed the Roman Empire was an emmer, but the most widely cultivated tetraploid wheat today is *Triticum durum*, another easy thresher.[30] I grow *T. aestivum* (hexaploid bread wheat) for our own consumption on the farm, but I use an electric chipper/shredder for threshing rather than a flail (the old way) or a combine (which costs thousands of dollars and uses lots of gasoline). I grew emmer wheat in 2012 and plan on growing einkorn and durum wheat in the future.

The preceding discussion on the origins of wheat highlights the ease of threshing, but we can also look at ease of growing and harvest. I grow wheat, spelt, barley and triticale for our own household. Growing it is not difficult. Tilling the ground is the same as any other crop and broadcast sowing by hand is simple. After sowing, I run my tiller over the wheat on a shallow setting to get the seeds under the soil, but I could just as well rake over it. Then I just leave it alone and it grows up over most weeds – an important benefit. I cut my wheat with a sickle and a wheelbarrow, so I do not have to bend over. I make a couple of swipes with the sickle and lay the grain stalks in the wheelbarrow. When the barrow is full, I use a two-foot piece of twine (I keep several in my pocket) to tie up the bundles. I leave my wheat to ripen as long as possible in the field, and put it in the barn right away after shocking. Then I thresh at my leisure, sometimes leaving it all winter. The key is keeping it safe from rats and birds.

The ease of growing, cutting, and threshing indicates the time spent growing wheat 10,000 years ago yielded an advantageous energy capture. Since grains have around 1500 kilocalories of energy per pound (1600 for wheat), growing grain (cereals) became an attractive proposition. The latest archaeological theories focus on people harvesting wild cereals (wheat, barley and rye) before the 1200-year cold snap of the Younger Dryas (10,800-9,600 BCE).[31] They then turned to grain growing - not just gathering - as the world warmed up because they already had experience with the benefits of cereals in their diet. This theory can be tested.

Using my hands to pull weeds and a shovel to dig and level, I can dig up 100 square feet in an hour, enough land to grow 4 pounds of wheat (I grew 5.5 lb./100 sq.ft. in 2010 and 3.0 in 2011). In addition to the hour to dig up the ground, I will put in another hour to sow, cut, thresh and winnow these 4 pounds, or 250 kilocalories of labor at 125 kilocalories per hour. For my 250 kilocalories of input, I get 6400 kilocalories of food, an EROI of 26:1. Of course the tools were different in the Neolithic (the term for the agricultural revolution of 10,000 years ago), but even if I arbitrarily halved my EROI to account for using a stone shovel and a sickle with microlithic blades instead of a steel shovel and sickle, I get an EROI of 13:1, still a good energy return.

Ian Morris mentions experiments with wild grain foraging from SW Asia yielding a ton of edible seeds from 2.5 acres for an EROI of 50:1.[32] This yield calculates to 800 pounds per acre, or 1.84 pounds of wild grain for 100 square feet, a little under half of my yields. This is not bad, considering there was no soil preparation nor sowing involved, only harvesting. In my present-day example, I get twice as much grain, but put in twice as much work. What stands out in my mind is being able to *get more output simply by putting in more labor.* This is significant and it really is the foundation of civilization. A final point is that Morris does not mention the technology used, but another series of experiments was conducted in eastern Anatolia in 1966 using a crude sickle with flint blades set in a wooden handle.[33] In this experiment wild emmer wheat was harvested at the rate of 6.25 pounds per hour, which would yield an EROI of approximately 80:1 (1600 kilocalories per pound * 6.25 pounds ÷ 125 kilocalories per hour for the labor to harvest). This seems a little high but my modern experience indirectly validates how easy it could have been to get wild grains from foraging. Also, a yield of 800 pounds per acre compares favorably to Roman yields of 1000 kg/hectare (890 lb/acre).[34]

The most important part of these experiments and my own experiences growing grain is the high EROI due to the kilocalorie density. It is easy to imagine a group of hunter/gatherers taking advantage of these energy-dense grains as part of their seasonal round. Then after a long period of colder weather lasting for 50-60 generations, the grains appeared in abundance once more and people not only harvested but grew the grain. It is also possible people were harvesting grain all through the cold snap of the Younger Dryas, but lived in dispersed communities for which we have little archaeological evidence.

Now consider what happens if I take my homegrown wheat, with an EROI of 26:1, and sell it to an office worker with an exchange EROI of 1:4 (as in my previous example). I am still getting an overall EROI of 6.5:1 (26:1 x 1:4 = 6.5:1) because of the energy density and ease of growing wheat. This 6.5:1 EROI is over **twice** my yearly average EROI from small-scale farming using minimal fossil fuel inputs and mostly hand labor. These EROI numbers for the last three years are: 3.52:1 (2009), 2.16:1 (2010), and

3.16:1 (2011), for an average EROI of 2.95:1 for the last three years. So wheat, with its high initial EROI of 26:1 is even better than the potatoes in my earlier example (initial EROI of 14:1) because it has a sufficiently high EROI. I still come out ahead, even with a disadvantageous price exchange.

When looking at my EROI numbers, the perspicacious reader should remember these numbers span good years and bad, as well as my gain in expertise and efficiency the longer I farm. For another perspective on this energy exchange consider the oft-quoted statistic that modern American agriculture with tractors uses 7-10 kilocalories of fossil fuel energy to produce 1 kilocalorie of food.[35] Using those numbers, I am 15-22 times more efficient than modern American agriculture even in a bad year (2010). In a good year (2009) I am 25-35 times more efficient. From a historical perspective and starting with a possible EROI of 50:1 foraging wild grain (per Morris), the history of agriculture is a history of reducing, rather than increasing EROI. In other words, as we moved from hunting and gathering to intensive farming, we have been going backwards. I have been able to reverse that trend only because I have foregone tractors for tillers and hand labor. I am more efficient only because I am comparing myself to inefficient industrial agriculture and not to hunting/gathering.

The idea we have been going *backwards* in food production efficiency (measured by EROI) over the last 10,000 years as society became more complex raises quite a few hackles in most social environments – be it informally in the pub or in more formal public meetings. The vast majority of people are invested in increasing energy capture and suggesting there is something wrong with modern energy addiction is anathema. Nevertheless, the modern usage of fossil fuels to grow food means we are "eating oil" every day. This is far, far different from the origins of agriculture. It is not just increasing complexity on a continuum, as Tainter suggests, but seems to be on a different continuum entirely. Perhaps a closer look at civilization is in order.

4 CIVILIZATION & SLAVES

Civilization is a much-abused term, often confused with culture, and people usually think of an "advanced" stage of development. It is rare for someone to look critically at what civilization really means. The word comes from *civis* and *civitas*, Latin for "citizen" and "city-state" respectively. Anthropologists usually start with characteristics of a state, cite a greater complexity and more centralization and then add the invention of writing and the presence of public works to get to their definition of civilization. The most important difference really is greater complexity and greater centralization. This means more energy capture to run the state.

Morris postulates a "hard ceiling" of 31,000 kilocalories per person per day that neither Western nor Eastern civilizations could break through until the Industrial Revolution.[1] By his reckoning, the Roman Empire reached this level in 1 BCE/CE (Before Christian Era/Christian Era rather than BC/AD) and hung on for 100 years until decline started. In his discussion of the Roman Empire collapse, Tainter cites a level of peace and prosperity throughout the first two centuries CE but argues that marginal return on investment had already declined, just not to the point where contining to invest was no longer worthwhile.[2] Both authors agree the Empire was declining after 100 CE.

The idea of a hard *internal* limit is intriguing. The history of the world up to the Roman Empire was increasing complexity, increasing energy capture, and increasing bureaucratization. The Romans had writing, monumental public architecture and a fearsome army. But the Empire could grow only so large and ran up against limits in the north of England, northern Europe, the Sahara in Africa, and the Persian Empire in the East. It is tempting to think better commanders (a Latin Alexander the Great, for instance) could have pushed the limits further, but both Tainter and Morris make good arguments for the inability of an empire to grow beyond a certain point.

Let us look at civilization from the perspective of capturing energy from other humans. We already know it is more advantageous to recapture energy indirectly from another human than directly from the environment. The question is not whether it is advantageous but how cheap it is. We can pay less to the farmer, for example, but at a certain point the farmer may just give up – a phenomenon we have seen in American farming since the 1960's. After some thought, it may become apparent the cheapest way to recapture human energy is slavery. This is an integral part of state level societies and especially important to civilization.

Slavery is a feature of chiefdoms as well as states, but the slavery is small-scale rather than the large-scale, institutionalized slavery we see in states, ancient and modern.[3] Warring chiefdoms provided a plentiful supply of captured prisoners which could be set to work, but the sheer scale and complexity of the Roman Empire, for instance, required massive institutionalized slavery. Prisoners of war became slaves, but citizens could sell their children into slavery and creditors could enslave insolvent debtors.[4] The foundation of Rome was its army, which provided slaves and conquered land, and in turn increased the wealth and complexity of the empire. One of the questions bandied about as an afterthought is whether slavery kept both the ancient Greeks and the Romans from developing modern technology. In other words, since human labor was cheap and plentiful, why put time and energy into developing a different energy capture? This is another subject for grad students to argue about in the pub after a hard day of seminars.

But is slavery integral to civilization? Are there any civilizations or even state level societies without slavery? By looking for states without slaves, perhaps we can discover how they managed without slaves. However, a search for civilizations without some form of slavery has proved fruitless so far in my research. There are states like the Incan Empire cited as having no slaves, but they did have a form of mandatory public service called *mit'a*, which enabled the emperor to shift labor around where it was needed to build roads.[5] This example points up the difference between *chattel slavery* (owning a person) and *corvée*, which is unpaid labor demanded from a citizen or resident.[6] We recognize this as *serfdom* in the European medieval period, when a feudal lord could demand work from his subjects and serfs belonged to the land. Some may argue slavery only includes chattel slavery, so serfdom or *corvée* does not count. However, the key point here is that slavery is not just ownership but energy capture.

Societies have slaves so they can get work done at the cheapest possible price. It is not entirely free, however, since slaves have to be fed and housed. If an emperor or lord can get work done without providing food or housing for the worker, it is a better bargain for the ruling class than actual ownership. In this sense, *corvée* and serfdom are more sophisticated than chattel slavery. In the Dark Ages after the Roman Empire collapsed, there was still precedent for chattel slavery, but over time serfdom became more important through the rise of manorialism and then feudalism.[7] As Cook calculated, by 1400 CE the energy capture of northwestern Europe had risen to approximately 26,000 kilocalories per person per day, or 84% of the energy capture of the Roman Empire.[8] This was accomplished through less centralization in feudal systems. Instead of an emperor, there were many kings and lords. Instead of an empire, there were many states and fiefs. Slavery remained legal but serfdom became predominant.[9] In a dark, dark era, we should expect the most efficient use of human labor (for the ruling class that is) would prevail. In a dark, dark future we might see it again.

Even when slavery or bondage <u>has</u> been declared illegal, it can still survive. For example, a caste system was integral to traditional Indian society and caste was clearly defined and rigorously enforced. The caste system survived the subjugation by the British and was only abolished in 1949, two years after the formation of the modern Indian state. Yet there are still an estimated 5-10 million people bonded as laborers, working their whole lives in quarries and rice fields for debts they did not incur. Most of these are *untouchables*, at the bottom of society.[10] This is an example of slavery being so important, it survives even when illegal.

Inequality – whether slave/owner, lord/serf, or wage slave/boss - is integral to stratified society. This stratification can be hereditary or incurred each generation. Since states and civilizations are more complex, they need more energy capture, which means stratification can be defined as *differential energy capture*. We can put slavery on a continuum of differential energy capture based on energy return on investment (EROI). In this schema, the different forms of slavery cluster on one end of the continuum because they produce more energy than they consume. On the other end lie the elites who command maximum energy capture in society and consume many times more than they produce. Everyone else lies somewhere in between. Somewhere along the line is the inflection point where the sign changes. This is the point at which a human changes from being a net energy producer to being a net energy consumer. Most of us now are net energy consumers.

The length of time it took feudal Europe to get close to the per capita energy capture levels of the Roman Empire (nearly 1000 years) indicates early agrarian states did indeed have an internal limit, even considering serfdom as a more sophisticated use of slavery. Cook notes the increased energy capture of northwestern Europe in 1400 CE also depended on wind, water power, and some coal use.[11] By this point, Europe is starting to look beyond agrarian sources of energy – human and animal. This indicates the internal limit might be lower than the 31,000 kilocalories per person per day postulated by Morris. It is even possible the Romans exceeded this limit temporarily because they were able to drain wheat and gold from Egypt, as well as gold from the Gauls and the Dacians.[12] This may be an early case of *overshoot* in complex human society.

Overshoot is an ecological term popularized by William Catton in *Overshoot: The Ecological Basis of Revolutionary Change* (1980).[13] It simply means increasing in numbers so much the carrying capacity of an ecosystem is exceeded. *Carrying capacity* is another ecological term which describes the maximum population of a given species which a particular habitat can support indefinitely. The key to the concepts of overshoot and carrying capacity is the word "indefinitely." This is the basis for our modern term *sustainability*, which simply means being able to continue using the same system more or less indefinitely. For further definitions of carrying capacity, one can turn to Joel Cohen's *How Many People Can the Earth Support?* (1995), where he examines multiple estimates of carrying capacity in detail, including biological, ecological, political and demographic definitions.[14] Cohen's book is quite comprehensive, but suffers from analytical impotence. In covering every eventuality in depth, he confuses the reader who would be satisfied with a good estimate that illuminates the problem. This is similar to the problem encountered by President Harry Truman when he famously said, "Give me a one handed economist! All my economists say, 'on the one hand . . . on the other'."[15] For my purposes, I am content to use the ecological definition since it has a biophysical basis.

In overshoot, the species may increase its population beyond the carrying capacity, but it is only temporary. A classic example from biology is a population of rabbits increasing beyond the carrying capacity of their habitat until they die off from starvation and/or disease (disease is more easily transmitted in overcrowded conditions). It is important to realize overshoot and dieoff do not happen in isolation. For instance, if a population of lynx depends on the rabbit population as their prey species, they will also exhibit overshoot and dieoff - just on a different timeline as they try to transition to voles and other prey. If the lynx population has risen <u>because</u> of the rabbit population increase, it is likely the lynx population will crash too, just not immediately. This is an important point. Species dependent on just a few food sources have a higher risk of precipitous decline (*crash*) than those species which are more diversified. This should immediately raise a red flag for us humans dependent on petroleum energy.

In the case of the Roman Empire, their peak of 31,000 kilocalories per person per day may have been a temporary overshoot of their habitat's (i.e. the Mediterranean Basin) carrying capacity. It is certainly plausible the Romans were so dependent on increasing levels of gold and grain from external sources (i.e. a "growth" economy) the Empire was unsustainable for decades or even centuries before they reached their peak. Their army expanded as far as they could and funneled resources to the center of the Empire, only stopping when they were halted by external forces, such as the

Germans and Picts in the north, the Persians in the east, and the Sahara in the south. In other words, Roman decline was due to external forces and their energy capture limit is not an internal limit.

The internal limit for energy capture in a society may be as low as 12,000 kilocalories per person per day, the level Cook calculated for early agriculturalists in SW Asia circa 5000 BCE.[16] These agriculturalists had animal and fire energy at their disposal, as well as trade networks. However, this was before the rise of large city-states, like Sumer and Babylon. It is likely early agrarian societies had some slavery, but without early writing we do not know for sure and the archaeological evidence is slim. For example, we may find prehistoric burials that exhibit violent executions, but the graves cannot reflect those people captured and kept as slaves. We may find burials where bones exhibit excessive lifelong toil, but no clear evidence the people were slaves rather than overworked family members. Without good evidence, it seems we are back at our continuum again, of capturing energy directly from the environment at a low level, but getting a higher level of energy capture by exploiting human resources. This is the key to civilization. Institutionalized slavery, whether chattel slavery or *corvée*, is necessary to get beyond low-level village agriculture to form cities, states and civilizations. In this context, an internal limit may just be an academic exercise, since in practical terms, we can exceed it through overshoot.

We have not had institutionalized slavery in the United States since the Civil War ended in 1865. Slavery still exists, but is underground (like sex trafficking) or is based on economic injustice (like fraudulent real estate loans). Consequently, we pat ourselves on the back and think we have somehow slipped the age-old pattern of enslaving somebody else so we can have a good life. However, this is just a delusion. Instead of human slaves, we have *energy slaves*.

Each one of us right here in the United States has a host of energy slaves at our disposal. These slaves all have various names, like "toaster" or "automobile" or "computer" or "electricity." They all consume incredible amounts of energy we tap into, without thinking, as we go about our daily business. If we use Cook's estimate of 230,000 kilocalories per person per day in the United States in 1970, we can quickly calculate how many energy slaves we use each day. Dividing 230,000 by 2500 (the energy equivalent of a person's daily requirement in food energy), we each have 92 energy slaves at our command – 91 if you discount yourself.

Of course, we might expect to have even more energy slaves in 2012, because surely we must be using more energy per person per day than we did in 1970. However, there have been some increases in efficiency, as well as some Americans actively trying to reduce their energy footprint in the last forty years. Even though considerably more energy is being used worldwide on a daily basis, the balance has shifted, with China, India and other industrializing countries using more and more of the world's energy output. This is due to their combined increase in population and their burgeoning development through economic activity (which takes energy).

In fact, the US has been static in energy consumption for over forty years. The Energy Information Administration (EIA - the statistics arm of the Department of Energy) reports US energy consumption has been about the same from the 1970's to the present. Their average from 1980 to 2010 is 334 million BTU's per person per year, or 230,439 kilocalories per person per day (a year equivalent to 365.25 days and 1 BTU = 0.252 kilocalories).[17] In other words, Cook's estimate for 1970 is still valid today and we each have 91 energy slaves at our disposal. In comparison, China uses 40,857 kilocalories per person per day and India 11,662.[18] This would be 16.3 energy slaves per person in China and only 4.7 energy slaves per person in India.

It should be remembered these figures are for the energy we actually use. They are not a measure of work. Many people confuse the two – some willfully and disingenuously, some because they do not know any better. Energy consumption is the measure that counts most, since it includes the heat we interject into the natural environment as well as the work we do. If we measure work only and discount waste heat and gases, we discount most of the heat energy we consume, which is analogous to mainstream economists discounting energy value as an "external." This is similar to Marx's famous dogma that everything nature offers us is *gratis* and we only produce value by labor.[19] In this sense, mainstream economists are closer to Marxism in their discounting of the externals of heat energy than they realize. I suspect most American economists would faint from apoplexy if they even entertained this similarity for a moment!

Nevertheless, most people follow the lead of mainstream economists in discounting our energy consumption; instead focusing on work, price and convenience. We live within a complex society that provides nesting levels of infrastructure which take care of our every want and desire, as long as we can pay the price. Most of us never bother to think about our energy usage. We have been lulled into oblivion because the infrastructure works so well to provide us with cheap energy. However, the era of cheap energy is over, so we will have to wake up.

5 CHEAP ENERGY & PEAK OIL

The Western world has been harnessing fossil fuel energy since the start of the First Industrial Revolution, 1750-1850. Although some coal was used during Europe's medieval period, the easily obtainable coal was found mostly in Britain and was exhausted by the 13th century CE. Even though coal could still be mined by digging shafts, it was not until James Watt perfected the steam engine in 1775 for pumping water out of mines that coal was extracted in great quantities.[1] Then, along with the steam engine adapted to multiple kinds of machinery and the coal to fuel it, Britain led the way into a new industrial world (and a new Empire!).

Even though the First Industrial Revolution changed the face of the world, the increase in energy capture was minimal. Morris notes that kilocalories per person per day in the West (which now included North America as well as Europe) only rose from 32,000 in 1700 to 38,000 in 1800. However, by 1900, the energy capture was up to 92,000 kilocalories per person per day in the West. Comparable levels for the East (China and Japan) were 33,000 kilocalories per person per day in 1700, rising to 36,000 in 1800 and only 49,000 in 1900. From about 600 CE the East had moved ahead in energy capture but fell behind in the 18th century.[2]

What really moved the Western world ahead of the East was the Second Industrial Revolution, from 1850 to the beginning of the First World War. This has been called the "technological revolution," with improved processes for making steel, improvements in production lines, and a greater understanding of chemistry and thermodynamics.[3] Although coal was the main fuel up to World War I, a signal achievement was the commercialization of oil as a cheap, portable and energy dense fuel. The first commercial oil well in the US was drilled by Colonel Edwin Drake at Titusville, Pennsylvania in 1859.[4] Although other commercial wells had been dug in Azerbaijan, Ontario, Poland and Virginia by this time, Drake's achievement was to use steel pipe to bore through the ground directly to the oil. Up until that time, oil was mainly a by-product of mining for salt. Soon, Drake's improved methods also generated investment in drilling, refining and marketing. Oil was cheap and there was plenty of it.

It is no accident oil became an integral part of the rise of the US as a world power. Unlike Europe and rapidly industrializing Japan in the latter half of the 19th century, America had little infrastructure to limit progress. There were no 600-year old buildings in New York and Boston, like in London and Tokyo. There was no transcontinental rail line until 1869. Finally, there was a great expanse of wide-open western land to move onto (once the original inhabitants had been killed off by the US Army). Along with large reserves of easily obtainable oil from southern California to Texas and Pennsylvania, the US had room to expand.

Soon after Colonel Drake's oil well changed the face of energy, the US fought a Civil War that tore apart conventional notions of what America was and could be. It is not hyperbole to say the Civil War swept away the social infrastructure. Even though the Civil War started as a war to preserve the Union, it soon became a war to end slavery. However, as we know from hindsight, it would have been extremely unlikely the US could advance further as a civilization without some form of slavery. The postwar Reconstruction Era bears out this argument.

From 1865-1877, the South struggled with a broken economy and various political factions seeking to gain advantage as the southern states were readmitted into the Union. There was a move towards urbanism both within the South and from the South to the industrial North. Voting rights were a main component of the postwar struggle, with 4 million former slaves raising the possibility of more voters and representatives from southern states in Congress than before the war. There were major disagreements about loyalty oaths and disenfranchisement for former supporters of the Confederacy.[5] Meanwhile, the states and territories west of the Mississippi provided a convenient dumping ground for damaged, embittered Civil War veterans. As a result, the Indian Wars of the plains, southwest and west coast increased in violence and rapacity, with the culmination of these genocidal campaigns in 1890 at Wounded Knee. Nevertheless, even though this period was fraught with social upheaval, by 1875 the energy capture of the industrial West (Europe and the US) had jumped to about 77,000 kilocalories per person per day.[6]

What happened during this time period was the demise of plantation agriculture and its replacement by sharecropping, the rise of urbanism and manufacturing, and the opening of vast amounts of arable land for agriculture west of the Mississippi. For instance, farm acreage in the US increased from 407 million acres in 1860 to 839 million in 1900, more than double the pre-war acreage. Farm mechanization in the US was well-advanced before the war, with the production of John Deere's wrought-iron plow jumping from 1000 plows a year in 1846 to 10,000 plows a year by 1857. Mechanical grain threshers had become commonplace in the East and Midwest by the 1840's and Cyrus McCormick had succeeded in perfecting his mechanical grain reaper by 1855. In the South, Eli Whitney's cotton gin had been invented in 1793, even though plantation agriculture still relied on slave labor until 1865.[7] Farm mechanization in the US was in place and ready to expand, first by horsepower and steam, later by gasoline and diesel.

It is a common misperception that the Homestead Act of 1862 was responsible for opening up the western United States, but of the 500 million acres of public lands disposed of from 1860 to 1900, only 80 million acres were distributed under the Homestead Act. About 108 million acres were sold at private auction, and about 300 million acres were given to railroads and states, which in turn sold much of the land to speculators and farmers. It is worth noting land speculation was a national problem from 1785 to 1860.[8] It is likely land speculation was integral to the rise of the US as a nation-state. However, after the Civil War, speculation became big business when it passed from private individuals into the hands of large corporations and the railroads.[9] Along with farm mechanization and cheap energy, big business helped build the US into a global agricultural power, as well as a global industrial power.

By 1900, US agriculture had coalesced into specialization by area. The Northeast specialized in fruit, truck crops and dairy production; the Upper South specialized in tobacco and the Deep South in cotton; the Midwest became the Corn Belt and a center for dairy products. In the West, the Great Plains became a gigantic wheat-production area while the intermountain area specialized in cattle and sheep ranching. In the Pacific regions of the Far West, fruit and truck crops became predominant, as well as grain production in eastern Washington and Oregon. During the time period from the Civil War to the turn of the century, wheat production increased fourfold, barley increased by six and a half times, cotton increased fivefold, the number of cattle on farms doubled, and hogs increased by 50 percent. Soon the problem became overproduction. US farm output increased by 53% between 1870 and 1880, while the population increased by only 26%.[10] During this period, exports could not keep up with production and farmers suffered.

In addition to overproduction, a series of financial problems occurred in the western developed countries. In 1873, Germany's decision to go off the silver standard caused a panic in the US and Europe because of falling demand for silver. This in turn triggered a depression that lasted until 1879 and was known as the Great Depression until a new depression overshadowed it in the 1930's. Panics and recessions continued through the 1880's to the eve of World War I and even after the war, with four recessions between 1918 and 1927.[11] Also during this time period, the US pursued global military objectives, such as the Spanish-American War. Clearly, the US was now a major player on the world stage, both influenced by and influencing global events. By the time of its entry into World War I in 1917, the US was vying with Britain for control of the seas. When World War II ended in 1945, the US had become the leading global power.

During the second half of the 19th century, US manufacturing rose to new levels, spurred on by increased use of interchangeable parts and streamlined production methods based on machines run by semi-skilled labor.[12] This increase made good use of the large number of immigrants pouring into the US who could be trained on the job. There were three great waves of immigration to the US in the 19th century and up to World War I. The first wave - 5 million newcomers from 1815-1860 - was greater than the whole US population in 1790. The second wave, from 1860-1890, brought in over 10 million more, mostly from northern Europe. The third wave - 1890-1914, totaled 15 million, mostly from southern and eastern Europe. In all three of these waves, more than 30 million in total, most immigrants settled in cities and provided labor for manufacturing. In 1870, the US was second only to England in production of manufactured goods. By 1885, the US was the world leader.[13]

The late 19th century was also the time of the robber barons who were more adroit at manipulating finance than actually producing goods. Robert Heilbronner provides the example of US Steel in *The Worldly Philosophers* (1953). In 1901, US Steel had real assets of $682 million, but had sold $303 million worth of bonds, $510 million of preferred stock, and $508 million of common stock. The "financial" company was nearly twice as large as the "real" company.[14] This financial play, with nothing more than "good will" behind the common stock, sounds incredibly modern to those of us who watched Wall Street perform similar sleights of hand in the early 21st century. Obviously, there was enough manufacturing going on in the late 19th century to provide a vast "cushion" allowing financiers to make money from money itself. Civilization in America was firing on all cylinders.

However, without some form of slavery, all this would not have been possible. The common myth of American "exceptionalism" maintains there is something unique and even divine about the United States. This myth asserts we have been able do something beyond the abilities of ALL previous civilizations and become an empire without slavery. Of course this is nonsense. A more parsimonious explanation is that we just threw more cheap energy at each and every problem. It is not hyperbole to say the US was a mess during Reconstruction, but the timely commercialization of oil and the rise of manufacturing after the Civil War (which required massive amounts of energy) argue for adoption of a *slave substitute* rather than a new form of civilization. After we outlawed slavery, we passed through a relatively brief period of "reconstruction" and then substituted energy slaves for real slaves. In addition to coal, steam power and farm mechanization, the US had plentiful reserves of cheap oil energy. This became the main driver for the rise of the US as a global power in the 20th century. In fact, during World War I, gasoline was so necessary to modern life there were wartime shortages. We are dependent on petroleum to power our economy to this day. We slipped a return to human slaves only because of our dependence on the energy slave of petroleum.

For the last 150 years, oil energy has been cheap and abundant. What has been touted as human creativity has really been the ability to throw massive amounts of energy at any problem. Witness the automobile as a solution to mass transport in a growing economy. It would be hard to imagine a more wasteful use of energy than a car traveling on an expensively constructed highway and carrying only one person. Yet this is the norm. As mentioned earlier, culture provided us with the ability to filter out the environment and gave us access to resources that were so plentiful we could invent ridiculous, wasteful things. Unfortunately, the downside has been our dependence on cheap oil energy to the exclusion of actually solving cultural problems. As long as oil was cheap, we could get by on this substitution. But now it is not so cheap.

Peak Oil

Petroleum, or "rock oil" (from the Greek *petra* – rock - and *elaion* – oil), is an easily transportable fuel with a high energy density. Coal has an energy density of 24 MJ/kg (megajoules per kilogram), while gasoline and diesel have nearly double that amount, at 47.2 and 45.4 MJ/kg, respectively.[15] (Crude oil has roughly the same energy density as diesel.) Coal is still an important energy source but it is not mobile, which is why gasoline and diesel-powered automobiles easily eclipsed the steam-driven car. Even in trains, which could transport coal to fire the boiler, diesel eclipsed coal because of lowered maintenance and operation costs.[16]

Petroleum, or colloquially *oil*, has assumed a greater and greater importance in our energy consumption over the last 150 years. In the US, field production of crude oil was estimated at only 1000 barrels per day in 1860, but had risen to 33,000 barrels per day in 1875, and 174,000 barrels per day in 1900. US production rose dramatically in the 20th century, and

US oil production peaked in 1970, at 9,637,000 barrels per day.[17] Using the estimates for energy capture from Cook (1971) and Morris (2010) provided earlier, as well as population numbers, we can see how oil became increasingly more important in providing energy. The percentages of kilocalories provided by crude oil per person per day jumped from 0% in 1860, to 1% in 1875, 4% in 1900 and 30% by 1970. Even though these estimates do not take into account production of US oil for export, the trend is clear, with oil assuming a larger and larger share of energy use for Americans in the 19th and 20th centuries. Some may see this as due to the increasing reliance on the automobile for private transport, but there are thousands of products made from oil in daily use by Americans every day. Oil is an essential ingredient of our daily life, from the toothpaste we use in the morning to the pillows we lay our heads on at night.[18]

There have been many volumes written on peak oil, but simply put, it is when production has peaked. Unfortunately, this peak can only be seen in hindsight. So, for example, the US reached peak oil in 1970, but we could not know it at the time. The usual graphic is to use the Hubbert Curve, which looks like your standard bell curve and was developed by geologist M. King Hubbert in 1956 for a presentation to the American Petroleum Institute.[19] He predicted US oil production from conventional sources would peak between 1965-1970 and the world peak would come in about "half a century" later (i.e. around 2006). The prediction for the US production peak was correct, but the waters have been muddied considerably since then for actually assessing the world peak of production. For a time, the peak was considered to be in 2005-2008, but now unconventional sources (e.g. the Bakken oil shale and deepwater Gulf oil) have come online, so there is always a bone of contention in trying to assess when the peak will actually occur. If we confine ourselves to conventional supplies we have likely already peaked.

When we have passed peak oil is less important than its effects. We can see these effects right now. For example, a consensus is building that oil is so important to the world economy that increases in crude oil prices serve as a drag on economic growth. As the price of oil goes up, it accounts for a greater percentage of the cost of doing business. If the price is too high, business is stifled and the economy stalls. As the economy stops growing or contracts, demand for oil goes down and so does the price. Then the lower price for oil allows business to grow again until demand increases and the oil price rises. As the price of oil again reaches a higher percentage of business costs, the economy stalls again and the cycle repeats. This price/demand cycle causes its own strain. In 2008, oil prices reached 7.5% of GDP in the US and triggered a major demand reduction. In 2010, Deutsche Bank predicted the next oil shock will come at 6.5% of GDP, which reflects their assessment of an increasing sensitivity to oil prices.[20] As I write this in 2012, the price of oil is approximately 5% of US GDP.

The most interesting aspect of our increasing dependency on oil energy is its ability to foster a growth economy and overshoot. Coal proved to be quite an advance in energy capture during the First Industrial Revolution and continues to be the principal source of electrical power generation worldwide.[21] However, when oil arrived, energy capture and growth scaled up to heights unknown and undreamed. Many scientists hoped for the same quantum increase with nuclear energy by the way, but after 65 years of nuclear weapons and power generation it has not lived up to its hype. We are still dependent on liquid petroleum for our profligate lifestyle.

Another problem rarely considered is displacement of cheap oil by expensive oil. We already picked the "low hanging fruit" long ago and so must now utilize oilfields that are more difficult to get to and maintain. This is what geologist Euan Mearns termed the "Net Energy Cliff."[22] As absolute EROI decreases from about 10:1 and approaches a 1:1 ratio, the energy that can actually be used by society decreases exponentially rather than linearly, due to relatively greater costs of infrastructure and supporting technology for smaller EROI's. We see this clearly as we transition from shallow wells in Saudi Arabia to deepwater wells in the Gulf of Mexico, to shale oil in Texas and tar sands in Canada. We can put the same amount of energy into each of these oil patches, but we extract exponentially fewer barrels from tar sands than from Saudi Arabian shallow wells. This differential is reflected in the worldwide price of oil. The lower EROI oil patches have a higher cost to drill and command a higher price at the retail end for the consumer. Anyone can grasp prices go up because it is harder to get oil now, but what is not usually appreciated is the exponential nature of replacing "easy" oil with hard-to-get oil, like tar sands and oil shale.

Peak oil is not just about production. We will likely never run out of oil, but we will run out of oil we can afford to get out of the ground. Currently, natural gas is touted as an alternate fuel, but the EROI of natural gas is only 10:1.[23] Since transportation is such a large component of modern life and few vehicles run on natural gas or propane, most uses of natural gas are for power plants, factories and residences that used to run on coal. However, natural gas may not be a viable substitute for coal because of the methane released in its extraction. Methane is a potent greenhouse gas which dissipates quickly, but traps 23 times more heat in the atmosphere than carbon dioxide.[24] In the overall scheme of things, the damage to the environment with natural gas is about the same as with coal.[25] Natural gas reserves may also be lower than expected.

Richard Heinberg, a fellow at the Post Carbon Institute, estimates we have only about 12 more years of natural gas supplies in the US.[26] In contrast, the natural gas industry estimates about 96 more years of supply at current usage rates, less if demand goes up (which is likely).[27] Even using the industry perspective, a substitution of natural gas for coal is unlikely to keep American civilization going past 2100. If we factor in inflated estimates of reserves and increased demand due to substitution for oil, it is likely we will reach peak natural gas well before 2100. In fact, we seem to be approaching *Peak Everything* – which is the title of Heinberg's 2007 book.[28]

Climate Change and Peak Food

Along with peak oil, peak natural gas, peak coal, peak water, peak phosphorous, and a host of other "peaks" we are approaching, we seem to be close to *peak food*. In March 2009, Sir John Beddington gave a speech to the UK Sustainable Development Commission, in which he warned of a "perfect storm" of food shortages, scarce water and insufficient energy by 2030, which will likely destabilize societies around the globe as people flee from the hardest-hit regions.[29] A week later Jonathan Porritt, Chairman of the Commission, published a comment on Beddington's speech in which he voiced agreement but collapsed the timeline to 2020.[30] Three years earlier, in 2006, a report from the UN Food and Agricultural Organization (FAO) had warned world food production would need "quantum jumps" to feed 8.9 billion people in the world by 2050.[31] Early in 2012, Secretary General of the UN Ban Ki-moon recommended a 50% increase in food, a 45% increase in energy, and a 30% increase in water by 2030.[32] It is unlikely any of these targets can be met, since modern food production depends on fossil fuel energy. The most likely scenario is Beddington's "perfect storm" - mass migrations and destabilized societies.

Climate change is already worsening the world's problems. As we spew more and more greenhouse gases in a futile effort to recapture our profligate lifestyles in the West, we warm the planet and change climate. As with peak oil, there are hundreds of books and articles on climate change so I feel no need to persuade anyone. The intelligent reader should already be aware of the problem. We have phenomena of melting glaciers and more open water in the arctic during the summer, as well as shifting migratory patterns of birds in the temperate zones. Climate change also affects the food problem by its impact on staple crops. A single example of changes in the rice harvest should suffice to illuminate the problem.

Rice is the staple food for over half the world's population. It grows well in wet areas not conducive to other crops, such as south China, Vietnam and the Philippines.[33] In experiments by the International Rice Research Institute (IRRI) reported in 2007, researchers found rice yields increased 0.5 ton per hectare for every 75 ppm (parts per million) increase in CO_2 concentration, while decreasing 0.6 ton per hectare for every 1° C rise in temperature. In other words, the temperature rise counteracts the beneficial effect of increased carbon dioxide for plants. Yield data were used in general circulation models (GCM - a special class of models developed for climate change) to predict yields under various climate scenarios. Not surprisingly, the results depended on which model was used, with one model predicting a net increase of 4% - 7% while two other models predicted net decreases of 4% - 13%.[34]

In another experiment on rice quality rather than just yield, the positive effects of elevated CO_2 did not compensate for the overall decrease in rice quality due to global warming.[35] Since global warming (climate change) is composed of several variables, it seems quality suffers and yields are likely to be lower – i.e. temperature trumps CO_2. It should also be noted that in the real world, these variables are interactive with each other, as well as with droughts, floods, etc. The effect of rising temperature on rice is just one example of the extremely complicated processes in the physical world. The simplistic approach of throwing more energy at the problem only exacerbates the difficulties. This was the approach of the Green Revolution, with its emphasis on more fossil fuels for fertilizer, mechanization and electricity to power irrigation. This did not solve the problem. There are more hungry people on the planet now than before the Green Revolution.[36]

On the one hand, we need more food to feed a growing population on the planet. On the other hand, energy scarcity and price increases make current production difficult, much less a 50% increase in the future. Climate change amplifies the problem. This is not a recipe for a happier, saner world. It is instead, a recipe for dieoff.

6 POLITICAL & FINANCIAL FAILURE

Many people are deluded. Whether they are liberal or conservative, Democrat or Republican, far left or far right in their political orientation, most of them seem to feel good times are "just around the corner." Their hope is if we can rein in the corporations, or the police, or the tax cheats, or the nasty demonstrators (pick your own outgroup), the American lifestyle will come back and everything will be just fine. This is a lie perpetrated on a daily basis by the government, corporations, media and even academics who should know better. Our current recession/depression is the first one driven by declining energy resources, so there is no precedent upon which we can rely. Faced with an entirely new situation, it is not so surprising many people buy the lie. It is not so surprising people just suffer and hope.

Instead of leaders who implement rational solutions however, we are saddled with overlords who borrow against the future and condemn our poorest citizens to perdition so the elites of society can get even richer and fatter. Instead of enjoying our lives, we spend most of our time in a fruitless search for money so we can buy overpriced goods that do not satisfy our needs, much less our desires. Simple pleasures, like eating quality food, are slipping away. On top of that, the price of oil is rising. Even though there are tremendous oscillations in the price of refined gasoline and diesel as well as crude oil, the price volatility is on an inclined plane and the overall direction is up. The cheap energy from petroleum is not so cheap anymore.

Since cheap energy is the foundation of the Growth Model, more expensive energy creates growth problems.

The Growth Model is the paradigm that both runs and ruins the political and financial worlds. It is almost impossible to find a politician or businessperson who does not believe *growth* (usually measured in GDP) is essential to a nation's survival. The emphasis on growth has grown from a post-World War II model developed to account for US economic expansion into a cult-like mantra trumpeted by every mayor in every little town across America.[1] From the President of the United States on down, the mantra is, "We need to grow our economy."

The usual formulation from economics is we need technology, capital and labor to grow. In a growing economy, these three variables intersect to create more goods and services and the general economy improves. As the general economy improves, the participants in the economy also improve their lives. Therefore, if a government focuses on the macroeconomic aspect of growing the general economy, all participants will benefit. To use President Kennedy's phrase from 1963, "A rising tide lifts all boats."[2] This is quite similar to the "trickle-down" theory of tax breaks for business and the wealthy later promulgated by President Reagan and which is still popular today.[3] Of course neither idea works, yet this fallacy has been integral to government and business since the end of World War II. The popularity of this lie is due to willful ignorance of another variable – energy.

The Growth Model discounts energy's role in formation of capital, use of technology and organization of labor. Energy is regarded as a given, similar to Marx's idea that everything we get from nature is *gratis*.[4] Most economists regard energy as an external, not only because it is complicated to track, but leaving it out of their market models makes things "tidy." However, as Reiner Kümmel put it so elegantly in *The Second Law of Economics* (2011), "Capital in the absence of energy is inert."[5] It is even easier to see how energy is important to technology and labor, as we see workers using ever more complicated machines rather than picks and hoes, and using ever more complicated machines just to get to work. These all require copious amounts of energy. Without accounting for energy, the Growth Model is invalid.

Even more shocking is the Growth Model postulates continued growth in the long term, which means an economy based on the Growth Model assumes infinite growth. This is not possible on a finite planet. The only way the Growth Model can work is with periodic "busts" that destroy capital, technology or labor (or all three). This means recessions and depressions are inherent in a growth model, essentially resetting the model at a lower point in order to grow again. Of course you never hear a politician or financial wizard say we need a depression in order to reset our economy. That would be political suicide – which is another problem with the Growth Model. It really is a con game, with intelligent people in command of powerful resources seemingly unaware their policies have a significant downside affecting the lives of millions. Energy is necessary for all economic activity. Disregarding it is intellectually bankrupt.

Now that we are hooked like crack addicts on cheap oil and the oil is not so cheap, do we have any chance to go backwards and rediscover cultural solutions we gave up and replaced with cheap energy? For example, would be able to retrace our steps, re-orient our society, make policy and order our affairs using a model based on constricting energy supplies and negative growth, i.e. a *constricting economy*? Unfortunately, it is not likely to work that way for a simple, yet significant, reason. Culture is an evolutionary adaptation and subject to the same mechanical problems inherent in our biological evolution.

Evolution by natural selection is a step by step process of small changes that survive over time. It is irreversible, even though biologists have sought for years to find evidence for reversibility. In order to go backwards in evolution, we would have to retrace each of these small steps. Even if we could retrace some small steps in human evolution, we still might face a time problem. Since these changes happened on a long timeline, the necessity of compressing the time for each trait reversal might render it impossible.

Culture is an evolutionary adaptation that enabled us humans to gain ascendancy over the physical environment. In giving up cultural methods of solving problems for the easy fix of throwing cheap energy at any and all problems, we embarked on a course of new adaptations to our cultural environment that were uniquely dependent on cheap energy. Each unique small step was dependent on an earlier unique small step, just as biologically adaptive traits are dependent on previous unique adaptive traits. So far, it seems impossible to work backwards in evolution.[6] Therefore it is likely to be extremely difficult or even impossible to work backwards in culture that is itself an evolutionary adaptation. In other words, the likelihood of retracing our steps back to an earlier time before cheap liquid petroleum has a low probability. Any changes will have to be new and different.

To make matters worse, we are losing our cultural buffer. Instead of being one remove from physical reality because of our human interactions, we benefit directly from increased inputs of energy – mostly fossil fuel energy. Instead of integrating physical energy through a cultural matrix that humans control, we just consume energy without restraint. Consequently, our cultural buffer has become "thin" and physical environmental limits are poking through larger and larger holes in the fabric of culture. For those who prefer visual imagery, consider culture as a transparent membrane we can see through and that provides a shock absorber between us and the realities of nature - a kind of see-through baby blanket that protects us from the outside world. This "baby blanket" of culture has become thinner and thinner. Soon we will have to wake up and deal directly with the laws of physics, just as most species already do in their daily lives. In a world dependent on cheap oil, a lack of cheap oil leaves a vacuum. Can culture fill this vacuum as it once did? Can civilization continue?

Based on our past history and the demands of civilization, we have two choices – *reinstitution of slavery* or *collapse*. Reinstituting slavery is unlikely because of the speed of communications and the knowledge base of modern humanity. People are just not going to go for it this time around. In addition, the traditions of slavery that stretch back millennia have been broken. To think the unthinkable - reinstituting slavery to save civilization – would require governments to force it upon people. This would take a great deal of energy during a time of decreasing supply. It is unlikely the benefits would outweigh the costs.

If slavery were forced on poor humans through the judicial system or instituted on a large scale against entire populations, there would likely be a dramatic loss of efficiency over current labor practices, which some already regard as near-slavery because of sociological pressures (think wage slaves, foreclosures and student loans). Recent forays into institutionalized slavery by the *prison-industrial complex* sheds some light on how inefficient slave labor can be. For example, in the fall of 2011, 105 prisoners from a Washington state correctional facility helped pick apples at an orchard in Quincy, Washington. They picked 1,217 bins of apples in 6 days, or an average of 1.93 bins per person per day.[7] Since I was a migrant worker myself and picked apples for 8 years in Washington, I can state with some credibility that this is inefficient and far below minimum work levels. Over my career picking apples, I never picked less than 3 bins a day, even on my first day. In my last two seasons, I averaged 8 bins per day. My experience is typical of migrant workers, whether Mexicans or Americans.

Forced labor is inefficient. State prisons are inefficient too, which is why many states now outsource prisons to private companies. The way private prisons make money is the subsidies they get from local, state and federal governments. This can include tax breaks as well as government contracts. In a world of shrinking government because of declinining oil supplies, it is unlikely governments will continue to pay private prisons at current rates. As private prisons cut costs and try to improve their bottom line by hiring out their prisoners to work in agriculture and industry, many will likely go out of business, leaving government once again to foot the bill for warehousing prisoners. Faced with rising costs and decreasing revenues, the most likely course of action for state governments is to simply reduce sentences for minor offenders.

Reducing incarceration by relying more and more on probation and parole makes good economic sense for cash-strapped states. For example, in the US as a whole in 2007, the average cost per person on probation was $3.42 per day while the average for parole was $7.47. If one compares this to the average cost to house a prisoner of $78.95 per day, it quickly becomes apparent that social sanctions agreed to by the prisoner (i.e. probation or parole) are more cost-effective than actually warehousing prisoners.[8] Reinstituting slavery on a massive scale would destroy the last shreds of the social contract that now keeps probationers and parolees agreeable to monitoring and trying to support themselves. Besides the reprehensible nature of reinstituting slavery, it would be economically inefficient and sociologically counterproductive.

Without cheap energy and without reinstituting slavery, civilization faces *collapse*. It only took Rome a hundred years to collapse. Since we live in a faster-paced world than the Romans, it is likely American civilization will collapse within a shorter time frame. Now that the world is linked through globalization, an American collapse (or European or Russian or Chinese collapse for that matter) will have a world-wide domino effect.

In a worldwide global system that is linked electronically, collapse in Europe or the US will spread quickly around the globe. If we look at the issue of collapse dispassionately, we may notice that institutions that work quickly can also fail quickly. In other words, the financial world operates at the speed of fiber optic cable and wireless radio waves. Energy supply routes are slower and dependent on trucks or rail or ships to get their products to market. Industry has products sitting in warehouses and agriculture has crops in the field. In this light, it is likely financial collapse will precede collapse in other sectors like energy, industry and agriculture. It is also likely politicians will have no constructive countermeasures to offer. Just as there were many emperors during the Roman collapse (four in 69 CE alone!), so too we can expect politicians to proliferate and fail.[9] It does not matter if there is a dictatorship or not – the laws of physics will once again take over. Civilizations around the world will collapse.

We are faced with a conundrum. We evolved as a species because of culture. We are a socially organized species that has increased our energy capture by leaps and bounds in the last 150 years. Now we face a new world where individuals will have to deal directly with the laws of physics. There is no precedent for how to deal with this problem. My suggestion is to embrace the laws of physics. Somehow, we need to get the laws of physics on our side. This is what I have been working towards for over 40 years. In the last 8 years I have developed a model for how to do it. The laws of physics are on my side precisely because I bend to them, rather than trying to organize a group dynamic to circumvent them. The next part of this book is how to deal directly with the laws of physics. By necessity it is individualistic in scope. However, once competent individuals come together as a group, they are much stronger than a group composed of needy individuals who require the group to hold them up. There is a necessary place for the group dynamic, but the laws of physics, just like evolution by natural selection, act on the individual. That is where we (you and I as individuals) need to start. In the next section, I begin by providing new ways to look at the problem in order to *change your mental landscape*. Then I recommend ways to *take physical action*. Hopefully, once you have integrated the mental and physical changes YOU will be able to *work in your community* to enhance your survival.

PART 2: THE SOLUTION

7 REALISM

The first step to solving a problem is to recognize the problem. The point of Part 1 is to get you to look at the problem. I am not worried about persuading you, nor am I worried whether you believe me. My main thesis is: We are now forced to deal directly with the laws of physics. It does not matter if you believe me or not. However, if you do think we are in a mess of trouble, it is worth your while to consider my solutions and pick and choose those that fit your situation. First you have to *change your mental landscape*. For most people this will be difficult.

Let us consider four approaches. I shall call them Plan A, B, C and D. **Plan A** is the modern narrative, business as usual. Plan A suggests we just go along with our lives and try to keep our jobs, trust in our leaders, and work to better ourselves. This is the plan favored by those who believe this is the best of all possible worlds (the Panglossians), as well as those who do not give a rip about other people and are even willing to sacrifice their children (the Molochites). Plan A is also the default plan for those who do not question their fate. This is the plan currently pursued by governments and corporations. It is the source of our problems and therefore not a solution. It assumes we will have all the energy we need – somehow!

Plan B, on the other hand, is for those who see the future and believe we can mobilize to save civilization. The term comes from Lester Brown and his decades-long work on sustainable development, first as founder and president of Worldwatch Institute, and currently as founder and president of Earth Policy Institute. Brown's Plan B has gone through several iterations, starting with *Plan B* (2003), *Plan B 2.0* (2006), *Plan B 3.0* (2008), and finally *Plan B 4.0: Mobilizing to Save Civilization* (2009).[1] His latest book is *World on the Edge: How to Prevent Environmental and Economic Collapse* (2011), which updates earlier analyses and solutions.[2]

Brown's Plan B 4.0 points out that by 2009 we had 1 billion hungry people in the world and that number will likely rise to 1.2 billion by 2015. We face water and arable land shortages that are exacerbated by climate change, peak oil, food riots, international conflicts, and failing states. Food security is the weak link undermining global civilization in the 21st century. Brown lists four main goals to solving these problems: 1) stabilizing population, 2) eradicating poverty, 3) restoring the earth's natural support systems, and 4) stabilizing climate.[3] These are all noble and worthwhile goals. However, they require governmental and corporate cooperation. This is the weak point in Plan B.

Brown admits saving civilization will require a mobilization far greater than the US achieved upon entering World War II. However, his recommendations are to: 1) get educated, 2) spread the word, 3) get politically involved, and 4) take action in an area that excites you, such as closing coal-fired power plants, tax restructuring, or ending fuel mandates that raise fuel prices.[4] Again, these are all noble solutions but they are just a pittance compared to the massive restructuring needed to save civilization. Nor will people who try to act be allowed to make any real significant change without pushback by governments and corporations.

Educating people, spreading the word and political action have achieved little over the last 40+ years. For example, I am fond of saying, "If **YOU** would have listened to **US** forty years ago **WE** wouldn't be in trouble **NOW**." This makes for a good button slogan, but it does little else. It points up the minimal effect talking about a problem has on changing people's behavior. Direct action to force change in the 1960's also failed. The failure of direct action is due to the incredible power of the police and every mayor's willingness to use it to quash dissent, but there is also a structural bias against direct action because of energy – both physical and social energy.

Modern civilization depends on incredible amounts of energy. As I mentioned earlier, here in the US we use 91 energy slaves per person on average. The amount of fossil fuel energy needed to power even the simplest communication network for coordinating street actions is not even considered because electricity is ubiquitous. Getting to demonstrations via subsidized subway or subsidized auto is not only ironic but ridiculous. Going to potluck-style meetings sharing food imported from foreign countries or transported across the whole nation while trying to formulate a marketing strategy for "sustainability" is equally ridiculous. It takes incredible amounts of energy to try and fight the system. It takes incredible amounts of energy to quash dissent. It is not just police wages, benefits and overtime. It also takes incredible amounts of energy to equip and clothe police officers, as well as develop software for communications and integration of tactics and strategy. Fighting the system (or preserving it!) is not cheap. It takes a lot of energy and this is reflected in the price of electricity and other forms of energy.

We should also consider *social energy*. Our modern civilization depends on participation of as many people as possible. Civilization is propped up by people who consume. In the US, personal consumption is 70% of GDP, with the rest of the economy made up of business investment, government expenditures and exports.[5] We can see how this plays out by looking at TV programs, newspapers and most websites. Advertising to hype consumption is everywhere. We must consume, consume, consume. Our social system needs us to expend social energy. We need to be constantly hyped up - wired on coffee, sugar and information overload. In fact, as I discovered in the 1960's, American society actually runs better on negative energy. Trying to tear down the system provides negative social energy of a greater intensity than the positive energy of those who just "go along to get along." This is significant.

Similar to Brown's example of the speed with which the US mobilized to fight World War II, the 1960's and 70's saw federal, state and local governments mobilizing quickly to deal with demonstrators. Whole industries in surveillance and weaponry were developed to deal with "the threat within." We can see the modern counterpart in the huge increase in government spending on Homeland Security since September 11, 2001. Paranoia is a growth industry. However, it only works one way. To try and get that same level of mobilization from corporations and governments to fight against themselves (who are not only the source of the problem but invested in keeping it going) is a nonstarter. Plan B would be a good place to start IF we could somehow convince the people with the power to do something different. But that is not likely to happen. Instead we are likely to get more repression. All in all, Plan B is a noble idea, but unworkable.

Plan C is the term coined by Pat Murphy in his book *Plan C: Community Survival Strategies for Peak Oil and Climate Change* (2008).[6] Murphy's categorization scheme is that Plan A consists of doing more of what we do now, using up fossil fuels as fast as we can and developing new energy sources (e.g. tar sands and nuclear). Murphy's Plan B is to try and keep the status quo by shifting to renewable energy sources. This is similar to Brown's Plan B since both Plan B's want to keep civilization alive as we know it. However, Murphy's Plan C focuses on community and curtailment. Murphy's meaning of *community* is a culture where relationships are more important than material goods and consumption as a way of life. He uses the term *curtailment* as more comprehensive than conservation and emphasizes drastically reducing consumption of fossil fuels and material goods in our daily lives.[7] Unlike Plan A, which is the status quo and requires centralization, or Plan B, which preserves the status quo but also requires centralization, Plan C is *decentralized* and concentrates on building local communities.

Plan C is workable, not because we have to convince any government or corporation to change their ways, but because we can just start at the community level. Plan C also envisions a constricted economy in direct contrast to the usual bromides of "growing the economy." To be fair to Lester Brown, his Plan B also incorporates community action but his focus on large solutions at the macroeconomic level makes Plan B unworkable. The takeaway here is that Plan C – starting at the community level and focusing at the level of householder economics – is something we can do right now. I would also argue that the individual can take action directly in his/her life with the community in mind, without having to work as a group. This is important.

As I mentioned before, the individual organism is the unit of evolution by natural selection, as well as the base unit of culture. The individual can move faster and more dramatically than the group. The individual can unite with other individuals into a cohesive group as needed, but then split off again as the circumstances warrant. This is known as a *fission-fusion model*. Chimpanzees and bonobos (our nearest primate relatives) use this kind of society to good advantage. Both species split into subgroups and come together into larger groups based on access to resources.[8] In the case of our primate cousins, this revolves around food patches and reproductive behavior, with mothers and their dependent children being the only stable grouping. In human society, mothers and their dependent children are the default group, but not necessarily stable. As our society fractures and collapses, we see single mothers already disenfranchised and poorer as a demographic group. This should be a clue to community and its value as a strategy.

Humans generally like being in a family. There is a broad narrative in western society that treats families as fodder for sitcoms and horror stories, but this would not be a common theme if the idea of "family" was not ubiquitous. Most people have a deep connection to their biological family. Those of us who do not are in the minority. Even a cursory examination of your friends and acquaintances will support this idea. The family is already well-established as a subgroup for most individuals. The key to creating community - and the key word here is *creating* - is not to remain stuck in the family thrust upon you by your genetic history and upbringing. Since we are large-brained hominids, we can create our own community of like-minded individuals. The question is how. As I have stated before, the key is to become competent as an individual and then bring your expertise to the community group you either create or join. If you want a snappy phrase, you can call it *informed tribalism*.

The advantage of this kind of creative "informed" tribalism is the flexibility of fission-fusion. You can join a group as needed, break off as needed and even belong to overlapping groups. Many people are already doing this with their social networks. In other words, you (the reader) probably already belong to a nascent community. You just have to use it more. Probably the greatest value of Plan C is to articulate what you already do subconsciously. Let us consider social networking and the fission-fusion model in the context of human social organization.

As mentioned in Chapter 3, there are four basic levels of human social organization: bands, tribes, chiefdoms and states. *Chiefdoms* and *states* both feature slavery, with the difference being the greater scale and institutionalization of slavery in the state. Since slavery is not one of our goals in dealing with the collapse of modern civilization, it is fruitless to try and create community on a state level. Nor is it advisable to move along the continuum of social organization towards the chiefdom level, because of its inherent instability due to jockeying for power to be the chief, as well as its dependence on bureaucracy, like a state. We might even theorize that centralized power itself is integral to the problem of collapse. That leaves *bands* or *tribes* as our preferred models of social organization as we try to create intentional communities.

Bands are a problem because they are associated with hunting/gathering and low population densities. Our default social organization thus becomes the tribe, with food resources accumulated by hunting/gathering, horticulture (non-intensive gardening) and pastoralism. However, bands can coalesce into tribes and tribes can likewise break down into smaller groups for specific purposes. Examples are the Native American tribes of the Great Plains, who expanded and contracted their group size based on feasts, political problems and resource gathering (and still do, I might add). Since both bands and tribes have strong familial components, there is a seamless flow between individuals, families, subgroups, bands and tribes. In practical terms, this is fission-fusion writ large.

So a band/tribal structure becomes our structural model for creating community, based on the histories of indigenous cultures that have dealt successfully with the demands of the environment. But why even plan an organizational structure in the first place? Why not just let it arise naturally as collapse worsens and the laws of physics dictate efficient organizational structures? The answer is Plan D. (I bet you thought I forgot about it, didn't you?)

Plan D is *dieoff*. It is based on the observable fact we are now in ecological overshoot and face a drastic drop in population once we cannot "eat" oil at our present rate. Fossil fuels have allowed <u>our</u> overshoot, unlike the Romans who plundered gold from the Gauls and Dacians to keep their society going. Here in the US, we have been plundering the world's fossil fuels since the end of World War II, using 10-20 times more oil than we produce and enjoying a very high standard of living based on mass consumption. Meanwhile 48% of the world's people live on less than $2.00 a day.[9] Nearly 1 billion people suffer from hunger while Americans struggle with obesity.[10] Even if the American lifestyle were not morally reprehensible, it cannot last because of the finite nature of fossil fuels formed millions of years ago. European civilizations are also culpable, but the main culprit is the US.

The logic is simple. We have too many Americans on the planet. It can be argued that IF Americans lived at the same level of affluence as say, Indonesians, we might be able to support 8 billion people by 2025, the projected increase.[11] However, 302 million Americans consume as many barrel of oil equivalents (BOE) per year as 4.8 BILLION Indonesians, a ratio of 16:1. [17,260 million BOE ÷ 302 million Americans = **57.15 BOE per American per year** while 839 million BOE ÷ 232 million Indonesians = **3.62 BOE per Indonesian per year**[12]]

There are 1.47 million kilocalories in a BOE, so converting to our previous measure of kilocalories per day, Americans consume 230,166 kilocalories of energy per person per day and Indonesians consume 14,579. The Indonesians are slightly above the energy capture level of early agriculturalists in SW Asia in 5000 BCE which were estimated to be 12,000 kilocalories per person per day (see Chapter 2).[13]

Using this same logic, if Americans lived at the same affluence level as the Chinese, we might also be able to support 8 billion people on the planet. China has a population of 1.318 billion people and consumes 13,380 million BOE per year or **10.15 BOE per Chinese per year**.[14] In this comparison 302 million Americans consume as many BOE as 1.7 billion

Chinese, a ratio of nearly 6:1. The upshot is we cannot support 8 billion people at the level of American affluence. In order for Americans to have a profligate lifestyle, other nations must suffer.

But are not other industrialized western nations also to blame? Up to a point. If we look at a modern European industrialized country - Germany for example - Americans still consume greater amounts of energy. In a year's time, 82 million Germans consume 2,480 million barrel of oil equivalents, or **30.24 BOE per German per year**.[15] This is only a little over half the energy consumption of the US, and it would take 570 million Germans to consume as much energy as 302 million Americans – 7 times their present population! The problem of overpopulation is not the number of people on the planet, but the greater energy use of <u>one</u> country, the US. It takes energy to do everything and the biggest energy user has the biggest impact, <u>far in excess of actual population numbers</u>.

It is unlikely the US will voluntarily wind down its energy use or curb its population, even though this would be the best course of action to transition into a cleaner, saner world. Instead we are already fighting wars for scarce resources, aided and abetted by other nations around the world worried about their energy supplies. This means there will be more resource wars in the future, more famines, more refugee migrations and more starvation. The result will be dieoff and I look for it to begin during the ten years from 2020 to 2030. To recap, here are the four plans (or scenarios) and their results.

> **Plan A** – business as usual – keep on doing the same thing – **leads to dieoff**
>
> **Plan B** – mobilize to save civilization through renewable resources and somehow get governments and corporations to change their ways – unlikely – **leads to dieoff**
>
> **Plan C** – create community, starting at the individual level – **our only hope**
>
> **Plan D** – **dieoff** – global population rises to 8 billion, then crashes to ½ -2 billion

(**NOTE:** As mentioned before there are many estimates of the real carrying capacity of the earth. I am using a low biological carrying capacity since we have already damaged farmland worldwide through industrial agriculture and poor management. The mismanagement will likely become worse as desperate nations try to adapt to the breakdown of industrial agriculture.)

The astute reader may be mentally calculating my timeline and realize we have only 8 to 18 years (from 2012 - 2020 or 2012 - 2030) to make major changes in how we carry on with our lives. This is a much shorter timeline than most energy analysts and pundits propose, but I think it better to "prepare for the worst and hope for the best." So how to prepare? Remember, the title of this chapter is "Realism." Plan C — create community — is our only hope.

Stay Where You Are

You already have a nascent network of community right where you are. There are friends, acquaintances, colleagues and even family all around you wherever you happen to live. You do not have to save money to buy a little spread in British Columbia where you will have goats and chickens and heat with wood. That was a good strategy in 1970. It no longer fits.

Both my significant other and I were back-to-the-landers in the 1970's, she in Vermont and I in northern Minnesota. There are many present-day advantages to having these life experiences, mostly because we embraced restraint while in our 20's, and are still comfortable with a much-reduced lifestyle. We also learned valuable skills when we had the youthful energy to experiment. However, the many failures of communes, collectives and communities in the 1970's tell the tale of good ideas gone awry. Some of these intentional communities still survive but are rarities. If you have an intentional community in your area, it would be worthwhile to visit and learn how it survived. The longer it has been going, the better.

If you have no intentional community to serve as a model, you will have to build one yourself. As mentioned, a fission-fusion model, with an overarching band/tribe structure offers not only flexibility but also continuity rooted in human history. This starts with the individual. The next step is to accommodate other people as they are affected by collapse and look around for food security. During this process of securing food sources, you are likely to contact like-minded people with whom you can forge community. Let us now look at ways to transition from changing your mental landscape into physical action. The key to making a seamless transition is *management* of what you already have.

8 WATER & FOOD SECURITY

Food, shelter and clothing are usually regarded as the three essentials to life. Water is taken for granted even though it is more important than food. You can do without food for some time, but not without water. In 1981, ten Irish political prisoners went on a hunger strike in Long Kesh prison in Northern Ireland because of their demand to be treated as political prisoners rather than criminals. They drank small amounts of water but no food. The longest any of them lasted was 73 days without food before dying.[1] In comparison, a person can only go 3-5 days without any water at all. Water regulates your body temperature, moistens your tissues, carries nutrients to cells, and generally keeps your human engine working smoothly.[2] Compared to water, food is just fuel.

In the Pacific Northwest where we live, there is plenty of water. Indeed, on the western side of the Cascades the problem is often too much water. As global warming ratchets up volatility in climate and weather patterns, we are getting later, colder, wetter springs, even as other parts of the US are getting earlier, warmer and drier spring seasons. The fire season in the arid western US starts earlier every year and the fires are more numerous and more dangerous. Meanwhile, in the Pacific Northwest we have more grey days and less temperature variance. This means we have to manage our water differently than someone in southern California, for instance. My water situation on the farm, with a well, septic system and irrigation for crops, is likely quite different from your own.

Most readers will not have their own well but will instead have a water supply managed by someone else, probably a municipal water district. This means you do not make the decision about whether there is fluoride or chlorine or other chemicals in the water. You also do not make the decision about what you pay for your water. However, you can manage the water you receive. This is where the idea of reduction of inputs becomes critical (or *curtailment*, to use Murphy's term).

There are plentiful ways to save water in the bathroom. Low-flush toilets are becoming the norm, but you can also save your urine for use on your garden (easier for men but still doable for women). The recommended dilution ratio for using human urine on crops is 20:1. Just to be safe, you may want to use your urine on ornamentals or tree crops. This is what I do. Urine, whether human or other mammal, is high in urea, which is 46% nitrogen.[3] It is a potent fertilizer and useful as an antifungal treatment for fruit and ornamental trees and shrubs. Industrial agriculture already uses bovine urea (separated cow urine) on crops like grain and blueberries, so if you are squeamish about this topic, think again. You can also just flush your toilet fewer times per day. If you save only one flush per day you will save between 1.6 (US standard since 1992) and 3.5 (old toilets) gallons of water per day.[4] Saving only a gallon or so a day may not seem like much, but neither is the actual drinking water requirement for a human. We only need two quarts per person per day for drinking – a gallon if it is a hot day.

Simple conservation while showering or washing hands is helpful too, as your shower and faucets run at the rate of 2.5 gallons per minute in standard homes hooked up to municipal water systems. Conservation while cooking and doing other household chores is another aspect of a conservation, or "reduced" lifestyle. The relevant phrase here is "Reduce, reuse, recycle."

In the larger scheme of things, better water management in the home will not reverse the damage done to freshwater supplies by industry and industrial agriculture. However, it does give you management experience at the individual and household level, as well as preserving your supply and saving money. If water is rationed in the future, you will be used to the idea of managing your water wisely and adjust accordingly.

Management can also be applied to food waste. Just as people can manage their water through wise reduction and conservation of use, so too they can better manage the food they are already buying. An ongoing study by anthropologists at the University of Arizona which started by tracking garbage in the 1970's has found that 40-50% of food produced in the US actually goes to waste. The majority of it is left in the field and 14% is wasted in the home after retail purchase. Coincidentally, food also accounts for 14% of the solid waste stream.[5] The most comprehensive report on postharvest food losses came in 1995 with the Economic Research Service (ERS) of the USDA breaking out retail and consumer food loss by food categories. For example, 32% of grain products were wasted in 1995, with 2% of that loss in retail and 30% in the home. The numbers were the same for fresh fruit and vegetables (each with 2% retail and 30% consumer waste) but if the fruits and vegetables were processed, the waste dropped to 1% at retail and 15% at the consumer level. Dry beans and meats/poultry/fish had low levels of waste comparable to processed fruits and vegetables, but eggs and dairy products were wasted at the higher rate like fresh produce.[6] Presumably, canning and freezing your own produce or produce you buy in bulk and in season (and therefore cheaper) would cut your food waste in half, just like industry processing.

The main culprit in the waste of your food and food dollar is likely your refrigerator. Having a big cold box in which to store a lot of "stuff" encourages buying a lot of "stuff." A refrigerator is like a backpack. No matter how big it is, it will get filled up. Then the resulting clutter makes it difficult to see what you actually have. Leftovers, bits and pieces, odds and ends – they all build up until they have to be thrown out. We all do it. However, you can trick yourself by filling up one shelf of your refrigerator with half-gallon plastic jugs of water. This will cut down on your tendency to buy more stuff, provide an emergency water supply if needed, and even out any fluctuations in temperature, since the water jugs act as a thermodynamic storage device for conserving energy. Your refrigerator will also run less, since you will have less uncontrolled air to leak out every time the door is opened. This idea also works for freezers. In short, better management of the food you already have will achieve significant gains However, real food security requires drilling down into how we actually get our food.

Food Security Through Risk Management

Food security is the focus of solutions presented in this book. It is translatable to all climates and all topographies. It starts with *risk management*. There are four levels:

1) Grow your own food – **1ˢᵗ party** management - the highest level of control and safety.

2) Buy from someone you trust – **2ⁿᵈ party** management – know your farmer.

3) Buy from stores with regulation by a **3ʳᵈ party** – certified organic, regular supermarkets and shops regulated by government agencies.

4) Don't worry – no management – lowest level of control and safety.

Growing your own food is obviously preferable if you want to control what goes into your mouth and stomach. Not only do you know the history of the food, but you get to choose the variety grown. Do you want heirloom St. Valery carrots? Not a problem if you grow them yourself, but try asking for them in a store and you will just get blank looks. When you grow your own food, you may get some untoward consequences, like drift from your neighbor's rose spraying, but you control much more of your immediate environment. There will always be a random chance of failure or mutation, vagaries of weather, etc., but you have greater control.

Buying from someone you trust is the next best option. Not only does the farmer get the <u>direct</u> sale from the consumer, cutting out the middlemen, but you have the opportunity to find out how the farmer grows food. Getting to know the farmer means you will find out what kinds of sprays he/she uses, how much energy is consumed with tractors and hand labor, what conservation practices are used, AND whether or not the farmer gets a fair price. You can even request specific kinds of produce or meats to be grown on contract. It is sometimes said the safest way to buy food is to know the first name of the farmer who grew it. (This could be you!)

Buying from stores regulated by a 3ʳᵈ party includes stores specializing in "certified organic" and all other food stores. It is important to realize that supermarkets, neighborhood grocery stores and even convenience stores have quite a bit of government regulation keeping them on the straight and narrow. So-called "natural food co-ops" are no longer the alternatives they once were and have adapted to the modern business model where profit is paramount. Since I was involved in food co-ops in Minneapolis from their beginning in 1970-71, I have some background in the co-op movement and I feel competent to be critical. Since I have been growing food using organic methods since the 1950's when I was a small child and have been an environmentalist since the late 1960's, I feel qualified to critique "certified organic." Regulation by a 3rd party, where you are not part of the relationship, is the problem. It makes little difference what organization is doing the regulating, because you have lost control.

The *lowest level of safety* is to not even worry about it. This is the level of dumpster diving or taking food handed to you on the street. Believe it or not, this may sometimes be safer than buying a meal at a fast food outlet. Those with experience working in fast food outlets or even in restaurants understand how things can go wrong under pressure. There are also larger considerations of chemicals and toxins added during processing that may be many times greater than the risk one takes by picking up an apple or an onion (i.e. an unprocessed food item) from a dumpster. The point here is that <u>control</u> determines the risk factor. Control and risk are in inverse proportions. The more control you exert over your own food security, the greater your safety and the lower your risk.

Most people rely on a third party to keep their food safe and there is a significant number of Americans who make a differentiation between third parties. For example, a lot of people assume buying at a food co-op automatically means their food is safe. This is a dangerous assumption, as you are just as likely to get a life-threatening toxin at a natural foods co-op as at a corporate supermarket. The differences between the two are mostly packaging. A little bit of my experience with food co-ops and organic food marketing may prove useful.

In 1970, I joined a buying club called the Ecology Co-op. It was run out of a church basement in Dinkytown, near the east bank of the University of Minnesota in Minneapolis. There was a master order sheet and we handed in our order each week and got the food a few days later. Everything was organic, a classification unregulated at the time (before state and USDA organic certification programs) and based on trust. When the order came in, volunteers like me separated out the orders into bags and boxes and marked each one with the member's name for pickup. The members paid for their order when they picked it up. This buying club also took food stamps. Back then the food stamp program was still focused on its original purpose of getting rid of excess agricultural commodities rather than denigrating and insulting poor people. It is interesting to note that Clifford Hardin, Richard Nixon's first Secretary of Agriculture, actually enlarged the food stamp program before he was replaced by Earl Butz in 1971.[7]

The Ecology Co-op had the usual problems: 1) not enough volunteers willing to do the actual work of distribution, 2) the necessity of ONE person being the gatekeeper, and 3) eventual breakdown as the organization became swamped by the logistics required to keep things straight. At one point, several of us went door-to-door to each of the members to try and get them more involved. This had predictable results, i.e. no results. Now remember, this was in the fall of 1970 when activism was at its peak in Minneapolis. The timeline makes it even sadder.

Several months earlier, Nixon had invaded Cambodia and the antiwar movement ramped up its efforts. During May 1970, four students were shot and killed at Kent State (Ohio) and two students were shot and killed at Jackson State (Mississippi), although this latter action started because of a civil rights issue. At the University of Minnesota, students went on strike and we were successful in shutting down the University for the rest of the spring and summer. Classes resumed in the fall. That summer, there were some difficult demonstrations in Dinkytown because of a vacant lot that had been turned into a "people's park" and was then torn down by the police (similar but on a much smaller scale than the People's Park riots in Berkeley the year before). Life was exciting but also dangerous. I had to run for my life more than once. ("Get that red-haired guy!")

There was another group of people in 1970 who had started a distribution "club," for want of a better word (rational solutions often go begging for the right descriptive word or phrase) at a community center. This was called "People's Pantry" and was run by a few folks who bought grains, beans, nuts and other foodstuffs in bulk and then weighed out as much or as little as you wanted. You could go in and buy just a pound or two of rice at just a little above the wholesale price of a 50-pound bag. This was a great benefit to all us "dirty hippies" who were suddenly able to eat well on the few pennies we could scrape up by selling beads or underground newspapers on the street corners.

There was quite a bit of "buzz" about eating natural foods at both the Ecology Co-op and People's Pantry and I was also reading quite a bit about nutrition at the time. Another seminal influence was the *Whole Earth Catalog*, which opened up a whole new world of ideas. I and my roommates became vegetarians that fall and I continued to be a vegetarian until 1981, with a few relapses (e.g. eating some venison on a canoe trip). 1970 was also when the environmental movement really took off with the first Earth Day being a major event. That spring I leafleted and sold books and buttons for Earth Day while I sold underground newspapers.

In the winter of 1970-71, several people came together to start the first food co-op in Minneapolis, called North Country Co-op. I was involved from the start, but was more interested in the grunt work rather than going to meetings – a bias I favor to this day. There was a natural progression from People's Pantry into North Country Co-op and a palpable sense of *intentional community centered on food*. The new emphasis on co-ops and actually doing physical work fit in well with the antiwar movement, and the bifurcation between mainstream culture and counterculture was obvious just through the bureaucratic nonsense people had to go through to set up a store. The red tape was unbelievable, but then things have not changed much. In 2008 there was an incredible amount of bureaucratic nonsense involved in expanding the Ferndale, Washington Farmers Market (which I started in 2006). It should also be remembered that those who study collapse of civilizations (such as Joseph Tainter, mentioned in Chapter 3), invariably point to the role of bureaucracy in furthering collapse. If anyone has lingering doubts about the waste of time and resources "working within the system," an objective look at the Democratic Party should dispel any notions about change from within. They are as phony as they were in 1968.

During my co-op years, I heard some criticism of starting from the retail side of food security. People asked why we did not start with farmer co-ops, such as the Finnish farmer co-ops started in northern Minnesota between 1900 and the 1930's. What people did not realize is that it is very difficult to start with nothing. In classical economics, *land* was considered as one of the three factors of production, along with *capital* and *labor*. Land is still important. Even in our technological world, where Americans use energy at an average of 230,000 kilocalories per person per day, it still takes some space to grow something. For us "dirty hippies" who did not have anything in 1970, it was more important to fit into the interstices of the prevalent economic system. In other words, as the hand of the status quo came down on us, we could squirt out between the fingers. Buying in bulk and passing along the savings worked – and it worked right away!

One should also remember the Rochdale Principles were part of the co-op movement from early on. In 1844, the first consumer cooperative was started in Rochdale, England. A small society of 28 members formed in this town and started renting a storefront, stocking it with the modern-day equivalent of $140 in staple food. They established some key principles which are still given at least lip service by food co-ops today.

1) Open membership
2) One person, one vote
3) Limited return on investment
4) Return of surplus
5) Continuing education
6) Cooperation among cooperatives
7) Concern for community (this was added in 1995).[8]

The key to the Rochdale idea is not necessarily the principles, which are often manipulated by the cliques that run present-day food co-ops, but rather that they started with almost nothing. The original Rochdale group saw a need, utilized what little they had, and got the job done. This is still a good direction for us as we move nearer and nearer to the collapse of a civilization hooked on cheap energy. Small groups using what little resources they have and focused on getting the job done stand a better chance of providing for their members. This is entirely different from food co-ops today, who have strayed far afield from their original model.

Here is an example of how good organizations go bad. In 1975, a schism arose in the Minneapolis food co-ops. A Marxist subgroup calling itself the Co-op Organization (CO) seized North Country Co-op, the People's Warehouse, and a few other stores by force. The response from the rest of the co-op community was to eschew violence, start a new organization, the All Co-op Assembly (ACA), and let the CO keep the stores they had seized (to be fair, some of the CO worked at these stores prior to takeover). They also boycotted the CO stores and started a new warehouse. Things came to a head the following winter (early 1976) when North Country Co-op was retaken with the help of the Minneapolis Police, who were glad to be on our side for a change. By the summer of 1976, the CO had run the warehouse business into the ground and court action returned what was left to the original warehouse board of directors.[9] The CO-run co-ops continued for several more years but then dribbled away as the Minneapolis and St. Paul co-ops morphed into what is usually called the "Whole Foods model." This is simply a patina of righteousness with no substantial difference from mainstream businesses.

As early as 1972, there were plentiful disagreements in the Minneapolis food co-ops. There was a lot of backbiting and nonsensical argumentation that wasted a lot of time. For example, I was selling sprouts to the co-ops at the time and was kept out of sales at one store simply so another person could sell sprouts. (So much for Rochdale Principles 2 and 6!) Also at this time, I sat for quite a long time at a co-op meeting listening to an endless discussion about whether the co-op should carry white flour and white sugar. After what seemed like hours, I finally piped up with, "Why don't we just vote on it?" Dead silence ensued and finally a friend of mine leaned over and whispered, "We don't vote anymore. We come to a consensus." (So much for Rochdale Principle 2!) Needless to say I got up and left. These two examples are indicative of where food co-ops were heading as early as 1972. The people running the store on a day-to-day basis were not above changing the rules as they saw fit, which naturally evolved into the rule by cliques you now see in present-day co-ops.

There was another problem that had surfaced by 1975, which I call the "business major from Oberlin syndrome" (named after a friend of mine who actually <u>was</u> a business major from Oberlin). Once the co-ops had been growing for some time and had a certain amount of gravitas and momentum, a growing demographic of young progressives started to drift into the co-op movement. By 1973, Nixon had wound down the Vietnam War and the draft ended. The actual end of hostilities on April 30, 1975 created a vacuum for social progressives looking for a cause, even with the growth of the environmental and women's movements. The co-op movement held out a lot of promise and these young liberal progressives were willing to put in copious amounts of organizing, as well as the real physical work of stocking shelves and running a store. Make no mistake, these liberals were doing what they thought was the right thing and were very dedicated. However, they suffered from two unwarranted assumptions: 1) it is possible to work within the system for real change, and 2) the American nation state has some validity.

Those of us who had been "shot at and missed – shit at and hit" over the years knew any change in the mainstream political and economic system had to be forced from without. Even when some legal changes were made (for example the Clean Air and Water Acts), they needed constant challenges to power from the bottom up. They were in constant danger of being whitewashed out of existence through their loopholes and the pitifully small fines that were levied quickly became just another cost of doing business. This cost was then passed on to consumers and citizens of other countries. As for the validity of the nation state, it was becoming crystal clear to many of us the US was collapsing under the weight of its inability to pay for its wars of aggression and the costs of empire. A lot of us were already fleeing the cities and heading back to the land in order to survive. Unfortunately, the "business majors from Oberlin" still had faith in the mainstream culture and never were part of the counterculture that started the co-ops. The results were inevitable.

As I mentioned in my preface, the commies fought the anarchists in the co-ops and the liberals won. After the Vietnam War ended, the focus of co-ops around the country (not just in Minneapolis) changed, from counterculture distribution of cheap healthy food to mainstream grocery stores that were liberal in outlook and catered to high-end consumers.

Some people may argue this is a good thing, but there is no longer anything revolutionary about the co-op movement. The main thrust of the co-op movement is now to become as much like Whole Foods as possible. Since Whole Foods usurped the food co-op model to begin with, this is more than a little ironic.

Whole Foods was started as Safer Way by John Mackey and Renee Lawson in Austin, Texas in 1978 with an investment of $45,000. Mackey was working at a vegetarian co-op in Austin, where he met Lawson. They started Safer Way as a supermarket and natural foods restaurant. Profit was their motivation from the beginning, rather than an alternative structure. Two years later, they merged with another store and adopted the name Whole Foods.[10] It is instructive to note that working in a co-op helped John Mackey see the business and social potential of natural foods. The success of Whole Foods today is a testament to the power of feeding people, as well as a movement's weakness to being co-opted by those whose aim is profit.

The Whole Foods model I find so egregious in modern co-ops is based on touting a store as "different" and "better" than corporate supermarkets, while using the same corporate business practices. For example, Whole Foods is focused on "certified organic" produce and brightly lit stores that use incredible amounts of energy to make the consumer feel good. Their large capitalization drives out small local stores and caters to a false sense of quality and equality. They have similar problems with *E. coli*-tainted foods as other supermarkets and have their own problems with wage levels, unions, and corporate responsibility. There is an extreme focus on marketing and their so-called community meetings are largely advertising venues. All of these criticisms can be made of food co-ops in the United States, from Bozeman to Bellingham (two co-ops I have had experience with in the last twenty years). I would be happy if these co-ops would just admit they are like corporate stores and cut the baloney.

The point of discussing the history of co-ops and their current problems is not to take cheap shots at egregious marketing or deception, although the co-ops I am familiar with certainly deserve it. The takeaway is that even a co-op movement started by well-meaning radicals can fail over time. Any system can have a florescence and a descent, no matter how righteous the individuals involved. However, when a <u>system</u> fails, it leaves a carcass that is not disposed of easily. So if the food co-ops are no different from Whole Foods or your local supermarket chain, why put them in a different category? They are still a 3rd party to your food security and you have more risk buying food from them than you do from a farmer. It is simple logic.

The same can be said for organic certification, which takes 3rd party certification to a new level. A brief history of organic methods versus "certified organic" may be helpful here. As noted in my preface, I grew up on a dairy farm in Minnesota, and we had a large garden every year. I started gardening at an early age and we did not use commercial fertilizers on our garden crops – just manure. Chemical fertilizers were used on cash crops, but the main fertility for the fields came from cow manure. Crop rotation was practiced as far back as I can remember and there was a mix of crops and animals on the farm. Without knowing it, we were following many of the organic methods codified by Sir Albert Howard and J.I. Rodale in the 1940's. This was before Earl Butz, Nixon's Secretary of Agriculture, started urging American farmers to plow up pastures and marginal land in order to plant "fencerow to fencerow" to grow commodities for international export markets. Back in the 1950's and 1960's commercial fertilizer use was increasing, aided and abetted by chemical factories who needed to market new products to replace their wartime products. However, the real uptick in commercial fertilizer, pesticide and herbicide use came in the 1970's. By this time farming had become as commercialized as other American businesses. In the time period from 1933 to 1970, farming changed focus from soil fertility generated on the farm and utilized by human labor to fertility inputs purchased from the nonfarm sector and utilized by machines.[11]

The number and size of farms also changed significantly. In 1935 there were 6.8 million farms in the US, but by 1970 this number had shrunk to 3.0 million.[12] Most of the reduction came in the period 1950 to 1970, when the number of farms dropped from 5.5 million to 3.0 million. After 1970, the number of farms continued to decrease at a slower rate until it hit 2.0 million in 1990 and then leveled off to about the same numbers today.

During this time period, 1950-1970, the size of farms increased from 205 acres to 400 acres.[13] Since 1970, farm size has not changed dramatically and in 2007 the average American farm was 418 acres.[14]

My family was part of this demographic of farmers leaving the farm and consolidation into bigger and bigger farms. The rise of corporate farming since 1970, with its emphasis on chemical controls, increased mechanization and low labor inputs, only accelerated a trend that had already begun decades earlier. In our case, it became harder and harder to make a living and we finally left the farm in 1965 and moved into town. Even then, we had struggled along for nine years after my dad died in 1956 before we finally threw in the towel.

By 1970, I was already an environmentalist and had started making plans to leave the city behind. When I did purchase some land in 1971 and started growing my own food, I followed the organic methods I knew from my childhood, as well as those I learned from the Rodale series of books and magazines, like the *Encyclopedia of Organic Gardening* and *How to Grow Vegetables and Fruits by the Organic Method*. These two books are still on my reference shelf.

The Rodale Institute got its original vision from Sir Albert Howard, a British agronomist sent to India to teach western agricultural practices to the Indians. He soon realized the indigenous Indian farmers had more to teach him than he could teach them, especially in dealing with animal and plant diseases. He utilized regular-sized farming plots in order to get a better overall integrative effect of fertilizer, soil and management variables, rather than the small "handkerchief-sized plots" still used today by most US experimental stations. His results proved the debilitating effects of chemical fertilizers on plant health and nutrition and his work is still relevant. His magnum opus, *An Agricultural Testament,* was published in 1940.[15] Although mainstream agricultural scientists dismissed his work, it was seized upon by J. I. Rodale in the United States, who started publishing the magazine *Organic Farming and Gardening* in May, 1942. This magazine is still published by Rodale Institute as *Organic Gardening*.[16]

The organic method's chief differentiation from chemical agriculture is its dependence on compost and organic matter. The organic paradigm is to "feed the soil" which is quite different from industrial agriculture's paradigm of "feed the plant." As noted, the period from 1933 to 1970 saw a decrease in farm-generated soil amendments in the US and an increase in fertilizers purchased in the marketplace. This followed the commercialization of farming and the application of factory-style business practices borrowed from the manufacturing sector. The result was that manure became a waste stream rather than a source of fertility. The resulting lack of fertility due to lack of manure necessitated purchased fertilizer inputs, which the manufacturing sector were happy to provide at ever-increasing prices. Soon this business relationship became a vicious circle and farmers were trapped on a treadmill.

As the US economic system became more and more addicted to cheap energy between 1945 and 1970, market pressures forced farmers to "get big or get out," a phrase first uttered in the 1950's by Ezra Taft Benson, Dwight Eisenhower's Secretary of Agriculture. Earl Butz, Richard Nixon's second Secretary of Agriculture, counseled something similar in the 1970's when he urged farmers to "adapt or die."[17] The result of these attitudes and policies were energy intensification, higher capital requirements, depleted soils, and degraded nutritional quality of the food produced on these depleted soils.

The antidotes to the inter-related problems of degraded soil and degraded food were organic methods. It was no accident that reduced capital needs and reduced fossil fuel inputs went hand-in-hand with the organic method. It was also no accident that organic methods were attractive to us "dirty hippies." It was a way to grow food that was nutritious and low-cost. It fell in quite naturally with the mindset and vision that started the original food co-ops. Organic methods are still our best alternatives for transitioning into a post-fossil fuel future.

While Earl Butz and his acolytes were spending so much time and energy changing mainstream American agriculture for the worse in the 1970's, more and more progressive small-scale farmers were adopting direct marketing to food co-ops and farmers markets. This movement grew rapidly in the 1970's and 80's until it became a problem of trust in what the word *organic* really meant. Until 1990, the USDA dismissed organic methods as nonviable and just ignored them. The trend, after all, was more mechanization and more chemicals, aided and abetted by the USDA's own policies. However, as organic products reached critical mass, the federal government decided it was time to take control of this new label – *organic*. In 1990 Congress passed the Organic Foods Production Act which established a National Organic Program (NOP) and empowered the USDA's Agricultural Marketing Service (AMS) to administer it. The National Organic Standards Board (NOSB) was set up to develop standards for organic production and what substances could be added to food products and still be "organic." Congress expected implementation to begin in 1993, but lack of funds and an extended public comment period pushed back implementation of the new label. The NOP actually went into effect in February 2001.[18]

The NOP established procedures for what constituted "organic" and the focus from the beginning was on marketing (administered by the AMS) and continued right through implementation. Dan Glickman, Secretary of Agriculture in 2000, admitted as much in his remarks on the final organic standards, "Let me be clear about one other thing. The organic label is a marketing tool. It is not a statement about food safety. Nor is 'organic' a value judgment about nutrition or quality."[19] In other words, the USDA turned the whole idea of organic methods and organic food on its head. What started as a soil building paradigm became a marketing tool.

The *organic* label owes a lot to the rise of branding in corporate culture in the 1990's. As Naomi Klein pointed out in *No Logo* (2000), by the mid-1980's management theorists realized successful corporations had to produce brands rather than products. The defining moment was the purchase of the Kraft *brand* in 1988 by Philip Morris for six times its asset value.[20] The reason for the higher price? The value of the brand name. This was not just a perfunctory share price add-on for "good will," a practice common since the 19th century. This was a new paradigm. The brand name itself was worth money. All through the 1990's and on up to the present day, we can see the results of this emphasis on branding in the business world. Brand names, logos and labels are everywhere. It is no surprise the USDA's Agricultural *Marketing* Service would use the logic of branding in developing organic standards after 1990. Whether or not they <u>intended</u> to co-opt the organic movement by developing the *organic* brand is beside the point – it worked.

Now the term "organic" is quite different from its original meaning, just as present-day food co-ops have strayed far afield from their original purpose. Huge corporate factory farms use massive amounts of energy to churn out products that are certified organic simply because they limit themselves to chemical synthetic additives allowed by the USDA. Small-scale farmers are going out of business, even as more and more "organic" foods fill supermarket shelves. The problem for the consumer is still one of trust. Even though something is labeled organic does not mean it is either safe or nutritious. It only means the farmer and processor have followed the paper trail set out by the USDA. A simple example from the county I live in is instructive.

In 2010, organic growers, food bank farms and home gardeners in Whatcom County in Washington state were hit by *aminopyralid* contamination. Aminopyralid is a chemical herbicide manufactured by Dow AgroSciences that targets broadleaf plants and is used to control thistles in hay crops, for example. When this hay was fed to cows, the aminopyralid remained active and passed unchanged through the cow and even through the composting of the cow's manure.[21] In Whatcom County composted dairy solids sold commercially as "organic" compost still retained traces of this powerful herbicide and resulted in contamination of broadleaf crops like beans and tomatoes in home gardens and on organic farms. However, the local food co-op in Bellingham continued to sell contaminated food as "organic" because the growers had followed all the rules formulated by the USDA. The state extension agents concurred these crops were still "organic" because procedures had been followed. The real issue of whether milk from cows fed hay grown with this herbicide was actually safe to drink was never addressed publicly. Nor was produce contaminated with this herbicide pulled off store shelves. The local food co-op and some organic growers in Whatcom County just ignored the issue and hoped it would fade away, which it did. I do not use dairy compost, so contamination on my farm was never a problem.

In the aminopyralid case, contamination of milk and produce was a real safety issue which the organic growers and the local food co-op just ignored. Yet at the same time, they advertised their product as safe <u>because</u> it was certified organic. This is deception pure and simple. For another example of deception consider the following quote from an article in the magazine *BioCycle* in 2011: "BioCycle happened across a commercial composter as well as a farmer who worked manure from a single horse into the soil in two hoophouses. Each reported experiencing problems with aminopyralid. The composter declined to go on the record because he was concerned about jeopardizing his organic certification."[22]

Once again, reliance on a *system* – in this case 3rd party certification – proved inferior to either 1st party or 2nd party management. If you cannot grow it yourself, you should find someone else you trust to grow it for you. Risk management is a straightforward way to deal directly with food safety. If you think in risk management terms, you may still end up buying from a grower branded as "certified organic," but you will be buying because you know and trust the grower. This is a very important difference. Know your farmer. Do not just wander into a supermarket or co-op and feel safe because of a label. It is a false sense of security.

Even if you are willing to buy directly from a farmer you know and trust, there is still a major structural problem because of overall low prices for food in the US. In fact, the real conundrum in small-scale farming is the price aspect of food security. Food prices are generally regarded as *inelastic* because of the size of the human stomach. (Physiology trumps economics.) This means you cannot count on increasing sales when you decrease price, unlike automobiles or widgets. Many farmers and gardeners, especially at farmers markets, fail to grasp the long-term implications of food price inelasticity. Short-term price reductions can give you a short-term influx of cash, but over time profit margins are whittled down to nothing. Soon enough, the farmer or market gardener is making far less than minimum wage for their labor. Meanwhile, the corporate farms that are part of an *extended infrastructure* – farm to factory to wholesaler to supermarket that are all controlled by just a few companies – use their market muscle to control prices and drive small-scale farmers out of business. Many corporate farms also get massive subsidies from the federal and state governments that are unavailable to small-scale farmers. All of these structural problems in the marketplace work against the small-scale farmer.

In addition to market advantages unavailable to small-scale growers, there are structural problems in getting fair wages for farmworkers. Farm work is seasonal and dependent on massive pools of illegal immigrants in many parts of the country. I worked as a migrant laborer for eight years in the Pacific Northwest and California. Most of my co-workers were illegal aliens from Mexico − or "undocumented workers" if you prefer the politically correct term. All of these Mexican nationals were being exploited and treated as subhuman, just as I was. Housing was deplorable, the greedy farmers often tried to cheat their workers, and the local townspeople and law enforcement targeted illegal aliens as a matter of course and according to their ingrained cultural behaviors based on white privilege. Since there was such a large pool of willing workers, wages were depressed. For example, I got $8.00 a bin for picking Red Delicious apples in Washington in 1978. In 1993, <u>fifteen years later,</u> the bin price was still $8.00! There is a very good reason that illegal aliens transition from farm work into construction, landscaping and other jobs as soon as possible. There is more money to be made.

This wage disparity also exists for the people who work on corporate factory farms, in corporate slaughterhouses and in corporate processing plants, especially when the business depends on illegal aliens as a significant part of its workforce. Documentaries and books abound on inequities in the workplace and we seem to be returning back to the "bad old days" profiled so well by Upton Sinclair in *The Jungle* (1906).[23] This book blew the whistle on dangerous and unsafe practices in American slaughterhouses at the turn of the 20th century and led to pure food laws. However, we still have plenty of unsafe food that is marketed to us in a deceptive manner. The small-scale farmer is squeezed by wage and price problems, as are those who do the work in the corporate food system. It may not even be viable to buy directly from the farmer for much longer, since small-scale farmers are going under and corporate farms are untrustworthy. In other words, we may be forced to grow our own food anyway. The time has come for a *paradigm shift*.

After years of banging my head against the wall advocating for a fair wage for farmers, I finally shifted my own paradigm in January, 2011. At a panel discussion where I was one of those on the panel, I suggested we give up trying to get higher prices paid to farmers and just concentrate on growing our own – starting with 5%, 10% or 15% of our food needs and then increasing the amounts as we learn more skills. Surprisingly, this elicited a generally favorable response from people in the audience – quite unlike the pushback I always get when I tell people they need to pay more for food in order to support the farmer.

It is foolish to make a big deal about one audience in one town in one year, but other attitudes indicate I may be onto something. Even the most progressive commentators on food pricing focus on low prices for poor people, even though this means the farmer becomes poorer than the people he is supporting. Even the most liberal-minded socialists have to be dragged, kicking and screaming, into any future scenario where the farmer makes as much money as a corporate manager or college professor. It just ain't gonna happen. Consequently, I suggest we just give up on fair prices for farmers. This means we are left to the mercy of corporate farms and big business – unless we grow our own food. To recap, the food safety aspect of food security is a relatively simple task, but incorporating living wages into food security quickly turns sour. Consequently, we need to start at the most individualistic level of risk management and "do for ourselves." It seems we have come full circle, back to the 1970's. As I am fond of saying lately, "Them dirty hippies was right."

9 ACCOUNTING FOR SUSTAINABILITY

Faced with a constricting economy due to constricting energy supply and increasing prices, we need to keep track of how much energy we use and what we get for our energy inputs. This means we need a solid accounting system that is: 1) small-scale, 2) adaptable to our own individual situations, 3) simple to use and 4) effective. The sustainable model I have developed over the last few years fits all four criteria. It starts with a spreadsheet.

I use a series of spreadsheets I developed myself. They enable me to effectively and sustainably grow food for my family while providing data for my research. My spreadsheets can also be simplified for the kitchen gardener (for your own household or a small community). They will provide useful information you need to decide what to plant year to year. If you are developing a market garden to provide you with a basic income, this system can be scaled up and expanded in many ways. It is infinitely adaptable and requires only motivation and simple computer skills. There are commercial software products available, but I don't feel they are worth the expense. It is better to create something tailored specifically to your own needs.

I first trained on Lotus 1-2-3 in 1985. By that time Lotus had already changed the face of accounting and Microsoft soon copied the look and feel in their own spreadsheet program, Excel. I use Excel, but those who want a free spreadsheet program can download a copy of Open Office Calc from Apache Open Office at (http://www.openoffice.org/). This is open source software, which means the source code is open to all for modification, distribution, etc. It works across all platforms and you can go back and forth between Calc and Excel. There is also a word processor in the suite called Write and other programs similar to the Microsoft Office suite. Since I use Excel, I will do all my examples in Excel and you can adapt the concepts and techniques to your own spreadsheet program.

Let us start with a list of what you want to grow. This is usually based on what you eat plus some new fruits and vegetables you want to try and think might do well in your area. You should also try some new varieties of what you already grow so you get an expanding database of what works well as the climate changes. This is where *diversity* becomes your friend and ally. I plant 20-30 different varieties of potatoes every year in order to keep the seed lines going. Every year different varieties rise to the top in the yield categories. Last year (2011) the top potato varieties were Bintje, French fingerlings and a new variety I developed from saving seed balls, which I then grew out in the field. This is the same process Luther Burbank used in the 1870's to develop the Burbank potato. His potato was used to develop the Burbank Russet, the signature potato of Idaho and the standard potato used in French fries (also known as "Freedom fries" from 2003-2006 when the US House of Representatives was on the outs with France!).

Diversity is one of the principle drivers of the organic method and it is based in evolution by natural selection, just like culture. Weather conditions change from day to day in most places. Now the climate is changing too. There are day-to-day differences in how you manage your crops, whether it is weeding or watering. There are random events every day that can impact your crops, like critters and sprays from your neighbors. Diversity through sexual recombination allows plants and animals to be better positioned to take advantage of new conditions in the environment. Diversity through random mutations serves the same function. Diversity in your choice of crops and varieties is a way for you to participate in the same flow. Diversity works in concert with feeding the soil to keep the mini-ecosystem in your garden functioning properly. Diversity should be part of your plan.

Here is a list of what I grew last year (2011). In 2012 I am adding some crops I usually grow but did not last year, like kohlrabi and rutabagas.

Apples	Artichokes	Arugula	Asparagus
Barley	Basil	Beet greens	Beets
Blackberries	Blueberries	Broccoli	Brussels sprouts
Buckwheat	Cabbage	Cardoon	Carrots
Cauliflower	Celeriac	Celery	Chard
Cherries	Cucumbers	Currants	Dry beans
Edamame	Favas	Fennel	Flour corn
Garlic	Gooseberries	Green beans	Kale
Leeks	Lettuce	Mustard	Oats
Onions	Parsley	Parsnips	Pears
Peppers	Plums	Potatoes	Pumpkins
Purple beans	Purple orach	Radicchio	Radishes
Raspberries	Rhubarb	Salsify	Shallots
Shell peas	Snap peas	Snow peas	Sorrel
Spelt	Spinach	Strawberries	Summer squash
Sunchokes	Sweet corn	Tomatillos	Tomatoes
Triticale	Wax beans	Wheat	Winter squash

This list of 68 fruits, vegetables, grain and dry beans includes some things with which you may be unfamiliar, like purple orach. Orach, *Altriplex hortensis*, is a member of the Amaranth family and is also called mountain spinach and saltbush. It is highly tolerant of salty soils and very hardy. I plant some every year, but it also comes up as volunteers. (We like volunteers!) Purple orach is a deep consistent purple, although there are a few reversions to green-leaved plants. It can be eaten raw, but I like it cooked. It makes a wonderful addition to pizza.

After making a list (and checking it twice!) you can now start looking at seed catalogs. I get at least twenty every year and most of them are just for reference. I buy the bulk of my seeds from Fedco, a cooperative in Maine, but I also get odds and ends from a handful of other companies. I also saved 46% of my own seed for 2012, including seed potatoes. Seed catalogs are not only full of things to buy but also practical advice. They are sometimes called "gardener's porn" and it is hard not to get carried away while looking at all the different varieties on offer. I suggest you order early, as the home gardener's market is growing every year and early orders have a higher chance of getting their orders filled. I have my orders in by December 31st, although I do extra ordering during the spring. I like to have enough extra seed in case of emergencies (like a breakdown in the overall system or companies going out of business).

After you get your seed, it is time for the data entry in your spreadsheet. In Excel or Calc you can use multiple tabs. My main spreadsheet has the following tabs: Main, Yield, Potatoes and Orchard. The *Main* tab has all my varieties and different plantings listed. For example, there is not just one row for Jade green beans, but a row each for the 1st and 2nd planting. There is also a different row for seed from different seed companies or my own seed. The *Yield* tab is how I keep track of my yield in pounds, dollar value and kilocalories. The *Potatoes* tab is just for potatoes since I like to keep track how each variety does. The *Orchard* tab is where I keep track of not only different tree fruits but the different varieties I grow. Currently, I have 45 fruit trees of various ages and 2 hazelnut trees I planted this year.

On the next pages are examples using real data. This is not speculative in any sense. These are all real numbers and based on accurate weights of produce as it comes in from the field. When I bring something in, it gets weighed right away. I write this weight and the item in a notebook I keep on a bench for just that purpose. At the end of each day, the notebook is taken into the house and I enter the data into my spreadsheet. As anyone who has done fieldwork knows, your analysis is only as good as your data collection. My data collection is rigid and precise. Everyone who helps me on the farm knows this. It has to be done right and it has to done right every time. That is why I have a high degree of confidence in my analysis.

Three items are denominated and sold in pints - cherry tomatoes, raspberries and blackberries - but all three weigh 12 ounces per pint on average and I have adjusted my spreadsheet totals accordingly. Corn is still counted by ears, but an ear of corn weighs about a pound. I had no sweet corn in 2010 and just a few ears in 2011 because of poor weather, so corn does not affect the margin of error in the following example. I calculated my margin of error for the three pint measures at 0.3%. This is well within a 95% confidence interval and so I regard my method of data collection as *robust*, or resistant to errors that violate assumptions. Robust data collection allows me to draw valid conclusions based on the data. In other words, I am not just testing my data, but I am also testing my data collection. It helps to be anal about all this stuff.

A few words are in order about precision, accuracy and validity. *Precision* is simply closeness of repeated measures. The classical example is shooting at a target and getting a close grouping, whether or not you hit the bullseye. *Accuracy* is how close the mean measurement comes to the real value, such as shots on target that could be well outside the bullseye but grouped so they are roughly equidistant. *Validity* is when your measurement is both precise and accurate. You can be precise but not accurate by grouping your shots on the edge of the target. You can be accurate but not precise by grouping your shots all over the target but equidistant from the bullseye, as above. However, if you have a nice tight grouping centered on the bullseye, you will be both precise and accurate, or *valid*. My data collection is precise because repeated measurements give the same results and accurate because they represent the true value of what is actually grown in the field. Because my data collection is both precise and accurate, it is valid.

In addition to robust and valid data, I also use a *median* measure as well as the *mean* and overall measures, like dollar and kilocalorie values per acre. The median is simply the point at which half your data is above and half below. It is the nonparametric counterpart to the mean. Nonparametric statistics are useful when you cannot assume your data is normal. For example, if you and I are sitting in a room with a bunch of people, we could ask everyone what their annual salary is and get a mean value. If, however, one of the people in the room is a billionaire software developer, the mean value will be wildly unrealistic. However the median will still represent "the true state of nature" as they say in statistics. I can use the median versus the mean to answer all kinds of questions, such as whether I should trim down the number of items I grow and sell. Questions like these are probably not relevant for home gardeners, but knowing where your median lies is useful in an overall look at your garden production.

Let us look at the *Main* tab of my spreadsheet *2011 Harvest Projections*. Notice there are 10 headings: Crop, Variety, Days, Planted, Est Harv, Act

Harv, Act-Est, Row Ft, Sq Ft, and Comments. Est Harv means estimated harvest, Act Harv means Actual Harvest and Act-Est is actual minus estimated, or how many days earlier or later the harvest is than expected. For those of you who don't need this much information, you could put in just the Crop, Act Harv and Sq Ft columns. These three headings would be easy to enter and keep track, while still giving you a broad overview of your crops. However, once you start using your spreadsheet, I think you will find that adding columns is quite easy (and even fun!).

The spreadsheet in Table 1 is a much smaller list of what I actually planted in 2011 and the original spreadsheet had 393 total rows. Notice the spreadsheet is sorted alphabetically by crop. This is useful in our present context, but during the growing season I sort by planting date. I also sort by the Est Harv column, for example, so I know what crops are approaching harvest time. The virtue of using the row/column format is you can sort your data by whatever category you desire. You may notice the bottom two rows have **Z** and **ZZ** in the Crop column. This is so I can use the speed key <Control A> to quickly highlight the whole spreadsheet and sort it. Since there are no values in these rows under the columns Planted and Est Harv, these two rows will always end up at the bottom of the spreadsheet where they belong. This is necessary to keep the integrity of the totals for the Row Feet and Square Feet. Simple tricks like this make data entry and spreadsheet management simple.

Crop	Variety	Days	Planted	Est Harv	Act Harv	Act-Est	Row Ft	Sq Ft	Comments
Artichokes	Violetto (Pinetree) - 6 plants	0	15-Apr-10	25-Apr-10	7-Jul	x	18	54	
Beans, dry	F.A. Kidney	95	12-Jun-11	25-Sep-11	19-Oct	x	113	338	
Beans, green	Strike (Fedco 2009) - 1st planting	53	6-Jun-11	8-Aug-11	23-Aug	15	205	615	
Beans, green	F.A. Jade - 1st planting	56	24-Jun-11	29-Aug-11	29-Aug	0	75	225	
Beets	Chioggia (Fedco 2010) - 2nd planting	55	24-Jun-11	28-Aug-11	17-Aug	(11)	45	135	
Broccoli	Premium Crop (Fedco 2010) - 92 plants	82	4-May-11	4-Aug-11	13-Jul	(22)	138	414	
Cabbage	Golden Acre OP (Fedco 2010) - 41 plants	62	12-Apr-11	23-Jun-11	29-Jun	6	62	185	
Cabbage	Red Acre (Ed Hume 2010) - 48 plants	77	14-Apr-11	10-Jul-11	16-Jul	6	72	216	
Carrots	Scarlet Nantes (Fedco 2010)	68	22-Jul-11	8-Oct-11	28-Sep	(10)	45	135	
Cauliflower	Snow Crown (Fedco) - 49 plants	70	18-May-11	6-Aug-11	27-Jul	(10)	74	221	
Celery	F.A. Utah 52 Improved (2008)	100	13-May-11	31-Aug-11	10-Sep	10	3	8	
Celery	Utah Improved - plants	0	8-Jun-11	18-Jun-11	x	x	14	42	
Chard	F.A. Volunteers - Ruby Red	59	23-Aug-11	31-Oct-11	19-Oct	(12)	75	225	
Corn, flour	F.A. Experimental - 4 varieties	85	10-Jun-11	13-Sep-11	18-Oct	x	237	711	
Favas	Windsor (Fedco 2010) - 1st planting	75	24-May-11	17-Aug-11	17-Aug	0	65	195	
Garlic	F.A. Chesnok Red (purple stripe) - strong	0	2-Nov-10	12-Nov-10	x	x	54	81	
Onions	Yellow sets (Magic Valley, ID)	100	1-Apr-11	20-Jul-11	16-Jul	x	276	414	
Pepper, sweet	Purple Beauty (Fedco) - 10 plants	74	13-Jun-11	5-Sep-11	13-Sep	8	20	60	Chinampa
Peppers, hot	F.A. Czech Black (2009) - 12 plants	65	13-Jun-11	27-Aug-11	13-Sep	17	24	72	Chinampa
Potatoes	F.A. Satinas	65	9-Apr-11	23-Jun-11	6-Jul	x	180	540	
Potatoes	F.A. Bintje	100	23-Apr-11	11-Aug-11	1-Sep	x	225	675	
Pumpkins	F.A. Pie (C. pepo 2010) - 43 hills	102	13-Jun-11	3-Oct-11	3-Oct	0	258	774	
Squash, winter	F.A. Delicata (C. pepo 2011) - 39 hills	100	13-Jun-11	1-Oct-11	24-Oct	23	117	351	
Tomato, det	Oregon Spring (Territorial 2010)	80	19-Apr-11	18-Jul-11	31-Jul	13	12	36	Blight 9/17
Triticale	F.A. Generic (2#)	0	24-Sep-11	4-Oct-11	x	x	225	675	
Wheat, winter	Generic hard red (Peaceful Valley 2011)	0	3-Oct-11	13-Oct-11	x	x	252	756	
Z					%Acre	145.0%	22,188	63,171	
ZZ					AVG	(2)			

Table 1 - Partial list of planting data 2011 (393 total rows in original). Estimated harvest based on seed packet Days to Harvest plus 10 days. Act-Est is the difference between actual and estimated and is calculated only for crops harvested as early as possible (unlike potatoes, for instance).

At the bottom right in Table 1 are the totals for the year from the complete spreadsheet. I planted 63,171 square feet, or 145% of an acre. I averaged 2 fewer days on actual harvest dates (Act Harv) than estimated harvest dates (Est Harv). Estimated harvest dates are based on the seed company's Days to Harvest number, usually available on the seed packet or in the catalog. I add 10 extra days to the number under the Days column and add this number to the planting date to get the estimated harvest date. I devised this system several years ago by adding a "fudge factor" of 23 days, but this proved to be too long. I dropped it down to 15 and then 10 days, which now works well to predict harvest dates.

If you look at the *Variety* column, you will see quite a bit of relevant information. The seed company is listed, as well as the year it was purchased. If there is no year, it is fresh seed sold for the current year. So, for example, I used 2011 Fedco seed for Purple Beauty peppers, but my own seed from 2009 for Czech Black peppers. By the way, my farm is called F.A. Farm (Food With **F**ull **A**ttention, **F**resh **A**bsolutely!), so my own seed has the prefix F.A. I also list the number of plants or hills when relevant and the genus/species for cucurbits. This is a reminder for me not to put two varieties of *Cucurbita pepo* together, for example if I am saving seed (they will cross-pollinate – more on this in Chapter 11 under Squash).

The *Days* column is just the listed days to harvest from seed packets or catalogs. Most companies will list this. For those who do not, you can sometimes get the info from a Web search. Days are listed as zero when I cannot find the number, the plants are overwintered, planted in the fall for next year's crop, or are perennials like raspberries. *Planted* is self-explanatory and the next three columns have already been explained. I list *Row Feet* as well as *Square Feet* because I still think in Row Feet terms, as do many other people. For example, if I say my potatoes are producing at a rate of 1 ¼ pounds per row foot, this means more to the average person than .4 pounds per square foot (with 3 feet between rows).

If you look at the *Act-Est* column, you will see that 2011 favored beets, chard (both are in the same family), cauliflower and broccoli. This was because of the long, cool spring. Other crops, like winter squash, took a long time to mature, even though planted late when it was warm. The takeaway here is there is a whole lot of analysis available because of the simple marking of dates. This information is enhanced by the Comments.

For example, in the *Comments* column you will see the word *chinampa* for the peppers. A chinampa was a raised bed constructed in a marsh or lake by the ancient Aztecs. It was the reason they could feed so many people in the Valley of Mexico (possibly as high as one million) by the time of the Spanish Conquest in 1519. The marsh or lake provided not only subsoil moisture and irrigation, but also muck for fertility, similar to the Nile flooding each year in ancient Egypt, which brought new soil and thus new fertility to the fields. I have adapted the chinampa to my area of northwestern Washington, where wet winters and cool late springs make excess soil moisture a problem. Chinampas allow me to control both surface and subsoil moisture, while enhancing early planting because the beds are higher and warmer in the early spring (each inch of rise in a raised bed effectively raises the temperature one degree Fahrenheit). The downside of a chinampa is it becomes dryer in July and August, but that is a small price to pay. For the Aztecs, the chinampa provided two out of the three necessities of intensive agriculture: 1) water, 2) fertility, and 3) labor. For the labor aspect, they utilized slaves.

Here is a sample row from Table 1. To save space, I limited the variety information (Fedco 2010 seed and 41 plants).

Crop	Variety	Days	Planted	Est Harv	Act Harv	Act-Est	Row Ft	Sq Ft
Cabbage	Golden Acre	62	12-Apr	23-Jun	29-Jun	6	62	185

The crop is cabbage and the variety is *Golden Acre*, a cabbage that yields well, is delicious and ready early. It also makes good sauerkraut. I planted 41 plants on April 12th and started harvesting heads on June 29th, six days after the estimated harvest date of June 23rd. I plant my brassicas on a 1 ½ foot spacing within the row, so I used 62 row feet and 185 square feet for this variety (3 feet between rows). I used leftover seed from 2010 for starting these cabbages and that is usually okay, as cabbage seed is good for four years, if your storage conditions are good. Notice there are no comments for this particular planting.

The next tab in my spreadsheet is *Yield* and Table 2 is based on this tab. At the bottom right of Table 2, you will find the figures 2,106,593 kilocalories of food energy output from 667,375 kilocalories of gasoline and human labor inputs, for an EROI of 3.16. If we accept the common metric that industrial agriculture uses 7-10 kilocalories of fossil fuel to produce 1 kilocalorie of food, I got 22–32 times more energy per kilocalorie of input in 2011, a year with a long cold spring and a summer with little sunshine. Unlike industrial agriculture, I am on the positive side of the energy ledger – even in a poor year. If we compare 2011 to 2009 (a good weather year and an EROI of 3.52), there was an uptick due to weather, but my methods are the key. For those of you who only want a simple Yield table, you could just use Crop, Weight and Sq Ft columns.

Table 2 is sorted by *Kcal/Acre*, kilocalories per acre. The first thing you might notice is that sunchokes (the old term is Jerusalem artichokes) have an incredibly high yield – over 20 million kilocalories per acre. This high figure was corroborated on a food bank farm I managed for a couple of years, where the sunchokes yielded at the rate of over 30 million kilocalories per acre in 2010. Sunchokes are an interesting crop. They are native to eastern North America and were extensively grown before white Europeans landed. They are well adapted to multiple soil and weather conditions and their upright stalks make them easy to find even in the snow. Sunchokes store their carbohydrates as inulin instead of starch, so they are a good food source for diabetics, since they do not stress the pancreas as much. [Garlic and leeks also have naturally high levels of inulin, by the way.] Inulin is indigestible by humans until it gets to the colon, where it is utilized by bacteria with the predictable result of producing gas. For this reason, people should ease into consumption of sunchokes, especially if they are currently eating a white flour/white sugar diet. As for myself, I eat them both raw and cooked and they only produce about the same gas as beans. Since they also store well and grow easily, sunchokes are a default survival crop.

Vegetable	Weight	Price	Total	Sq Ft	$/Sq Ft	$/Acre	Kcal/lb	2011 Kcal	Kcal/Acre	Median
Sunchokes	106.00	$ 2.50	$ 265.00	75	$3.53	$153,912.00	333	35,291	20,496,974	
Pumpkins	1,160.88	$ 1.25	$ 1,451.09	774	$1.87	$ 81,666.21	117	136,303	7,670,991	
Prunes (all)	275.50	$ 2.00	$ 551.00	450	$1.22	$ 53,336.80	275	75,804	7,337,851	
Apples	1,109.99	$ 2.00	$ 2,219.98	1,800	$1.23	$ 53,723.52	237	263,043	6,365,646	
Beets	313.82	$ 1.75	$ 549.18	484	$1.13	$ 49,425.86	194	60,811	5,473,010	
Celery	113.81	$ 1.75	$ 199.17	68	$2.93	$127,584.36	72	8,181	5,240,679	
Garlic	80.22	$ 8.00	$ 641.76	576	$1.11	$ 48,533.10	757	60,700	4,590,422	
Potatoes	1,824.25	$ 1.50	$ 2,736.38	7,446	$0.37	$ 16,008.12	349	637,430	3,729,040	
Leeks	41.38	$ 2.50	$ 103.44	150	$0.69	$ 30,038.25	275	11,397	3,309,743	
Basil	7.70	$12.00	$ 92.40	20	$4.62	$201,247.20	171	1,319	2,873,152	
Cabbage	1,347.07	$ 1.25	$ 1,683.83	2,363	$0.71	$ 31,040.07	112	151,174	2,786,771	
Kidney beans	13.88	$ 8.00	$ 111.00	338	$0.33	$ 14,305.21	1,530	21,226	2,735,482	
Rhubarb	138.25	$ 2.00	$ 276.50	240	$1.15	$ 50,184.75	97	13,410	2,433,960	
Delicatas	63.06	$ 1.75	$ 110.36	351	$0.31	$ 13,695.88	180	11,351	1,408,719	
Brussels sprouts	62.88	$ 2.50	$ 157.19	392	$0.40	$ 17,467.06	196	12,326	1,369,735	Kcal/Acre
Carrots	32.81	$ 1.75	$ 57.42	175	$0.33	$ 14,293.13	130	4,256	1,059,441	
Green beans	200.25	$ 3.00	$ 600.75	1,225	$0.49	$ 21,362.18	140	28,101	999,232	
Purple beans	39.81	$ 3.00	$ 119.44	258	$0.46	$ 20,165.49	140	5,587	943,256	$/Acre
Cauliflower	126.38	$ 1.75	$ 221.16	725	$0.31	$ 13,287.68	114	14,344	861,801	
Onions	196.25	$ 2.00	$ 392.51	3,759	$0.10	$ 4,548.42	151	29,700	344,164	
Tomatoes	94.47	$ 3.00	$ 283.40	1,725	$0.16	$ 7,156.34	81	7,671	193,706	
Spinach	6.13	$ 8.00	$ 49.00	225	$0.22	$ 9,486.40	106	649	125,616	
Totals	9,682.64		$20,965.44	41,250	$0.51	$22,139.50	Total Kcal	2,106,593	5,756	

$ 2.17 ←per lb
218 ←Kcal/lb
94.7% ←% Acre

$0.010   Avg $/SqFt   Avg $/Acre   Total Kcal
  Avg $/SqFt $0.51   ←$/Kcal   Kcal/Acre

Total Kcal	2,106,593	Kcal/day
Kcal/Acre	2,224,491	Kcal/day
	2,106,593	Kcal Out
	667,375	Kcal In
	3.16	EROI
	51.07	Kcal/sq ft

Table 2 – Partial list of yield data 2011 (73 rows in the original). Total poundage under Weight column reflects weight adjustment for items denominated in pints (12 ounces per pint of raspberries, blackberries and cherry tomatoes). Other amounts in pounds.

Other crops that yield at a high rate of kilocalories per acre are quite surprising. For instance celery, pumpkins, prunes and garlic can yield over 4 million kilocalories per acre, or equivalent to a good wheat yield. It should be noted the yield data in Table 2 is based on my particular abilities as a farmer and soil steward, so yield numbers will likely be different for other farmers. However, the whole point of this exercise is to show you what works and how we know it works. Success in a poor year can be seen as a minimum value for good years, but also point out how to deal with the extreme weather we are likely to endure in the future.

We might expect potatoes to do well most years, but last year was a poor year for me with potatoes. That was because of my rotation, early harvests, other work commitments and a generally crappy spring. I harvest a lot of new potatoes and that destroys yield numbers since you only get about half the yield by taking the spuds early. The role of crop rotation in 2011 was particularly significant, because as you rotate your crops you will eventually get a poor "fit" with a crop location every so often. Crop rotation is necessary to keep pest levels down and I use a six-year rotation of 1) grain, 2) favas, 3) root, 4) fruit, 5) pea and 6) leaf. (More on crop rotation later.) In 2011, I had to put my potatoes into an area of relatively poorer soil, so along with taking new potatoes and a crappy spring, the deck was stacked against potatoes. In comparison, I produced 8.9 million kilocalories of potatoes per acre in 2009. By the way, it should be remembered that kilocalories per acre is a normalized number. I do not have a whole acre of potatoes. Pounds per acre, dollars per acre or kilocalories per acre are all normalized to a common metric that can be used by everyone. Kilocalories per square foot would work just as well, but using the acreage metric allows comparisons to industrialized agriculture.

The columns in Table 2 should be self-explanatory, except for *$/Acre*, dollars per acre. As stated, normalizing to an acre is a common metric and I calculate it by multiplying *$/Sq Ft*, dollars per square feet, by 43,560, the number of square feet in an acre. If you are more used to hectares, you can easily convert dollars per acre to dollars per hectare by multiplying again by 2.47, the number of acres in a hectare. If we look at the dollars per acre column, we see tremendous opportunities for certain crops like sunchokes, celery, basil, and chard. However, the high dollar value is not viable if you cannot sell it, so crops like sunchokes will have only a limited market. We can also look at certain crops, like chard, and see that we can afford to drop the price. Thus, if we can sell a lot of chard, we could drop our price from $6.00 per pound to $4.00 per pound and still have a high dollar per acre value.

The *Kcal/lb*, or kilocalories per pound, column is based on information from a single source, http://caloriecount.about.com/. It is important to be consistent, so I default to this one source on the Web that has virtually any food I can grow. The only food I have been unable to find at this site is orach. This information is as current as I can make it. I am writing in the summer of 2012 and just checked my numbers. As with any data collection or sourcing from an outside source, you have to make decisions. So, for instance, I used a generalized winter squash measure of 180 kilocalories per pound for delicata squash because they are not listed on the website. A person can quibble about these numbers, but the point is we can measure our energy outputs just as surely as we measure our inputs. There will be a certain amount of error viewed in the short term, just as you might work hard one day and expend more kilocalories of energy than the average of 125 kilocalories per hour. However, over the long term it evens out.

By the way, inputting daily weight into your spreadsheet is simple. Just put an "equals" sign into the cell and then a plus or minus after each number. Ounces are simply 1/16, 2/16, 3/16, etc. So an input of 12 pounds and 3 ounces would be = 12 + 3/16. When you hit <Enter> the result will be 12.1875. If you restrict the cell to 2 decimal points the result will be 12.19. You can enter as long a string of numbers as you wish, although the menu window where you see the numbers will become unwieldy. In that case, you can just input your cumulative result and add more numbers.

As with Table 1, let us take a single row and analyze the information it reveals. I have listed the information on two rows for space purposes.

Crop	Weight	Price	Total	Sq Ft
Rhubarb	138.25	$ 2.00	$ 276.50	240
$/Sq Ft	**$/Acre**	**Kcal/lb**	**2011 Kcal**	**Kcal/Acre**
$1.15	$ 50,184.75	97	13,410	2,433,960

The crop is rhubarb and the 2011 yield was 138.25 pounds. Last year's price was $2.00 per pound for a total of $276.50. The square footage was 240, so $276.50 divided by 240 equals $1.15 per square foot. Multiplying $1.15 by 43,560 square feet in an acre equals $50,184.75 per acre. There are 97 kilocalories in a pound of rhubarb, so the total kilocalories for 2011 are 138.25 times 97, or 13,410.25 (rounded to 13,410), with a yield of 2,433,960 kilocalories per acre.

Rhubarb is a crop with a high dollar per acre and a kilocalorie per acre value above the median. It comes through in crappy weather and the year-to-year numbers back this up. If you add in low maintenance because it is a perennial and its ability to thrive in partial shade, it is a necessary crop. Rhubarb can be frozen without blanching (although I do add a cup of sugar per gallon freezer bag) and I recently ate some that was sitting in our freezer for two years. It was still excellent. The bottom line on rhubarb is that it is not only good as an early spring tonic, but as a cash crop

Now let us drill down a little further into Table 2 and look at the median measure. The *median* for kilocalories per acre is 1.4 million for delicata winter squash. As noted, the median gives a better measure of the "middle" than the mean because of data with wide discrepancies (*outliers* in statistical parlance). In fact, since I produced 2.1 million kilocalories on .95 acre, the *mean* is 2.2 million kilocalories per acre, or half again as much as the median. What this indicates to me is I could increase my kilocalorie yield potential by focusing on crops that lie above the median and growing fewer crops below the median. Based on this one year alone (and do not forget it was a poor year!), I might decide not to grow spinach, tomatoes, and onions. But I like those crops so I will continue to grow them. However, I may drop them out of my sales lineup and just grow them for my own use.

We can use the similar logic for the median dollars per acre as we did for median kilocalories per acre. This median was $20,165.49 for purple beans. In this case, the price per pound is $3.00, which I have found to be a solid price for sales at local farmers markets over the years. This is one indication our overall pricing scheme is robust, even with some unrealistic prices like kidney beans at $8.00 a pound (nobody is likely to buy at that price unless it is for seed). In other words, since we know subjectively that $3.00 per pound works for fresh beans and this price provides us with the median, the subjective and objective measures corroborate each other for the price of beans.

Another indicator our overall pricing is robust is that it is common to shoot for $20,000 - $40,000 an acre in sales of vegetables and fruit directly to the consumer. This is a figure that comes from experience with other Whatcom County farmers and it may even be lower than other parts of the country. In other words, there is greater potential for more money per acre in produce than beef or corn, for instance, where the gross sales are in the hundreds rather than the thousands of dollars per acre. Of course this presupposes you can actually sell what you grow - the most difficult part of farming. Even in industrial agriculture, overproduction and depressed markets are problems.

What the median for dollars per acre really tells us is which crops are worth selling. Some of these crops are basil, celery, apples, and prunes. It is no coincidence crops like apples and basil have a certain cachet based on smell and appearance and thus can yield more dollars per acre. There are multiple variables in every decision made on the farm (as in any business) and the median is another tool which gives us more information. Table 2 represents the information I use that comes from my daily data collection in the field. When I have a question, I can turn to these numbers, which I know to be valid indicators. Both these tables are simple to set up. You the reader can set up a similar system that fits your individual purposes with just a few keystrokes.

The next two tabs in my spreadsheet are not strictly necessary, but they are useful to me. The *Potatoes* tab records yields for specific varieties of potatoes, including fingerlings. Since I regard potatoes as the staple crop for northwest Washington after the collapse of the American empire, I grow 20-30 varieties each year and keep track of each variety's yield. There is precedent for this view, since potatoes were introduced into Washington in the 1830's (then part of the Oregon Territory) and there were around 2,000 potato farms in the Yakima Valley by the 1900's.[1] The Ozette fingerling potato was a staple crop of the Makah by 1792 in their settlements on the Olympic Peninsula in Washington and probably introduced to the Makah by Spanish traders from South America.[2] Potatoes also fed the loggers and settlers in Whatcom County.

Table 3, on the next page, is based on my *Potatoes* tab and we can track 3 varieties of potatoes from both 2011 (a poor year) and 2009 (a good year). The columns are similar to Table 2, but also include *Cwt/Acre* (hundredweight per acre) for comparison to the US national averages from 1930 to 2005. From 1930 to 1935, the US national average was 66 hundredweight per acre, but it then started to increase about 3% per year. By 2005, the US average had reached 390 hundredweight per acre.[3] My particular yields do not average anywhere near this figure, but I am stingy with my irrigation and do not use chemical fertilizers. Potatoes pumped up with water do not necessarily have any more solids and nutrients than a potato grown with minimal or no irrigation. Likewise, pumping up the fertilizer does not necessarily increase nutrient levels. Nevertheless my yield levels were generally better than potato growing before the era of chemical agriculture.

Table 4 is also on the next page and the data is from my *Orchard* tab. In this table we can see my apple yields are comparable to the national average for commercial orchards, which was 611.9 bushels per acre in 2009 (there are 42 pounds in a bushel of apples).[4] Apples do quite well in Washington and I don't have to spend a lot of time tending my trees.

In Table 3 we see Chieftains were the best yielder in 2009 (a good year) but did poorly in 2011 (a poor year). There may be complicating factors, since the seed potatoes were bought commercially at a local farmers co-op (WFC = Whatcom Farmers Co-op), but using my own seed potatoes usually produces better yields than commercial seed potatoes since they are acclimatized. It is likely Chieftains just cannot handle poor weather. The Bintjes actually did better in a poor year (2011) than a good year (2009), but I had them in a very good spot in 2011, where I made compost years ago. The salutary effects of compost-making last a long time, which is why I move my compost piles around to get an extra fertilizer "bump."

Year	Variety	Sq Ft	Yld	Yld/Sq Ft	Yld/Acre	Cwt/Acre	$/Sq Ft	Total	Rating	Kcal/Acre
2011	F.A. Bintje	402	298.88	0.74	32,386	324	$1.12	$448.31	BEST	11,302,560
2011	F.A. Satimas	540	195.75	0.36	15,791	158	$0.54	$293.63	Good	5,510,885
2011	F.A. Chieftains	390	52.75	0.14	5,892	59	$0.20	$79.13	Poor	2,056,227
2009	F.A. Bintje	1,140	571.19	0.50	21,825	218	$0.75	$856.78	Good	7,617,023
2009	F.A. Satimas	640	405.75	0.65	28,507	285	$0.98	$608.62	Good	9,948,955
2009	Chieftains (WFC)	325	357.06	1.10	47,857	479	$1.65	$535.59	BEST	16,702,219

Table 3 – Selected varieties of potatoes from 2011 and 2009. Rating based on yield per square foot.

Apples	Weight	Price	Total	Sq Ft	$/Sq Ft	$/Acre	Comments	Lb/Acre	BU/Acre
Gravenstein	446.87	$2.00	$893.73	225	$3.97	$173,026.13	Picked 9/2	86,513	2059.83
Spartans	146.06	$2.00	$292.13	225	$1.30	$56,555.40	Picked 10/22	28,278	673.28
Goldens	215.75	$2.00	$431.50	225	$1.92	$83,538.40	Picked 10/24	41,769	994.50
Jonagold	196.06	$2.00	$392.13	225	$1.74	$75,915.40	Picked 10/31	37,958	903.75
Apples (all)	1,109.99	$2.00	$2,219.98	1,800	$1.23	$53,723.52	Yield 545# 2010	26,862	634.96

Table 4 – Selected varieties of apples from 2011. Sq Ft based on 15 x 15 foot grid.

The *Satina* potatoes did well in both a good and a bad year, but had 80% greater yields in a good year (2009). This is expected since Satinas are a very nice potato overall - consistently good yielders but able to excel under the right conditions, early to harvest, resistant to scab and quite tasty. Satinas are one of the first new potatoes I harvest each year.

In Table 4, we see four apples trees and four varieties, which represent 90% of my 2011 harvest. Three out of the four are mature trees already on the property when we arrived in 2004. I planted the *Spartan* tree in 2005 and it is already doing quite well. I have since planted 43 more fruit and nut trees, 22 of them apples. Some of my 2007 grafts are coming on this year, so I am looking forward to new varieties. In this table, we can see *Gravensteins* were a very productive apple and they produce well every year. They can be harvested over a month earlier than other apples, which allows me to do cider pressing in two lots. My square footage of 225 square feet per tree is based on a 15 x 15 foot grid, a standard of 200 trees per acre for semi-dwarf trees. In Washington and elsewhere you may find many other planting systems, but I like this system. In addition, it was in use during my eight years as a migrant worker, so I know its advantages and disadvantages from both a picker's and a grower's perspective.

As mentioned, the national average for commercial orchards in the US was 611.9 bushels per acre and my average for 2011, including young trees, was 634.96 bushels per acre. This is quite good, but I am in an area with plenty of soil moisture and Washington is an excellent place for apples - on both sides of the Cascades. I also more than doubled my production last year over 2010. On the other hand, when I look at my records for 2009, I see I produced 1,048 pounds in a good weather year versus 1,110 for 2011. A good year for apples is more about bloom and pollination than about sunshine in summer and 2010 had a worse spring than 2011. This year, in 2012, we had both good bloom and excellent pollination, so I look forward to a good harvest.

If we look back at Table 2 for a moment, we can see my apples produced at a rate of 6.4 million kilocalories per acre. This is 70% better than my potatoes in 2011, and comparable to an average potato year, when potatoes can be expected to produce around 6-8 million kilocalories per acre (the comparable figure for wheat is 3-4 million kilocalories per acre). Apples also have a high dollar value per acre, so apples are clearly a good crop for the future. They are also relatively easy to pick, as long as you feel confident on a ladder. I fell more than once while I was a migrant worker, so I am quite careful now that I am in my 60's.

These four tables represent the main tabs in my primary spreadsheet. I also have a corn log in this spreadsheet for the times I have sweet corn, and a squash tab so I can keep track of squash pollination and isolation. I have spreadsheets for expenses and tax purposes, keeping track of planting dates year-to-year, seed orders and calculating fertilizer (I make my own organic fertilizer). This discussion of spreadsheets is intended to provide you, the reader, with a simple view of just how powerful it can be to keep track of your data in a systematic fashion. Spreadsheets are the way accounting is done nowadays and I highly recommend them. If you want to know how to manage energy efficiency, you have to collect data and put it into a framework so you can make sense of it. An unintended benefit of this system is you have produced an objective measure of sustainability - another reason I walked you through it.

10 FARMING AS IF ENERGY MATTERED

In the preceding chapter I presented some examples of how to set up spreadsheets for measuring sustainability. Since most readers come from a non-agricultural background, perhaps these examples will serve as a kind of mental template on how to organize your planting, make sense of how your crops do at harvest and decide what to grow. Now it is time to take direct action in the field. This will require manual labor, but there is a hidden advantage to the use of the human body as your primary engine. This is because of the positive feedback loop of using human energy to grow the food which feeds the human body which grows the food, and so on. There are both qualitative and quantitative advantages to using human labor, something most people do not recognize. Not only is manual labor in the garden quite relaxing and conducive to family quality time, it is a more efficient use of energy. The human engine can grow its own fuel.

Modern agribusiness acts as if energy use does not matter. If the farmer can afford it, he is encouraged to buy it. The operative paradigm is the one used by Marxist and capitalist alike – everything we get from nature is free. Coupled with this false paradigm is the trend in modern agribusiness that follows modern business in general – get rid of the human whenever possible. My approach is entirely the opposite – we need to use the human first and then add machines only as needed. For example, I do not have a tractor. When I need some heavy tilling done, I hire somebody. I do nearly all of my tilling with a BCS walk-behind rototiller. There are other brands, but in my neck of the woods, this is the tiller that is most popular and easiest to get and maintain. I know, by keeping track of my gasoline consumption, that I can grow a lot of food with very little fossil fuel energy. Here are my usage statistics from the past several years.

Year	Lb	Hr	Gal	Kcal Out	Kcal/lb	Kcal/Hr	EROI	Acres	EROI/A
2007	8,029	3000	21.25	1,263,389	157.3	421	1.21	1.00	1.21
2008	11,851	3000	27.50	2,246,938	189.6	749	1.81	1.29	1.40
2009	15,685	3000	22.25	3,789,138	241.6	1,263	3.52	1.47	2.40
2010	7,426	2000	17.25	1,712,922	230.7	856	2.16	1.12	1.93
2011	9,654	2000	13.25	2,106,593	218.2	1,053	3.16	0.95	3.32

Table 5 – Energy inputs and outputs 2007-2011.

In the above table, the columns are largely self-explanatory. In 2007, for example, I grew 8,029 pounds of food using 3000 hours of labor and 21.25 gallons of gas. My kilocalorie output in 2007 was 1,263,389 kilocalories, which calculates to 157.3 kilocalories per pound or 421 kilocalories per labor hour. The EROI is calculated by dividing output by input in kilocalories as follows: 1,263,389 kcal ÷ (3000 hr * 125 kcal/hr + 21.25 gal * 31,500 kcal/gal) = 1.21.

Acres is how many acres I actually harvested (1.00 in 2007) and so the EROI per acre for 2007 is 1.21 for 2007. The acreage I harvest each year is different from the acreage I till and plant because I need to plant some acreage for green manure and cover crops. There are also some crop failures and this acreage is not included in harvest acreage. However, the gasoline and labor for ALL areas are included in the overall yields. This gives a truer representation of how much energy is consumed and how much energy is produced overall, which is the main focus. Very often, corporate and government statistics split out inputs and outputs into multitudinous categories, which not only fail to provide the overall picture, but allow obfuscation and covering up of discrepancies in a jumble of numbers. It is important to be honest and stay focused.

Notice how my yearly labor has decreased from 3000 to 2000 hours. I am trying to reduce it even further. As noted earlier, labor is calculated at 125 kilocalories per hour and includes time spent at the computer and doing seed starts (relatively low kilocalorie inputs), as well as tilling, weeding and shoveling (relatively high kilocalorie inputs). It is axiomatic that a farmer does not just grunt and strain all day long, but rather moves from task to task. Most people do the same and it is also axiomatic that just as much energy is expended by a typical human on weekends or after work as during work. The common myth of working from sundown to sundown in the fields under a broiling sun has little basis in reality. Over a year's time, the grunt work is counterbalanced by other tasks that do not expend as many kilocalories. Besides, part of the objective here is to work efficiently so a person can sweat and strain less and less.

We can see from the EROI/Acre column in Table 5 that I have become more efficient over the years (1.21 in 2007 to 3.32 in 2011), even with poorer weather, less fossil fuel use and fewer labor hours. This is because of management. *Management* is what separates good farmers from mediocre farmers. In a micro sense, this means managing time and pennies, because "Seconds make minutes and minutes make hours," as well as "Pennies make nickels and nickels make dollars." In a macro sense, management means choosing what engines will do the job and how your overall operation is run. I am efficient because I manage my time and pennies well, but more importantly, I am using the most efficient engine on the planet – the human engine.

The human engine is a marvel of efficiency. Because we are bipedal, we can carry things while we work, from buckets to babies. We also move very efficiently because we are bipedal. As we step out, our legs store up energy in a pendulum motion which is transferred to the ground and helps us take the next step. The metabolic rate for this energy transfer can be measured in relationship to body mass and adjusted for morphology and speed. When this is done, humans only use about 68% of the energy of chimps walking on their hind legs (their normal gait is knuckle-walking), and only 77% of the energy of chickens, who are bipedal when not flying.[1] Quadrupedal animals expend even more energy, as I mentioned in the previous discussion of horses. Human running takes almost twice as much energy to move a given distance as walking, but unless your work is playing professional sports or some such pursuit, your work is done at an efficient walking pace.

As well as the pendulum action, we move efficiently because we walk on a "narrow trackway" unlike geese and chickens. Our width has a lower ratio to our leg length and we do not waddle, which takes energy to counteract side-to-side motion. We also carry our weight centered over our hips and the shape of our pelvis allows us to move forward in a smooth linear motion, unlike chimpanzees. When chimps walk upright, they have a distinct "rolling" motion like a sailor used to the pitch of a ship and who suddenly walks on land. Bipedalism is a very efficient way to move forward at relatively low speeds. High speed motion is an entirely different affair, with quadrupeds like the cheetah and gazelle attaining speeds impossible for us. The downside is the tremendous amount of energy it takes to run at high speeds. However, even while running, humans expend less energy than geese do while walking, which is why geese have to eat constantly.[2] All in all, the human organism is an efficient engine, running or walking.

In addition to our efficient bipedalism, we have dexterous hands with opposable thumbs. This allows us to do things like peel an orange, construct a stone tool to crack open a bone for marrow, or skin an animal and tan its hide for clothing. Coupled with our extremely large brains (much larger in relation to body mass than our nearest chimpanzee and bonobo relatives), we can invent all kinds of new tools – tractors, computers, etc. Of course the tractors and computers use incredible amounts of energy to operate and we end up paying high prices (both in dollars and in greenhouse gas emissions) for using these tools. If we then use our extremely large brains to actually look at the downside of all our new tools (like tractors and computers), we can easily calculate how much energy we are wasting and even measure the results in the pollution of the atmosphere, land and water. Sustainability is based on measurement and the further we get from using our bodies, the more energy we use and waste to produce smaller and smaller returns.

Energy use matters. It is clear the way to use energy most efficiently is to use the human body as our primary engine. The way to do this is simple - so simple it gets no respect. For example, we build factories to produce chemicals which we then pour on the land to control weeds. It is simpler and more efficient to just go out and pull the weeds by hand. The real conundrum is not the energy comparison - there really is no justification for the high energy usage in chemical agriculture. The real conundrum is an economic system based on wasting energy. This results in pollution, global warming and economic exploitation of farmers at home and abroad. The best way to quash this nonsense is to grow your own food. Once you decide to do so, the best way is to use human labor. So how to do it?

Soil Preparation

You might be surprised at how much work you can get done with a shovel and a rake. For example, let us suppose you want to grow 5% of the food you eat, a very small start. Based on a daily requirement of 2500 kilocalories and a standard of 200 or more kilocalories per pound overall, you will need around 4500 pounds of food per year. Five percent of that would be 225 pounds of food. Using my standard of growing 10,000 pounds per acre you could grow this amount on 2.25% of an acre, or a plot about 30 feet x 30 feet. This is a very small garden. You can dig this up in an afternoon, even starting with hard-packed sod. I have dug an area this size in less than 2 hours. The key is to make sure your shovel is sharp and use boots with a stiff sole. [By the way, the best preparation you can give your children and grandchildren for the future is to teach them how to use a shovel.] Sharpening your shovel with a file is relatively simple. Just bevel it about a quarter-inch on the back side and do a quick swipe on the front edge to take off the burr.

As you flip over the sod or soil, cut the clumps with your shovel. Chop, chop, chop – it's simple. After shoveling, rake and chop the clumps some more. You can do it all in one afternoon or turn the sod over and let it sit for a week to let soil microorganisms break down the biomass. The key is to just do the task. If you are grunting and cursing you are missing the point. It should be a relatively pleasant task.

If you have a tiller at your disposal, you can till it up in less than an hour, but you will have some difficulty if you start with sod. This is where the shovel is actually superior. I break new ground with my tiller every year by extending already tilled areas, but I run over it with my tiller and then let it sit for a while to let the soil microbes break down the biomass. Using a shovel can get the sod-to-soil process done in a day. If you are tilling up a garden spot that was used the year before, a walk-behind tiller can be a very efficient use of energy. I can till up about $1/10^{th}$ of an acre in an hour

(4,356 square feet or 66 x 66 feet) using less than a quart of gasoline. It takes about 2 gallons of gasoline and 10 hours per acre for the first tilling of the year. This calculates to 63,000 kilocalories for the gas (31,500 kilocalories/gallon of gas x 2 gallons) plus 1250 kilocalories for the labor to run the tiller (125 kilocalories/hour x 10 hours), for a total of 64,250 kilocalories to till up an acre of ground previously worked the year before. For your 30 x 30 foot plot this would total about 1327 kilocalories in energy use using a tiller. It would take you almost 11 hours of shovel work (at 125 kilocalories/hour) to equal this energy footprint, so digging up a small plot by hand uses much less energy than even using a tiller.

If you want to hire someone with a tractor to work up your garden, that is a relatively low-cost procedure and in the grand scheme of things, a relatively small waste of energy. Getting someone to till up even a 100 foot x 100 foot plot will use up less than a gallon of fuel and take less than an hour. If you make one or two fewer trips to the grocery store over the course of a year, you will recoup that savings in energy. This brings up a larger point. Using a tractor for very basic tasks has a relatively small impact on the ecosystem. Mindless driving in automobiles has a far greater impact than even industrial agriculture. Restricting your daily usage of fossil fuels is a big step towards a cleaner, saner world and the benefits can be quite substantial. You can curtail your fossil fuel use in a number of ways, but driving less will have the biggest impact. If you want to use a tractor to do the preliminary tilling, go right ahead. After the ground is worked up, you will then find you can do a lot simply by using your hands. By the way, your tractor operator will probably use a rototiller mounted on the back of the tractor, but a plow, disk and harrow will work too. Either system will give you nice soil in which to plant.

Where a tractor becomes a wasteful use of energy is in the embedded energy for its manufacture. *Embedded energy* is the energy used to mine the ore to make the steel, tap the trees to get the rubber, transport raw materials, put the machine together, etc. This embedded energy can be compared to the energy in the fuel. For example, David Pimentel estimated the energy needed to produce an acre of corn as 412,146 kilocalories for the machinery (including combines to harvest the corn as well as tractors and implements to till and cultivate) and 406,073 for the diesel to run the machinery. The embedded energy for the machinery was first calculated in total and then prorated over 10 years.[3] Although some tractors do last longer, increasing maintenance costs argue for a 10-year life span as a valid estimate. Since the difference between fuel energy and embedded energy is only 1.5%, you can just measure the fuel energy of a tractor and double that amount. This will be a good approximation of the real energy cost of using a tractor.

A walk-behind tiller has a similar 10-year lifespan and uses similar materials in its manufacture. However, it is only about 200 pounds versus an average tractor weight of 6-7 tons, or an average of 13,000 pounds (combines are even heavier). Therefore, we can estimate a tractor consumes about 65 times more energy in its manufacture than a walk-behind tiller, so there is only 1.5% of the embedded energy in a tiller as in a tractor. This is such a small amount it would likely be masked by human factors in the use of the tractor (driving the tractor on the road to the field, excessive idling, etc.). In other words, if the tractor fuel use is the same as a walk-behind tiller for tilling the same area of land, it still uses nearly twice as much energy overall.

At this point the astute reader may object that a tractor should be able to till more ground per gallon of fuel. However, if we discount the embedded energy and restrict ourselves to fuel consumption comparisons only, the tractor still cannot decrease fuel usage by a significant amount. Tractor manufacturers tout the fuel efficiency of their newer machines, but if a tractor uses 406,073 kilocalories of fuel per acre, this is the energy contained in 11.6 gallons of diesel (35,000 kcal/gallon) or 12.9 gallons of gasoline (31,500 kcal/gallon). In 2011, I used 13.25 gallons of gasoline in my tiller, or 417,375 kilocalories of energy. However, included in my gasoline usage was the amount needed to till up half an acre (1.45 acres tilled, .95 acres productive) for cover crops and green manures that increase biomass, cycle nutrients and feed the soil for future years. Accounting for this extra land, I used only 9.1 gallons of gasoline, or 287,845 kilocalories per acre - 29% less fuel than the tractor average. Pimentel's comparisons, it should be noted, were only for acreage that produced a marketable crop. In short, even on a strictly fuel basis, a tractor cannot compete with a walk-behind tiller. The tiller does use some fossil fuel, but allows you to maintain a human scale. My tiller uses significantly less energy per acre than a tractor. To be blunt, if you are riding on it, it is probably not sustainable.

Planting

Once the soil is prepared, planting is more about paying attention than actually working hard. If you want to plant things in blocks or circles instead of in neat rows, go right ahead. It is more important to make sure you plant at the proper depth, as listed on the seed packet. There are many books on how to grow a garden, but I recommend the guides by Steve Solomon and Eliot Coleman. Specifically, I like Solomon's *Gardening When It Counts* and Coleman's *The New Organic Grower*.[4] Both of these books have bibliographies so you can follow their recommendations and build up your own research library. Solomon maintains the online Soil and Health Library at www.soilandhealth.org, which is a wonderful source of classic and out-of-print titles. Donations help him maintain the library, so don't be cheap.

In thinking about what to plant, you should take into account what you like to eat, what would be cheaper to buy from someone else, and what grows well in your area. For example, tomatoes are difficult to grow and can be purchased from local farmers for a very cheap price when tomato season is in full swing. However, there is nothing quite like picking and munching your very own tomatoes. Potatoes, on the other hand, have very little romance and glamour about them, but they are easy to grow and harvest, as well as producing a high kilocalorie yield per acre (6-8 million kilocalories per acre vs. 2-3 million for tomatoes). In my own life, I do not eat tomato products every day, but I do eat some form of potatoes nearly every day. I also have a much more symbiotic relationship with potatoes and am invested in growing many different kinds of spuds – not so much with tomatoes. Personal preference is important.

The time of year is another consideration. Your growing season may be much more inclusive than you realize and four-season gardening is becoming more popular in many areas of the US. This usually requires hoophouses and special techniques. It may be worth investigating as you become more proficient in growing crops, but simple techniques are available to the beginning gardener right away. For example, if you build a *raised bed* that is 10 inches high, your effective temperature has been raised by 10 degrees Fahrenheit – one degree for each inch of rise above the surrounding ground level. This means you can get some crops planted a week or even a month earlier in the spring using raised beds.

Hay bale culture is similar to raised beds but even easier. You just lay out a line of bales, end to end, and shovel six inches of dirt on top of them. However, a word of warning is in order. As the hay bales start to break down they heat up and will kill germinating seeds. If you lay your bales out in the fall, the winter rain and/or snow will take care of this. You can also just lay the bales out two weeks before you actually plant and water them well. They will heat up so much it will be uncomfortable to stick your hand in the bale. When it cools down, add the soil and plant. This method works best with shallow-rooted crops like salad mix. Hay bales are relatively cheap and sometimes you can get them for free. However, they do have quite a bit of embedded energy in their manufacture, about 156 kilocalories per pound, or 7800 kilocalories in a 50-pound bale.[5]

If the 50-pound bale is 18 inches wide and 4 feet long, the 7800 kilocalories is spread over 6 square feet. This is 1300 kilocalories per square foot of energy just to set up this growing method. Digging the soil or trucking it in increases the energy input further. Since salad mix is only going to produce about 39 kilocalories of energy per square foot with repeated cuttings, the bale is only going to produce 234 kilocalories in a season and it will last only 1-2 seasons. By strict objective measurement of inputs versus outputs, hay bale culture would not be worth it.

However, the value of using resources that might otherwise go to waste and the ability to grow food in an otherwise untenable location is a case where the subjective trumps the objective. For example, I raised the soil level on one area of my farm by over a foot, simply by laying out 400 free bales and letting them break down for two years. The farmer who grew the hay was using rented land and had no place to dump the bales without extensive transport costs to his home place. I used the bales to build soil, something that takes about a thousand years using only natural processes.

As I mentioned earlier, an older twist on raised beds is the *chinampa*. Chinampas allow me to control moisture and weeds. The standing water in the channels on either side of the chinampa in late spring promotes algae growth, which is a negative in ponds but a plus if you are concentrating nutrients for the use of plants. Filling the channels with plant debris over the summer not only keeps weeds down but provides something for the algae to eat in the winter and spring when the rains return. In other words, pond scum is good.

My chinampas are constructed with varying widths, 4-6 feet, and varying lengths 35-100 feet. I also tried them with a north-south as well as east-west orientation. The east-west orientation seems to work slightly better, but this is a subjective interpretation, as I have not done a comprehensive trial yet. As a general rule, you can increase your sun exposure to the middle of your crop rows by using a north-south orientation, but it can be too much in a hot summer and cause burning and shriveling of your plants as well as an increased need for water.

Another advantage not immediately obvious is that digging a channel and throwing the dirt on the chinampa increases the height twice as much as bringing in soil from another area via wheelbarrow or truck. Consequently, you can do most of the work on the chinampa without bending over, since you are standing in the dug channel. This saves time as well as making it easier for people like me who are getting older. Chinampas require some shovel work to construct, but if you till the soil first, shoveling is much easier. Once the chinampa is done, you can climb up and till the top, which is why some of my chinampas are wider than others and slope on the ends. All in all, chinampas are an improvement over raised beds and allow you to get into the field earlier than you thought possible. It helps to widen your planting window in the spring.

In the fall, you can extend your crops by putting an old window over the top of some crops, raising it up above the plants with boards or even bales. This is a very effective *cold frame*. It is quite nice to go out into your garden in early December, brush snow off your cold frame, lift up the window and harvest fresh salad mix. In some areas, like the western side of the Cascades where I live, you can even leave much of your produce in the ground over winter and harvest as needed. Examples are cabbage, broccoli, Brussels sprouts, carrots, beets, rutabagas, and potatoes. Brassicas and root crops work best for storage in the field.

Here are some crops you can plant in August for fall crops and hold over winter in the Pacific Northwest on the western side of the Cascades: arugula, carrots, chard, kale, kohlrabi, mustard, parsnips, raab, radicchio, rutabagas, salad mix, and turnips. Depending on where you are, you may be able to hold some of the hardier crops all winter, like kale. Other crops can be planted early in spring and then just left as long as possible, like Brussels sprouts and potatoes. Potatoes especially hold well in moderate winters where the ground does not freeze hard, but you have to get them out of the ground before early spring warm-up causes them to break down. This is right around February 1st on the western side of the Cascades. There is an upside to losing a few of your potatoes stored in the ground however, as many will sprout and come up as volunteers. In fact, one of the things to consider when designing your planting areas is where you might have volunteers. However, before we go on to different crops and crop varieties, now is a good time to talk about soil and fertilizer.

Building and Improving Soil

As mentioned previously, I build soil as part of my farming practices. So just what is *soil?* In the usual geological definition, soil is disintegrated rock. However, soil is also the living matter within the disintegrated rock – humus, microbes and other organic matter living and dead. There is also water and air within soil, upon which the living organisms depend.[6] So what is *humus?* That is a little more difficult, but the most parsimonious definition is organic matter that is stable and will not break down any further. "Organic" in chemistry simply means carbon-based, but popular use of the term "organic matter" means matter (or "stuff") that was once alive and is now decaying or has finished decaying. So if a mole in your lawn, for example, dies and decays, the process continues within the soil as the molecules of the mole disintegrate and the elements are absorbed by other plants, animals and fungi. This process of decay and recycling of elements has an end point when it becomes humus. The humus is still chock-full of nutrients usable by plants and animals in your lawn, but is a stable compound. This is a useful concept.

Consider what happens when you make *compost*. You put decayable items into a box or frame and just leave it for a year or more (cold compost method) or manage it through aeration, water and agitation (hot compost method). The first stage is when you get red worms, which signals the early phase of decay. The second stage is marked by grey earthworms, which feed on compounds that have formed in half-decayed organic matter. The third stage is when the compost is done. There is a much milder smell, the *tilth* (or "crumb") of the soil is more friable, and the worms are gone. What you have is essentially humus because it is stable. Some may accuse me of oversimplification in this three-stage description, but I have good luck building soil based on this paradigm.

First of all, if we just wait the thousand years it takes to build an inch of topsoil naturally, we fall into the trap of fighting for pieces of a shrinking pie of arable land. However, by understanding what happens in the compost decay process, we can utilize it to our advantage to not only improve the soil we have now, but also rehabilitate depleted soils and make new soil where there was little or none before. Since humus is what we need to grow food and since we can make it through the compost process, it behooves us to use compost extensively.

What people usually think of when they see the need for more compost is to get all kinds of biodegradable "stuff" and make big piles. Then they turn it, water it and screen it at the end. This way of thinking naturally lends itself to using dairy solids, human sewage, or wood pulp as a source where you can make large amounts. Of course, the trap is in thinking large and using lots of machinery (and energy!) to work the compost. It is much simpler to do the compost on site and let the worms and microbes do the work. This is why I adjudge the *cold compost method* to be superior. I simply put my compost in stackable wooden frames made from scrap 2 x 4's, set up at the edge of the garden, and leave it for a year. Then I screen it into a wheelbarrow and use it where needed. Sometimes I just take the frames down and pitch it as far as I can.

Sheet composting is another method that has multiple advantages. Laying down a goodly amount of hay, straw, or other thick organic matter in a "blanket" over a patch of ground not only enriches the soil as it breaks down, but it smothers weeds and lawn. Some hardy weeds may survive, like quack grass and canary grass, but they are much more manageable and the clumps can be dug out with a shovel. *Lasagna mulching*, or layering up various kinds of biodegradable matter, works well too and you can even use soil as the top layer, similar to hay bale culture. You can use cardboard or newspapers, but there is glue in cardboard and ink in newspapers that may be harmful to your soil. I use neither, but you may decide to do so after some research. The key is to do your homework and not blindly follow someone else's advice.

Another interesting method is *hugelkultur* ("mound culture" in German), where you lay down rotting wood, woody vegetable stalks, or roots (like cabbage roots or bolted chard stalks) either in a pit, a raised bed, or even just right on the ground and cover it with soil. This is a very good way to fill up a raised bed. When you add the soil on top, it fills in the spaces and gets the decay process going as you use the top layer of soil. One downside to this method is sometimes the roots will regenerate once they have soil and moisture on them, but this is easily manageable when weeding your plants in the raised bed. More problematic is if you fail to put in enough soil and the soil level sinks as your new plants are germinating. Tamping the soil around the roots as you fill the raised bed helps with this problem.

Some people may only want to modify the soil they have; for instance if they have a lot of clay. Once again the answer is to add more organic matter to the soil. Over time the soil will achieve a balance of 5-7% organic matter, which will provide a fertile medium for growing food, as well as bring pH to a neutral level around 6.8-7.0. The key here is to add a balanced soil amendment, rather than a highly concentrated source of one element at a time. This is why I do not recommend dairy solids as a nitrogen source. They are just too concentrated and more of a waste stream than a soil amendment. The balanced approach would be to take bedding from the barn with the manure and urine already mixed in - the old way to do it. This is already a mix of what are called *brown* and *green* compost ingredients.

The brown ingredients have a relatively high carbon to nitrogen ratio. Hay and straw are around 50:1, with 50 times more carbon than nitrogen in their chemical composition (the brown). Cow manure has a much lower ratio of around 12:1 (the green) and the optimal ratio when making compost is 25:1. When you mix the bedding with the manure and spread it out on your fields, you get something approximating the optimal ratio. It may not be "just right" but it is closer to the optimal ratio than just spreading highly concentrated dairy solids or even straight manure. It also works faster than straight hay, like I use, and my sheet mulching with hay takes two years to break down. The hay alone works fine in the end – it just takes longer. The same cannot be said about the dairy solids or liquids because they work faster than the balance of bedding/manure and quickly create problems in the soil because they break down so fast.

This idea of using a balanced approach is critical to understanding why soil tests are a waste of time and money. Conventional wisdom says soil tests are one of the beneficial things the USDA pushes on people. It is not true. Soil tests are flawed in both theory and method. Soil tests are based on Justus von Liebig's contributions to chemistry and agriculture and reveal a shift to a machine-age bias introduced into farming in the mid-19th century. They also utilize a sampling method that defaults to monocropping on large acreage. The procedure is to take random samples in a field and mix the samples together. Then you fill up your container out of this accumulation of samples. This sampling procedure gives you an overview of the whole field, but you lose the natural variability in soil that often occurs within a few feet. More tests are not the answer. If you tried to do 80 soil tests for 80 different crops the cost would be prohibitive and would only be valid for that year. As you rotate crops the next year, you would need 80 more tests. This is why soil tests default to "vegetables" as a category, rather than differentiating between tomatoes and corn, for example. This makes a single soil test affordable to a gardener, but it is a gross measure, when a finer one is needed. It is no accident that soil tests are based in reductionist chemistry and not holistic soil stewardship.

Fertilizer

Justus von Liebig was a German chemist who lived from 1803 to 1873, a critical time period for industrial Europe and the world.[7] As a young boy he lived through the "year without a summer" in 1816 caused by volcanic ash in the atmosphere from the eruption of Mount Tambora a year earlier. Excessive volcanic ash and sulfuric acid in the atmosphere can increase the earth's reflectivity and thus reduce the amount of sunlight available to grow crops. Germany was especially hard hit in the global famine of 1816 and von Liebig's experiences shaped his life. As an organic chemist, he was responsible for many innovations, but the two most important were the Law of the Minimum and the simplification of crop nutrient requirements to three basic elements: nitrogen (N), phosphorous (P) and potassium (K).[8]

The Law of the Minimum was actually formulated by Carl Sprengel in 1828, but popularized by von Liebig in mid-century.[9] It simply states that plant development is limited by the one essential nutrient in short supply. The usual example is a wooden water barrel with staves of varying lengths, also known as "Liebig's barrel." If you fill such a barrel with water, you can fill it only to the top of the shortest barrel stave. So it is with crop yields. If nitrogen is in short supply, it does not help to add more phosphorous and potassium. The extra P and K will be wasted. Modern fertilizer applications still use this principle. There are even applications of this law in economics and resource management, where the growth of markets are thought to be restricted by the input in shortest supply.

After the Law of the Minimum and the discovery of synthetic urea by Fredrich Wöhler (also in 1828), von Liebig concluded there was no distinction between elements produced by natural processes using a living organism (i.e. "organic") and those produced by chemical means in a laboratory. He further concluded you could pare down necessary elements to just nitrogen, phosphorous and potassium.[10] Not only was this a necessary prelude to making fertilizer from cheaper ingredients, but it reflected a major change in scientific thinking, away from vitalism and towards materialism.

Vitalism posits a "life force" that is vital to a living organism and makes it different from non-living entities. Consequently, there is a difference between nitrogen produced by a cow and excreted through urine and the nitrogen in ammonia produced in the lab by the interaction of nitrogen and hydrogen gases in the presence of a catalyst. *Materialism* quashes this dichotomy by saying only matter and energy exist. Materialism has been the mainstream view of science since Liebig's day and is integral to evolution by natural selection. Nevertheless, there are interactions we cannot track, or even observe, that can make a difference in the complex of nutrients both used and produced by plants. For example, pharmaceutical vitamins are often touted as a substitute for eating a variety of fresh foods. However, a diet rich in a variety of fresh foods is rich not only in those reductionist vitamins, but all the other molecules that have become incorporated into the DNA of each plant or animal domesticated and consumed by humans over millennia, in synchronicity with the human digestive system. This is the most basic meaning of *coevolution*, wherein we humans evolved right along with our domesticates like maize, wheat and potatoes. It is ironic that coevolution, rooted in materialism, is better served by eating whole vital foods rather than vitamins devoid of their context. Predator/prey relationships are usually cited as examples of coevolution, but the term is also relevant in an agricultural context.

While it is true you can grow lots of corn with chemical fertilizers rather than manure, the corn may be lower in nutrients and less resistant to pests simply due to lack of other nutrients plants need and which manure has. We can see over time that organic methods feed the soil and provide long-term benefits, while chemical methods strip the soil of essential nutrients and provide only short-term benefits. We can also see how dependent chemical methods are on energy from fossil fuels. The *balance* is not there anymore once you strip fertilizer down to three elements – N, P and K.

The answer to this conundrum is *holism*, another major paradigm in anthropology, alongside culture and evolution by natural selection. Holism simply states that not everything can be broken down (or reduced) into its essential elements. In other words, systems or organisms need the *integration* of their parts as surely as they need the parts themselves. The emphasis is on whole systems, or as Aristotle said, "The whole is greater than the sum of its parts."[11] Of course there are disagreements about holism among anthropologists and biologists, but that is par for the course. The main point is holism provides a counterpoint to *reductionism* (everything can be reduced to essential elements) and allows us to account for irreducible interactions we may not be able to comprehend but that nonetheless work. By using manure and bedding on our fields we are using a whole product with multiple benefits for soil health, rather than a simplified reductionist product that just gives us increased yields. In a very real sense, von Liebig threw the baby out with the bath water. Now we have a gigantic fertilizer industry that is directly responsible for pollution and global warming, as well as indirectly responsible for mass starvation as indigenous farmers and farming methods are forced off the land.

A balanced, holistic approach to fertilizer is to <u>start</u> with balance. In other words, rather than get a soil test which says you are deficient in one element and then just adding that element, the holistic approach is to start with a balanced fertilizer that also contains trace minerals. This may provide more of one element than actually needed, but the balance is already there from the beginning and other plants and microbes can use the excess. These other plants, or "weeds," will provide an important source of organic matter for the future as they break down. In other words, using a balanced fertilizer enhances the composting process already at work in your soil. It also mitigates the chances of more excess elements simply being flushed out of the soil into rivers and streams because of an increased likelihood of the elements being used by "something."

The idea that weeds serve a purpose in holding nutrients in reserve is not new, but it is unfashionable, even among organic farmers. Another unfashionable idea is to use weeds as *nutrient accumulators*. Consider the lowly thistle and its long taproot. The thistle thrives in poor soil because it digs deep for nutrients. If you pull the thistle out of the ground and lay it on top of the soil, you have now accessed minerals and nutrients you normally could not get to because they were deep in your soil. By pulling the thistle out by hand, you are cycling nutrients. This is a very beneficial use of weeds and should not be dismissed. First they are weeds, then they become mulch, then compost, and finally humus.

Liebig started out by dismissing the role of humus and reducing a complex web of soil fertility down to three elements: N, P and K. In this process he also dismissed the role of calcium (Ca), magnesium (Mn) and sulfur (S), as well as trace minerals. Calcium and magnesium can be added back to soil by liming, and sulfur is added in the production of phosphorus and potash fertilizers. *Trace minerals,* though, are still dismissed as an afterthought. If a farmer is using animal manures instead of chemical fertilizers, it is likely the fields are getting some trace minerals, as well as primary nutrients. This "masking effect" is probably the reason problems with chemical fertilizers did not surface until the 1970's. Until that time, there were still plenty of family farms and they had not gotten rid of their animals yet. My current theory is that animal manures were still compensating for the dearth of nutrients in chemical fertilizers until the animals were replace by monocropping in the "Earl Butz" decade.

So should we be embarking on a massive shift back to integrated animal agriculture? Not necessarily. First of all, it takes significant time, money and land to raise animals. The time element is a major problem. Animals like consistency and need care. Throwing the food over the fence and filling up their water trough is not enough. You have to observe them, make them move around, milk them in the case of cows and goats, and generally devote time to them. As for the money problem, it was true in the 1950's and it is true now that if you are <u>not</u> raising the feed for your animals, you are not covering your costs. I see many small-scale farmers subsidizing their animals out of their part-time jobs or even from sales of their produce. Finally, it takes land to raise animals. Cramming a few goats into a suburban backyard is not good for the goats, nor for you, nor your neighbors. Having enough room per animal is key to disease prevention and this also means fencing and other capital costs. Some people feel the manure value alone is a good tradeoff for all the attention animal husbandry requires, but I do not buy it. I grew up on a dairy farm and raised my own hogs and sheep, as well as taking care of cows and calves. The downsides are huge and the upsides are small. Raising animals is only valid if you really, really have a desire to do so. As a business decision, it does not pencil out.

So where do we get the fertilizer to add back fertility to the soil? After all, every time we sell an ear of corn or a tomato, fertility leaves the farm or garden. Even eating your own produce does not completely cycle nutrients back to the soil unless you are dumping your septic tank onto your fields. We can use cover crops and green manures to access nutrients already in the soil, but unless we bring in outside fertility by soil amendments, we have a net loss of fertility. This is why making your own organic fertilizer becomes so important. I use the recipe method and am indebted to Steve Solomon for my basic mix (*Growing Vegetables West of the Cascades* and *Gardening When It Counts*).[12] The difference is in my substitutions and calculating by pounds rather than volume.

For nitrogen I use soymeal and start with a 50 pound bag. This has an N-P-K ratio of 6.5-1.5-2.4, and this ratio means the meal is 6.5% nitrogen, 1.5% phosphorus, and 2.4% potassium. Multiplying these amounts by 50 pounds means I have 3.25 pounds of nitrogen, .75 pounds phosphorus and 1.2 pounds potassium. For phosphorus, I add 20 pounds of bone meal, which has an N-P-K ratio of 3-15-0. By the way, these percentages of phosphorus are *available* phosphorus. Rock phosphates have only about 20% of their phosphorus available immediately. The unavailable phosphorus will become available over several years time in the soil, but in calculating your fertilizer mix, you should concentrate on available phosphorus. This is why industrial phosphate fertilizers have been treated chemically so plants can access the phosphorus.

For potassium I use 10 pounds of sul-po-mag, which is a naturally-occurring compound of sulfur, potassium and magnesium. The N-P-K ratio is 0-0-22. Sul-po-mag also has trace minerals because it was formed from ancient sea beds, a good source of trace minerals. It was originally called langbeinite, after A. Langbein, who first described it in 1891.[13] Along with the sul-po-mag, I also use 10 pounds of greensand, which has an N-P-K ratio of 0-0-3. The greensand adds trace minerals as well as potassium, again because it comes from ancient sea beds. When I mix all these together (I use a wheelbarrow), I get a mix weighing 90 pounds that has a total of 3.85 pounds of nitrogen, 3.75 pounds of phosphorus, and 3.70 pounds of potassium, or 4.28% N, 4.17% P, and 4.11% K. Rounded down this is a 4-

4-4 fertilizer and is balanced between all three principle elements. Organic fertilizers are usually in a low range like 4-4-4 or 5-5-5, unlike popular lawn fertilizers which are 10-10-10 or 15-15-15 and can burn your lawn if overused. A low ratio gives you a bit of insurance. Table 6 provides my calculations and current prices in 2012.

Product	Lb	Price	Price/lb	N	P	K	Mix	N	P	K
Soymeal	50	$ 19.29	$ 0.39	6.5	1.5	2.4	50	3.25	0.75	1.20
Bone meal	50	$ 40.13	$ 0.80	3.0	15.0	0	20	0.60	3.00	0
Greensand	50	$ 37.96	$ 0.76	0	0	3.0	10	0	0	.30
Sul-Po-Mag	50	$ 23.90	$ 0.48	0	0	22.0	10	0	0	2.20
Cost/lb			$ 0.53				Totals	3.85	3.75	3.70
Cost/sq ft			$ 0.014				%	**4.28**	**4.17**	**4.11**
Cost/acre			$615.65							

Table 6 – Calculating fertilizer costs and ratios. Final ratio (rounded down) is 4-4-4.

Notice this fertilizer costs $.53 a pound and $.014 per square foot. This is based on using 1 gallon of the dry mix per 100 row feet and a dry gallon weighs 8 pounds. Since I have 3 feet between rows in my garden, a dry gallon actually covers 300 square feet. My costs are actually a bit lower because I also add 4 quarts of agricultural lime (for calcium), 3 quarts of dolomite lime (for calcium and magnesium), and 2 quarts of gypsum (for sulfur and calcium) per fertilizer mix (all cheaper than the N-P-K sources). This has proven to be a very good mix over the years. You may be shocked at how expensive organic fertilizer is per acre. However, remember you should be able to generate $20,000-$40,000 per acre in produce, unlike a conventional farmer growing corn and generating $1,000-$1,200 per acre.

If you do not feel competent making your own fertilizer, there are several companies selling balanced mixes. They will cost at least 50% more than making your own, but they are convenient. Some of their nutrient sources may be questionable however, so do your homework before you buy. There are other ways of adding fertility to the soil that you may not have considered. For instance, think of a pumpkin as a bag of fertilizer.

Pumpkins like rich soil and are heavy feeders. As such, they sit on top of the nutrient chain, similar to us humans sitting on top of the food chain. Therefore, if you drop a pumpkin on the ground and let it break down, it will deposit the nutrients the plant has accumulated in the fruit and seeds. This can be a considerable amount, as pumpkins are rich in nutrient food value. Some of the pumpkin flesh and seed will be eaten by rodents and birds, but presumably they also poop on site. Most of the pumpkin flesh and seeds will decay and become available to microorganisms in the soil and eventually the plants in that patch of soil.

The takeaway here is you could buy a truckload of pumpkins when they are cheap (cheaper than $.53/lb. – your homemade fertilizer cost), dump them on your fields in the fall and let them break down over winter. In the spring you will have already-fertilized soil. I do this already and can report good results with cabbage, onions and volunteer pumpkins. The volunteer pumpkins are earlier than my other pumpkins and readily outcompete the weeds. Once again, we can get multiple benefits from using an integrated, holistic approach that feeds the soil, rather than treating the soil as a factory and just feeding the plant. **Plant to improve your soil, not just to grow food.** The extra benefit will be better food.

Cover Crops and Green Manure

Another way to improve your soil is through cover crops and green manure. The terms are often used interchangeably, but a cover crop's primary goal is to *prevent erosion*, while a green manure's primary goal is to *enrich the soil*. As with mulch, cover crops and green manure have multiple uses. They also hold moisture in the soil and control water flows on the surface. They promote symbiotic relationships in the *rhizosphere* (the soil or plant root zone) between fungi and plants. They give microorganisms and "critters" habitat and something to feed on. They also provide cover for various predators who feed on the bugs and slugs and rodents.

Cover crops/green manures do not have to be planted. You can just let the weeds grow. As I mentioned earlier, thistles go deep for nutrients with their long tap roots. While they grow, they accumulate nutrients and if you pull them out (ideally before they flower!) and lay them on top of the soil, they become mulch and then compost, chock full of nutrients. However, if you do plant cover crops/green manure, there are advantages and disadvantages to consider.

Most cover crops are planted in the fall, although I do use buckwheat as a summer cover crop. Several years ago I got a bag of cover crop mix containing rye and vetch. This mix was slow to come up in the fall, but really took off in the spring. It grew quite rapidly and was hard to turn under without a tractor. In other words it is suited to machine cultivation, rather than hand cultivation (including a walk-behind tiller). A better alternative that comes up faster, grows higher and is easier to turn under with a tiller are favas. I prefer a small-seeded variety called Banner, although I have used another variety, Diana, which I did not like. I am also experimenting with fall-planting a large-seeded variety, Windsor, that is usually planted in the spring. Some crops, like barley, have a *facultative* property, which means you can plant them in either spring or fall. I am hoping the Windsor will overwinter and give me an early crop of large-seeded favas.

Planting grain and legume cover crops in the fall gives you multiple options. If your winter wheat does not look good, you can plow it under in the spring and the soil will have increased tilth and added fertility. With fall-planted favas, you can till them under in the spring or leave them for fresh pods or dry seed. It is usually best to till in your legumes at the peak of their flowering stage, as the plant changes from feeding the nitrogen-fixing nodules to filling the pods for the plant's seeds. For grain crops tilled under in the spring, you can just till them in when it is convenient. However, you should be careful with winter rye, as it has *allelopathic* properties, meaning it releases chemicals into the soil to suppress weeds around the plant.[14] This property of rye makes it attractive to researchers looking for a substitute for chemical herbicides, but best results for weed suppression come with combinations of other crops. This is why a rye/vetch mix is a popular cover crop/green manure. If you use this combination you should try to turn it into the ground 4-6 weeks before you plant something else.

A brief note on legumes and nitrogen-fixing bacteria is in order. The whole process is quite fascinating. A common soil bacterium, *Rhizobium*, invades the plant root and starts to grow within the root cells. The plant feeds the bacteria and within a week, nodules have formed on the roots. By 2-3 weeks, the nodules can be seen and turn from white to pinkish red as they start to fix bacteria. What the bacteria in the nodules do is to take inert nitrogen gas in the air (N_2) and convert it to useful ammonia (NH_3), which all living organisms need to manufacture amino acids proteins, and other necessary compounds. The plant feeds the bacteria and the bacteria feed the plant – a *symbiotic* relationship. As the plant changes modes from flower production to pod fill after fertilization, the nodules are cut off from nutrients and sometimes even discarded into the soil.[15] At this point, the nitrogen is free in the soil to be used by other plants. Tilling in your favas or other legumes at flowering thus provides the most nitrogen.

Planting a fall crop of grain after a summer of growing a legume, such as soybeans, allows the grain crop to take up the available nitrogen and store it in the biomass. This short-circuits the natural cycle of soil microorganisms converting the nitrogen into a methane (CH_4) byproduct as they eat through the organic matter in the soil. While this is the ideal scenario, methane production is a natural process that occurs in healthy soil, even though methane is about 23 times more potent as a greenhouse gas than carbon dioxide. The problem with methane is not with natural methane production in forest and field, but rather the production of gas from landfills, seepage from hydraulic fracturing, and holding animal manure in anaerobic conditions in lagoons.[16] As with most environmental problems, the industrial scale causes the problem, rather than the actual chemical. On the up side, methane has a shorter life in the atmosphere, about 12 years instead of the 200 years needed for carbon dioxide to break down. All in all, using a cover crop to produce nitrogen produces more benefits than harm.

Another reason farmers favor cover crop mixes is because two or more crops allow a symbiotic <u>physical</u> interaction. For example, with an oat/pea/vetch mix planted in the spring, the oats come up first and get pulled down by the peas, which are then pulled down by the vetch. This forms a mat you disk in during the autumn. Notice again how this mix is suited more to a tractor scale than a human/tiller scale. In the case of our fall rye/vetch mix, the rye serves as a nurse crop to protect the vetch from frost damage There are many ways to look at cover crop combinations, but since I operate on a human, rather than a tractor, scale, I like to keep things simple. I plant favas, vetch, or crimson clover by themselves.

The use of cover crops fits in well with crop rotation. As I mentioned earlier, I use a six-year rotation, but I am not a slavish adherent. There are multiple variables to deal with, so it is disadvantageous to be too rigid. In my rotation, I start with grain and then go to legumes like favas for the second year. The reason for favas <u>after</u> grain is because you always get volunteers if you let your favas seed out. These are easier to handle while cultivating and weeding your row crops than letting a broadcast grain grow up and walking through the young grain crop pulling volunteers.

The third year is a root crop, like potatoes or onions, etc. The fourth year is a fruiting crop, like squash, sweet corn, or tomatoes. The fifth year is another legume to build up nitrogen again and the sixth year is a green crop, like lettuce, cabbage, chard, etc. Notice how the legume crops are separated by two other crops. This means one out of every three years I am putting back nitrogen into the soil. I also keep my fertilizer costs down by not fertilizing my legume crops. Over several years of building up my soil, I find I can get away with this lack of phosphorous, potassium and lime during one out of three years. Here is the rotation in a nutshell:

grain---------favas---------root---------fruit---------pea---------leaf.

I started out this chapter talking about farming as if energy matters. This quickly became a discussion about soil and fertility. In animal husbandry, the farmer is facilitating the animals doing the real work. The cow or sheep grazes the pasture and the farmer takes the milk or meat. The chickens scratch around all day and the farmer takes the eggs and meat. The farmer is like an overlay on a natural process. We can treat the soil in the same respectful fashion. The microorganisms and plants in the soil are doing the real work. Hopefully, we can be efficient and go about our day by doing pleasing tasks that facilitate their work.

We control what comes up as much as we can, but we do not need to worry about weeds as much as the chemical companies would have us believe. If you were to visit my farm, you would be surprised by how beautiful the crops are, yet how "messy" some areas look. It is like triage in the garden every day and I never get to everything. In fact, I purposely bite off more than I can chew every year so I am forced to come up with efficient solutions. [Back when I was a youth soccer coach I used *performance under pressure* as a coaching strategy. I do the same to myself.] The bottom line is that I get great results by doing what I can in a reasonable manner, using just a little bit of fossil fuel energy. We do not need tractors except occasionally. What is essential is to manage the soil properly by feeding it. **Feed the soil instead of feeding the plant.** The soil feeds the plant.

11 CROPS & CROP VARIETIES

N ow it is time to get down to the nitty-gritty of specific crops. As mentioned previously, there are quite a few books on how to grow a garden and they usually give you information on specific crops. I will provide some information you may not find elsewhere because it is based on my own experience. I will use my list of crops and start with apples, a crop I have experience with both as a migrant worker and as a farmer.

Apples

There are a multitude of heirloom varieties of apples available, even though there seem to be only a few available in grocery stores. My favorite is the Spartan because it is delicious and stores well. The tree is vigorous and a consistent yielder. It also does well against coddling moths. I use *spinosad*, an organic spray marketed under various labels, to spray my apples, pears and plums, but I am not as rigid on spraying as other people. The reason is continual use of one spray promotes resistance in the pest. Typically, I am late on the first spray after petal drop, since I have 20 different kinds of apples and they all bloom at different times. It is hard to include the early bloomers' petal drop with the late bloomers, so I just wait for the last petals to fall. This opens up a window for the pests on the early trees. I mitigate this somewhat by cleaning up apples in the fall and promptly cleaning up branches from winter pruning, since coddling moths like woody debris and moldy apples for their eggs.

I also typically wait too long between sprays (should be 10-14 days), but I want to continue using spinosad year after year, so I limit my spray to less than the maximum number of six sprays per season. I usually only do four sprays. This lackadaisical approach means some apples will have blemishes. I use these for cider. The Spartans have a bit of built-in resistance to coddling moths, and some of my other apples seem to as well, like Yellow Transparent, Akane and Ben Davis.

My only other spray is a combination dormant oil and lime sulfur spray in midwinter. The dormant oil spray is to coat overwintering insects and thereby suffocate them. The lime sulfur spray is for peach leaf curl in plums, but it also has a preventive effect for other bacteria, insects and fungi. I do not worry about other pests because 1) sharing is okay as long as it is less than 10% and 2) using organic methods and feeding the soil makes the soil healthy, which then makes the plants growing in the soil healthy. The attitude of sharing a small amount with the pests and feeding the soil may require some explaining.

We live in an extremely complicated and interactive environment. Without insects we would not have birds that feed on the insects. Predator/prey relationships are complex. Trying to get every last little bug off your apples or other produce is not only anti-evolutionary, it is inefficient. It has been said that building the US interstate highway system cost as much for the last 5% of the system as for the previous 95%. It is axiomatic that getting the last little bit of pollution out of a smokestack quickly achieves diminishing returns. It is the same with the food you grow. If you are satisfied with a small "bite" for the bugs, you will have much less work to do and considerably lower costs of production.

In the same vein, understanding we are part of a complex interactive web allows us to approach prevention in an indirect manner. Feeding the soil instead of feeding the plant is the basis of organic methods and when we do that the soil is healthy. When the soil is healthy, the plants in the soil can fight off bugs and viruses easier. It is similar to your body's immune system. If you have a healthy immune system, you can fight off disease and bacterial "invaders" to a greater extent than if your immune system is compromised. It works the same way with the soil. I see this on a daily basis in the field, which is why the organic method of feeding the soil works so well. Part of this is refraining from using synthetic fertilizers and pesticides, but balance in adding nutrients to the soil is important too. A balanced fertilizer, making your own compost and growing out biomass in the field all work well to keep the soil healthy.

In addition to feeding the soil in your orchard, you must attend to your apple trees. They require water and will go deep for it, but in the first year you need to pay attention to the water needs of your new trees. If you do your own grafting, you will likely be paying close attention to the water needs of your grafts, so extending this to treess in their first year should come naturally. After the first year in the orchard, you can treat the young trees the same as the older trees. Pay attention and water as needed. I do not irrigate my orchard at all, but I have a special situation with a water vein directly underneath. The climate in western Washington also allows me to get away with no watering. Even though it is hot and dry during the summer, there is plentiful soil moisture because of the winter rains. I do not even need to water our lawn to keep it green. This is what is called "dry farming" and the advantages are that your apples are more flavorful. If you taste two apples of the same size, one from an irrigated and one from a dry-farmed orchard, you will likely notice the dry-farmed apple is more flavorful. That is because the irrigated apple is pumped up with water, so there are actually fewer nutrients per the mass of the apple. In an industry that values yield and not taste, this is the inevitable result – large apples that are tasteless. Most people do not know what an apple should taste like, since they have only had apples from industrial orchards sold in the supermarket. When you grow your own apples, you will see and taste the difference.

Another important aspect to growing apples is to *prune* your trees sensibly. When I was a migrant worker I also pruned during the winter, so I learned how from the orchardist who employed me. I use what is called the "modified central leader" system, which is the way orchards were maintained in the 1970's in Washington. I like this system because it is easy to pick and allows a lot of sunlight into the center of the tree. However, there are many other pruning systems. Once you are committed to having apples, you really should go to a local orchardist and apprentice or pay to learn techniques. You cannot get what you need from books or even instructional videos.

Thinning your apples is usually not as much of a problem as you think. Most of my 19 different varieties self-thin and my habit of not watering my orchard helps the trees achieve a balance between the load on their limbs and what the roots can take up. I dislike thinning anyway. Back in my migrant worker days I was lucky enough to be able to pick peaches instead of having to thin between cherry and pear seasons. More of a worry than thinning is cutting off suckers – or water sprouts. Again, I do not have too much of a problem here because I do not irrigate my orchard – water sprouts are a function of excess water compounding pruning that is too vigorous. I like to prune heavy one year and then lightly for two years, so that may have some bearing on my sucker production, but it really is not a problem. As with most of my solutions, they are built upon balance, so I get balance as a result.

Artichokes & Cardoon

The *artichoke* is a strange vegetable. If you gave one to a person who had never seen one and said, "Here – boil the hell out of it and peel off the leaves one by one so you can eat the little tiny bit at the bottom of the leaf," he or she would surely think you were crazy. But the artichoke is quite good once you get past all the work of preparing it. The same goes for *cardoon*, which is an old Roman/Greek vegetable and the ancestor of the artichoke. With cardoon, you eat the stalks instead of the flower bulb. The taste is also quite good, but it takes a lot of preparation. First you strip the feathery edges off the stalks with a sharp knife - the strings too, if the stalks are not young and tender. Then you cut them to size and keep them in a pan of cold water and lemon so they do not brown. Then you boil them, also in lemon water, for twenty minutes or so before baking them. I like to bake them with sautéed onions and topped with parmesan. This is the kind of dish that elicits responses like:

"This is really good."

"Yeah, I know. I like it too."

"NO, I mean this is <u>really</u> good."

Growing artichokes and cardoon is relatively simple, although you have to start them indoors. Even though they are perennials, they can be grown as annuals in cold weather climates. I also like to *vernalize* my seed. This is just subjecting the seeds to some "chill hours" so they think they have passed through a winter. To do this, I wrap them in wet paper towels, place in a plastic bag and put them in the refrigerator for two weeks. Then I start them in transplant mix.

A word about transplant (starting) mixes. There are many recipes but I have good luck with ½ garden soil, ¼ compost and ¼ peat moss. I also throw in some perlite to lighten up the texture. I make up 20 gallons at a time, or two 5-gallon buckets of soil, one bucket of compost and one bucket of peat moss. I bought some coco coir to replace peat moss a few years ago but it is not as good. (Harvesting peat for the nursery industry adversely affects Canadian marshlands.) It also comes from Sri Lanka, so the energy/travel miles across two oceans negate any environmental upside. If California starts producing coco coir I will go back to it.

I use the cement floor in my barn for mixing and just dump out the buckets and mix with a hoe. This is the same technique as mixing my fertilizer, which I do in a wheelbarrow, since it is of lower volume. I also add a pint of fertilizer mix and a half-cup of lime per 5-gallon bucket of mix, so for 20 gallons that comes out to 2 quarts of fertilizer mix and a pint of lime per batch. Plants do not need nutrients when they are just coming up because they feed on stored carbohydrates. However, it is often necessary to "hold" your starts when you cannot get into the field right away (wet soil) or if you are swamped with work and do not get to plant your starts on time. This is where the little bit of fertilizer in your transplant mix becomes valuable. The little bit of lime sweetens the mix and allows greater absorption of nutrients. When you are starting artichokes or cardoon, figure on 8-12 weeks from planting to the field.

Since we are on the transplant topic, it behooves you to build one or more *cold frames*. It is just fine to use a kitchen table or windowsill with a southern exposure to start your plants, but you need to harden them off. This is where a cold frame becomes really valuable. The easiest cold frame to build is just an old window and frame attached to a rectangular box where the back is 12 inches higher than the front. This increases the sun exposure because the angle of the glass approximates the angle of the sun. (This is the same principle as passive solar heating – the best angle is equal to the latitude of your location.) You can use plywood or regular lumber. Attach the window frame to the back with a couple of hinges and put a handle on the front so you can open the lid easily. Keep a couple of scrap pieces of wood around to prop up the lid for ventilation on sunny days. You would be surprised how easy it is to "cook" your starts.

After your starts are up and healthy (usually 2-6 weeks depending on the crop), you put them out into the cold frame for two weeks - after all danger of frost is past, of course. For the first couple of days, make sure the frame is closed up for the night. If you are really worried the first night or two, you can put a blanket over your frame. After a while, you will see the plants are used to the outside weather and then you can leave the frame open all night. Two weeks is a good average in the cold frame, but you can also transfer starts out of the cold frame and onto a nearby table where they can sit for weeks. Just keep them watered.

Many people like to use a cover over their starts, like a plastic dome or plastic wrap. This just provides a perfect environment for mold. Your plants need several things – moisture, sun, warmth, and air. Some people like to use a heated cable bed or heat mat under their starts and I do this for early starts like cabbages. Cable beds and heat mats work quite well, but you still have to do the rest of it. Some people like to "bake" their soil to get rid of errant bacteria and kill any weed seeds. I do not bother. Baking your soil is a messy, time-consuming process that yields little return. Trust in the quality of your transplant mix, especially if you are using your own soil and compost. Finally, do not expect all of your seeds to germinate. Artichokes and cardoon usually have a germination ratio of only 50%. Other seeds like cabbage will be around 90%.

Arugula and Other Mustards

Arugula is often dismissed and despised as "yuppie fodder." However, it is a sturdy plant, yields well and provides winter greens. I quite like the buttery, peppery taste. Like all the mustards, it gets hotter when the weather is hot, but if you plant it in the fall and let it grow over the winter, it will have a milder flavor. My significant other and I eat arugula and mustard salads all winter and we like to joke that when spring comes we have to go back to "wimpy" salads with lettuce. Most plants that winter well produce more plant sugars when the weather gets cold — sort of like an antifreeze solution. This makes them sweeter. Carrots and parsnips are the usual crops people notice are sweeter after a freeze but it works for mustards too.

Asparagus

I cannot emphasize enough how wonderful home-grown asparagus is — even eaten raw as you weed the bed. It is well worth the trouble to grow and provides a burst of springtime flavor in April and May when you need it most. Since it is a perennial, you should think a bit about your plans for the next 10-20 years (or more). Usual width between rows is four feet, but you might be able to get away with a narrower spacing, especially if you put in your plants 1 ½ feet apart rather than 1 foot. Usually you will be able to buy 2-year-old roots and they are hardier than 1-year-old roots. However, you can also start asparagus from seed. I added a row this year from a purple French variety I could only get as seed. I started them in my transplant mix and left them a long time on an outside table before planting in the row mid-July. They are doing well.

Weeding asparagus can be a real pain. Asparagus needs rich soil and weeds respond to rich soil faster than asparagus. This is why mulching is important. The mulch helps keep the weeds down and keeps the soil moist and cool. I like to mulch between the rows and even cover the rows over winter. However, this is best done after the ferns have died down. Even with mulching, there is no substitute to getting on your knees to weed.

The ferns are the way the plants get nutrients for next year as well as for reproductive processes, so you should let the spears go once they slow down to pencil thickness. By that time you should have already gotten 6-8 weeks of nice fat thumb-width spears, so you will have certainly gotten your share of the crop. If you have planted all-male spears from the nursery, you will likely see no red berries in your row. The all-male plants are a recent innovation in asparagus growing and I have mixed feelings about them. I would like my asparagus to spread to fill up my patch, so I am now planting from seed so I can get both male and female roots.

Whether you plant purchased roots or your own starts, you should not take any spears until the second year in the field - and then only a couple if you cannot resist. It is better to wait until the third year. When you plant, you should use a balanced fertilizer and add extra phosphorus. This is where rock phosphate comes in handy, as only 20% will be available the first year. The rest becomes available over time, so putting down rock phosphate is a cheap way to get slow-release phosphorus for the future.

Barley

Anyone who drinks beer can appreciate barley. It was even postulated by botanist J. D. Sauer in 1952 that beer was the reason for domestication of wild barley around 9000 BCE at Jarmo (in Iraq near Kirkuk and excavated by archaeologist Robert Braidwood 1948-1955).[1] This theory could not be proven because the same equipment could just as well be used for breadmaking as for brewing. Nevertheless, the theory still survives and it makes for a pleasant tale. There was even a Sumerian goddess of beer named Ninkasi, 5000 years after the first domestication of the grain.[2] If beer was not the prompt for the Neolithic Revolution, it certainly contributed to the rise of civilization.

Barley is quite the flexible grain. It does well in both desert and maritime environments, at high altitudes like Tibet and near sea level like the coast of Washington. It can be planted early when fields are still a little wet and the usual dictum is, "Plant your barley in the mud and your wheat in the dust." The downside is the groat which requires extra threshing. *Malting* (sprouting the grains until just before they break the husk), *roasting* and *sparging* (running hot water over the sprouted, roasted grain) release the sugars into a liquid, which is then called *wort*. Pitching yeast into the wort produces an alcoholic beverage first called *ale* (without hops in the old nomenclature) and now called beer when hops are added. Hops were first domesticated in Germany in the 8th century and became popular in the Middle Ages to clarify ale, since there was a real pollution problem in Merry Olde England and the rest of medieval Europe.[3] So-called "small beers" of low alcohol content could be drunk throughout the day with little negative effect on the peasant way of life. This was preferable to water from the open sewers in use at the time. Beer was a health drink. Some say it still is and I would concur, as long as it is a microbrew and not the usual mass-market sludge.

Barley also makes for a sweet addition to bread, and you do not have to worry as much about the groat. If you only use 10-20% of the whole kernel in your flour mix, the extra fiber does not detract from the texture at all. However, if you want to use your barley for soup, you will have to find some way to *pearl* it. I have not discovered a small-scale method yet, so my alternative is to grow hulless barley. I have two spring varieties with which I am experimenting.

Barley exhibits a *facultative* property, meaning you can plant it either fall or spring. This is important for ongoing climate problems. If you can plant in both fall and spring, you double your chances of getting a crop. In some years the fall crop will be your mainstay; in others you will have to depend on your spring crop. So not only should you be diversifying by planting multiple grain crops to see which ones do well in a particular year, you should also be planting these crops in both seasons. Some crops may not take to this and I am in the midst of ongoing wheat experiments. Barley generally does quite well either in spring or fall planting.

Another planting trick is to till in your barley field after harvesting. This allows the grain you have dropped (using your primitive harvesting methods such as a sickle) to provide the seed for next year. You can even fertilize the ground to give your grain a boost. I developed this idea of *semi-permanent* grain production because of the problems of perennial wheat. Over the last decade, several researchers have started working on perennial wheat. However, the researchers seem to be stuck and they are always 10-20 years away from a perennial wheat that has good yield. The reasons for developing a perennial wheat are to keep the soil covered, bind the soil with a much more extensive root system, and cut down on tillage. The semi-permanent solution uses a little bit of tillage, but it does keep the soil covered while the crop is growing. Tilling after harvest also stimulates microbial processes in the soil. There are pluses and minuses in both systems, but right now we can grow an annual grain and then grow it again in the same spot − thus the *semi-permanent* label. The main downside is lowered yield in the second year. However, you can till your field after harvest and let the grain come up over winter. Then in the spring you can decide whether to keep the grain or till it in as green manure. Once again, flexibility is the key.

Basil

If you are only going to grow one herb, I suggest basil. It smells like summer and pesto is a wonderful alternative to marinara sauce on pasta. It can be difficult to get basil started, but purchased starts are usually available from people who have greenhouses. You get a tremendous amount of leaves from each plant so just pinch off the flowers as they form and the plants will thrive until frost. Around here, they seem to like the morning fog and afternoon sun we get in September and early October. Of course warm summers are enjoyed by basil, but are not strictly necessary. Once it gets started it adapts quite well. I particularly like to grow purple basil as well as sweet basil and Thai basil. The purple basil provides a nice color compliment to a tomato and cucumber salad. There are a lot of basil varieties and they all have their advantages.

Speaking of greenhouses, hoophouses and the like, I find them to be too much bother. I put up a simple *hoophouse* several years ago and a strong wind came up the next day and knocked it flat. I have also noticed the difference in flavor between food grown under cover and food grown out in the wind and rain and sun. I suspect weather stress promotes stronger flavor. My reasoning is that stress prompts plants to produce compounds that help maintain upright posture and counteract extremes of heat, cold, light and moisture. We notice these compounds when we taste the crop. Over time, we have come to recognize these compounds as part of the flavor profile of the plant. Using greenhouses and hoophouses allows the plant to put energy into growth rather than produce the necessary compounds to deal with environmental stressors. Thus the bland hoophouse tomato. Great for early harvest. Not so good for flavor.

Beet Greens, Beet Roots and Chard

Beet greens are a very nice salad green for spring. They come up fast and after you cut them a couple of times you can leave them to develop their roots. A very good variety for this dual purpose is Early Wonder Tall Top. Many people like Bull's Blood because of its deep red leaf color, but I like the taste of Early Wonder better. You can also leave Bull's Blood for later root production. For beet greens, just cut off the leaves at 4-6 inches tall, just like cutting your lettuce for salad mix, making sure you do not cut into the leaf crown. They will grow back.

What is commonly thought of as beet seed is actually a multigerm cluster containing 2-5 seeds, although some seed companies break apart the clusters. Breaking apart the clusters reduces the viability of the seed somewhat, so it is not uncommon to get poor germination. An easy way to get around this difficulty is to plant double rows. I use a seeder for most of my planting and I just go down the designated row on one side of the centerline and back on the other side, 4-6 inches apart. You can use a string if you like, but I find it to be too much bother. After all, I have been planting straight rows for over 50 years and if you are not on a tractor scale, the straightness of your rows is less important. It is good to have straight rows for your tiller, but a tiller is more forgiving than a tractor when cultivating between rows.

Thinning is usually advised with beets because of the clusters. However, I find beets, carrots and onions all crowd together just fine and do not need much thinning. It is more important to weed than to thin. Also, since I use a seeder, the seed plates provide a nice space between plants and this saves on thinning, as well as the amount of seed used. I have planted a whole acre of 60-80 crops by hand but a seeder makes for a lot less work. Some things still have to be planted by hand, like large-seeded favas, but a seeder will work for most of your seeds.

My favorite beet is the Chioggia variety, although Detroit Dark Red is a variety I grew in the 1950's that is still around. Both of these beets are fast-growing and delicious. The Chioggia has a candy-apple red outer color and alternating white and red bands inside. It also does not stain like the dark red beets. I make pickles every three years or so and sometimes I plant Cylindra (or Forono) for this purpose. They grow up like cylinders, rather than spherical, and they fit handily into pint jars when making pickles. Beets can be left in the ground over winter if your winters are mild like here in northwest Washington. The Detroit Dark Red beets hold better than the Chioggias, which tend to blow up in size more. The Detroit Dark Red beets

169

are also the best for *borscht*, one of our winter staple foods. Another good winter keeper is Red Ace, which is a hybrid. The other beets mentioned are heirlooms. Some people like golden beets, but I feel their flavor is not as good as the red beets. To each his own.

Chard is a beet developed for its foliage rather than the root. It is called silverbeet in England, but there are more colors than the standard white-ribbed, green-leaved chard like Fordhook Giant. I grow Golden and Ruby Red chard as well and I let the plants overwinter here and there. As a result, I have volunteer chard in several places each year and I just let some come up, as well as doing a small planting just in case. This year I have chard in my cucumber patch, as well as in a raised bed and on the sides of two of my chinampas. Chard is a wonderful green and we especially like it baked in frittatas (a frittata is like a quiche but not in a shell). It is also good sautéed with onions and served over pasta.

Blackberries

Blackberries grow wild in the Pacific Northwest and they can become quite a nuisance. When I was competing in *orienteering* (point-to-point running with map and compass – sometimes called "the thinking person's sport" and "cunning running"), the blackberries were often marked as "Fight" on the contour maps because you had to fight your way through. Blackberries are one of the reasons orienteers prefer long pants and long sleeves. Nevertheless, how can a person complain about delicious berries growing along ditches and roads that can be eaten out of hand, made into tarts and jam, or thrown into a bag and frozen for a quick treat or cereal topping in January?

Back when we did farmers markets, we sold blackberries in August and put a sign up saying, "Of course you could, but will you?" This usually got a laugh from customers and pre-empted the inevitable comment, "$3.00 a pint? I could pick them for free."

Broccoli

Broccoli is more important for its shoots than for the main head. The shoots can be harvested until the plant stops producing. This is dependent on how hard your winters are. You can even let the plants hang out all winter and then let them seed out for bee feed. Like all the brassicas, they are biennials and so flower and produce seed the second year.

Bees are an integral part of your garden. You need them for pollination and many agricultural crops need bees to pollinate. Having your own bees is not necessary if you have plenty of wild bees. I provide plentiful bee feed from early spring to late fall just by letting crops like broccoli and mustard seed out. The bees love it and I can usually identify 4-5 different bee species in the garden. I also plant borage just for the bees, but the diversity of plants on our farm is the main reason bees do so well. A main component is letting broccoli overwinter.

Most of the broccoli varieties I like are hybrids. I especially like Arcadia because it comes up fast in the heated cable bed, transplants well, grows fasts, tastes great, and hangs on for a long time producing side shoots. Other good hybrids are Marathon, Premium Crop and Green King. Waltham 29 is a good open-pollinated heading variety usually listed as a fall broccoli, but it does well up here because of our cool summers. If you have hot summers, you might be forced to split out your broccoli into spring and fall crops. Up here in the northwestern corner of the Pacific Northwest, I just plant in April and keep planting until September.

Sprouting broccoli may or may not produce a main head (Calabrese does but Purple Sprouting does not) and it has been selected over the years for a sweeter taste. We find the stems to be sweeter too and sprouting broccoli can be cut further down the stem than the side shoots from heading varieties. When we were doing markets, the broccoli *connoisseurs* invariably asked for sprouting broccoli. One of the sprouting broccolis I especially like is just called Purple Sprouting. It needs overwintering to produce sprouts, so it just hangs out all summer, fall and winter, getting bigger and bigger. Then in February or March, it puts out an abundance of purple sprouts, which are quite delicious as they come in late winter when you really need nutrients.

Brussels Sprouts

Little cabbages in wintertime – that is what Brussels sprouts are. You can see why a French person might call you *mon petit choux* ("my little cabbage") as a term of endearment. (Or maybe not - such are the vagaries of language.) Brussels sprouts seem especially susceptible to aphids, which disappear after the first frost, so I wait until winter to indulge in the little cabbages. Sometimes I get a few Brussels sprouts in September from a hybrid called Gustus, but usually I have to wait until late October or November (first frost where I live is historically on October 10th). Since I have a surplus of brassicas year-round, I do not mind the wait. The open pollinated varieties I like are Falstaff (purple in color) and Roodnerf. Brussels sprouts hang on for a long time in areas with milder winters because they stand up above the ground-clinging frost. Like kale, they provide fresh taste and nutrients in the dead of winter. I like them best just steamed and slathered in butter, but they take well to curry and can be roasted with herbs too.

Buckwheat

Buckwheat has an odd-shaped seed and is not a grain. In fact it is often called a *pseudocereal* in order to distinguish it from real grains like wheat and rye. The etymology of the name seems to be a corruption of the Dutch word *beuk* (beech – seeds from the beech tree have a similar shape) and the fact it can be used like wheat (i.e. for flour).[4] Buckwheat is simple to grow and will often outcompete weeds. As such it makes a great summer cover crop and is reputed to change insoluble phosphorus to a more soluble form. In other words buckwheat makes insoluble phosphorus available to other plants and soil microorganisms as well as itself. This could be important in the years to come when we may have to worry about peak phosphorus. Other plants reputed to have this capability are rye and clover.

I sow buckwheat like my other grain crops. First I find out how many pounds per acre are recommended. In the case of buckwheat it is 50-75 pounds per acre. Then I multiply these numbers by the fraction of an acre I am planting. So, if I am planting 450 square feet of space the calculation is $50 * 450 \div 43,560 = .52$ pounds or $75 * 450 \div 43,560 = .77$ pounds. In this case I would just weigh out ¾ of a pound and broadcast as I walk along in my prepared seedbed. Then to till in the seed, I set my tiller on a shallow setting and go over the seedbed once. This puts the seed under the soil, away from birds and surrounded by soil moisture to speed germination. This year (2012) I have been irrigating briefly after planting to increase soil moisture, as we went the whole month of August without any measurable rain. Buckwheat can be sown any time during the summer and it will be worth it. You can get 3-4 crops a year if you like, but I usually just do one. A word about sowing by hand. It is not difficult to get into a rhythm of flinging out the seed. Marking off your area into two parts so you can go out and back is the best. This also enables you to restrict your natural tendency to throw out too much seed. You will be surprised at how little seed it takes to sow a field. Start out with small amounts. You can always go over it again.

Harvesting buckwheat is simple. You just walk along with a bucket and strip off seeds from the stalks. If you want to use both hands, just hang the bucket on a strap around your neck and use a cross strap around your midsection to keep the bucket stable. (This also works with picking other crops like raspberries.) You do not even have to bend over to harvest it! The problem is what to do with the grain that still has a hard husk. If you grind it into flour without hulling, it is hard on your flour mill motor and leaves excess fiber in the flour. My solution is to use a hand-cranked mill set at a coarse grind. The buckwheat readily grinds into flour and hulls, which can be sifted out using a regular kitchen strainer. In other words, you go from the husked grain right to the flour, bypassing the intermediate step of husked whole grain.

You might think this technique would work with barley and oats, which also have a groat that must be. However, the unique characteristic buckwheat has to "flour" easily when ground is the deciding factor. I tried grinding several kinds of barley and oats to test this and they did not "flour" as readily. The ground meal has virtually the same consistency as the husks and needs considerably more grinding to make it "clump" into flour. In other words, there is not enough difference in the consistency of the endosperm and the hull in oats and barley to make it work.

Cabbage

You should eat more cabbage. It is easy to grow and easy to start your own transplants. If conditions are right, you can get it out to the field in only four weeks. You can plant it in the rain and it holds on all summer and fall. In the maritime climate in the Pacific Northwest, it lasts in the field most of the winter. You should also consider making sauerkraut (lacto-fermented cabbage), another food item that should be considered a staple. I like sauerkraut unpasteurized because the enzymes are still alive. This means when I jar up my kraut, I just keep it in a refrigerator all winter. I have plenty of refrigerator space, but if you do not have room in yours, just can it using any of the recipes found in canning books. If you have a root cellar that is below 50 degrees Fahrenheit, you can probably get by leaving your kraut uncanned. Just leave the jars closed loosely so bubbles can work their way out. Fresh or stored cabbage also provides the other crucial element in our winter *borscht*.

Two varieties of cabbage I have found outstanding are Early Golden Acre (early) and Danish Ballhead (late). For red cabbage, I like Red Acre. These are all heirloom varieties, but there are abundant hybrids out there to try. I am not a big fan of Savoy cabbage and have not had good luck with Chinese or Napa cabbage, but many people like to grow these. If you are going to make kim-chee, you will need to grow Napa cabbage. You can also shred these varieties fine for a good salad extender in the summer when your lettuce is bitter and bolting. And of course, what would a summer picnic be without cole slaw?

Carrots

Speaking of cole slaw, you will need carrots in your garden. Carrots need a certain measure of heat in the soil to germinate well, so I plant my carrots around June 1st. You may be able to get yours in earlier where you live. Two varieties I am partial to are Scarlet Nantes and Red-Cored Chantenay, as they are quite dependable and consistently flavorful. Carrots are another crop, like beets and potatoes, that can be left in the ground most of the winter and harvested as needed. For fall/winter harvesting, plant around early to mid-August.

Cauliflower

I have always liked cauliflower. It tastes great and looks like a brain. It is easy to grow in maritime climates and I start transplants the same time I start cabbage and broccoli, around mid-to-late February. Varieties I like are Snowball and Snow Crown. The last couple of years I have grown purple cauliflower and the two varieties I like are Graffiti and Purple of Sicily. Some people like Cheddar, which has a pleasing orange color.

Celery and Celeriac

Celery and celeriac are well worth the effort and I like to grow them in raised beds. Celeriac is often called celery root and that is what it is. The texture of the baseball-sized root is crunchy and I prefer it raw and sliced as an appetizer. It is also good in soups. I have yet to find a consistent celeriac and the only consistent celery I have found is Tall Utah.

Cherries

Back when I was a migrant worker, I started the year with cherries in Yakima, Washington, although one year I did try the cherries in Lodi, California. The season would start with Vans, then Bings and finally the real moneymaker - Lamberts. We used to start picking at 4:30 in the morning - when we could just see - and were done by noon. Even then the cherries were sticking badly since it was usually 100 degrees Fahrenheit by 9:00 am. Then it was off to town for lunch and beers. The rest of the afternoon was spent lying about in the shade, sweating and drinking beer. It was a little better in Hood River, Oregon, but the real fun picking was at Flathead Lake, Montana. The cherries were sometimes as big as half dollars and the trees were loaded. It was also quite scenic with the lake on one side and the Mission Mountains on the other. The downside was the cherries often split because of the usual morning rain and the morning heat that followed.

We have several cherry trees but they struggle every year because of cool weather and wet soil. I am partial to Bings, but we also have a Van and two Rainier trees. Most sweet cherries require a pollenizer, or "rooster tree," but Vans and Bings together take care of our pollination. Sour cherries are another alternative and most sour cherries are self-fruitful, so you can have a single tree. Flowering cherries are also wonderful ornamentals, but they too will struggle if they get "wet feet" from waterlogged soil and cool springs. As one of the growers I used to work for was fond of saying, "Cherry trees are just looking for an excuse to die on you."

Corn (Maize)

Corn, or maize, is a problem in maritime climates, even though it can produce a tremendous amount of kilocalories per acre, grows up above the weeds, and you can easily double up on the number of plants per acre. In fact, the reason the Green Revolution was so successful increasing corn yields was because of corn's natural affinity for crowding. Just add more fertilizer and water and pack 'em in together.

The main problems with corn come from the overdependence on yield and the market-induced overemphasis on sugar in the American diet. Even though corn was first hybridized in 1906 and the first commercial variety introduced in 1921, hybrid corn did not gain popularity until the 1930's.[5] Although field corn (to be fed to animals or made into high fructose corn syrup) is the bulk of the corn grown in this country, the home gardener really only needs to consider sweet corn and flint/flour corn.

Most everyone is familiar with sweet corn, but the difference between flint and flour corn can be confusing. Flint corn has a hard *pericarp* (outer shell) covering the *endosperm* (the tissue surrounding the embryo in the seed that is composed of mostly starch but some protein and oil). Flour corn has a softer, thinner pericarp. Dent corn (most field corn) is midway between the two with hard sides covering the endosperm and a softer top which collapses during drying, or dents. Popcorn is just flint corn that holds some moisture inside which explodes, or pops, when heat is applied. Sweet corn has a gene that retards some of the sugar to starch conversion of the endosperm, which is why we eat it in the immature stage when it is still sweet. In the mature stage, sweet corn usually has a wrinkled pericarp.

Grits, polenta, and flour can be made from flint corn, but some people prefer flour corn. On my farm I am breeding a couple of varieties of flint corn for our maritime climate that are intended for polenta or cornbread rather than making tortillas. Tortillas require a complicated process of *nixtamalization* because untreated corn is deficient in free (i.e. usable) niacin. Without some way of compensating, using corn as a staple puts a population at risk for pellagra and other vitamin-deficiency diseases. In addition, corn lacks essential amino acids, so other foods like beans need to be eaten with corn. The solution is to use lime (calcium hydroxide) and ash (potassium hydroxide) to make an alkali solution which reacts with the corn and changes the protein matrix of the endosperm. This makes the niacin available for the human digestive system and makes the *masa*, or corn dough, hold together so it can be rolled out into tortillas.[6] Once the tortillas are made, a delicious filling of cooked beans provides a complete meal with necessary amino acids and vitamins. Corn is the reason the Mayans and Aztecs could build empires.

Sweet corn is easier to grow and eat. Not only do you harvest it immature in less than 100 days, but you do not have to worry about raccoons getting your crop while it dries on the stalk. Nowadays, there are many sugary-enhanced varieties, which are sweeter than the early hybrids. For the sugary-enhanced hybrids, called SE in the seed catalogs, I prefer Kandy Korn and Bodacious. There are also good white varieties and even varieties with both white and yellow kernels. A good variety of the latter is named Peaches and Cream. I have tried some open-pollinated varieties of sweet corn but have had little luck so far.

The best kind of sweet corn for our cooler climate seems to be Golden Jubilee, an old variety that is not sugary-enhanced and usually categorized as SU in the seed catalogs. This variety has increased vigor and points up the tradeoff between increased sugar content and lowered adaptability. The new supersweet varieties, called SH2, and those with an X in their name are much sweeter than even the SE varieties, but have more problems under variable conditions. Personally, I do not even like the taste as they are too sweet. The corn conundrum is being forced to rely on hybrids for sweet corn, even though you can grow open-pollinated varieties for polenta, grits or tortillas. I am working on an open-pollinated sweet corn.

Cucumbers

Pickles are a necessary ingredient for the good life. This means growing cucumbers. I have been successful in adapting a pickling variety called National to our crappy cold springs and I can usually make enough pickles to last a year. I use a basic recipe of 1 quart of white vinegar to ¾ cup salt and 2 quarts water. I let the cucumbers soak overnight in water in the refrigerator, drain them, pack in sterilized jars and pour the boiling vinegar solution over the cucumbers. I use either fresh or dried dill, depending on what I have. I also add a clove or two or raw garlic in each jar. These pickles last at least two years on the shelf.

This brings me to another point. You can make chutneys and other relishes, pickled beets, dill pickles, and other canned goods for multiple years to tide you over bad years in the garden. Typically, I make enough green tomato chutney and pickled beets to last me three years, since they both are time-intensive. Dill pickles, on the other hand, are easy to do, but some years the pickling cucumbers are "iffy" so I like to make extra.

For slicing cucumbers, I like the Marketmore and Straight Eight varieties. I have more problems saving seed from the slicers than the picklers and I have no clue why this is so. In fact, some years the slicers do better than the picklers (2011) and some years the picklers do better than the slicers (2012). We cannot figure out all the things going on in the garden, so it is best to just plant enough and even do multiple plantings. This is a case where redundancy is your friend.

Currants and Gooseberries

We have black currants and they are a wonderful crop. I got them from a neighbor so I never knew the variety. They make good *crème de cassis* (a dark-red sweet liqueur) and jam. Currants need to be watched closely when they are ripening, as you only have a short harvest window. Around here, they are ripe around July 25th. We also have gooseberries, which also make great jam. Again, since they were donated, the variety remains a mystery. Gooseberries are a bit more forgiving on harvest dates and are ready about the same time.

Dry Beans

Dry beans are a necessary ingredient for feeding yourself from your own garden. They pack a lot of nutritional punch, at 1530 kilocalories per pound, and complement other foods (like corn tortillas) in necessary amino acids. There are an incredible number of dry bean varieties available and I grow around 15 of them. My standbys are Kidneys and Cannellinis, but I also grow Vermont Cranberry, Bird Egg, Arikara, Jacobs Cattle, Pintos, and others which I am adapting to our climate. These are all bush varieties and I find them easier to manage than pole dry beans because of the labor involved in setting up poles or wire fences.

The main problem with dry beans is letting them hang on long enough in the field. This is why my standbys are Kidneys and Cannellinis. They are both ready by mid-September in a good year, when we still have some dry weather in the maritime Pacific Northwest. The last couple of springs have required late bean planting, so having a shorter growing season is important. In 2011, for example, I only harvested planting seed for several varieties. This raises a couple of issues. Theoretically, the survivors from a poor year have been naturally selected for hardiness, but the overall vigor may be reduced. Currently, I am saving multiple years of seed, so I can replant with another year's seed if need be. Bean seed lasts quite a long time and the pinto beans I grow originally came from a Y2K survival seed pack. The seeds in this pack were over 10 years old when I got them and the only viable seeds were the pintos.

Beans are inbreeders, so I grow multiple varieties in rows next to each other. However, I get some variation and independent seed breeders report crosses when beans are grown this close together. It is up to you. Since the main emphasis of my research program is adapting to climate change, I want variation and the occasional cross because it widens the gene pool. Most bean varieties are different because of color patterns and shape differences. Taste is another factor, but it depends on your taste buds. If you plant close together, you might just get a beneficial "taste" mutation.

Shucking your dry beans is tedious but not a real problem. Just put the pods in large cardboard boxes that you can hold on your lap while you watch TV and shuck into the box, putting the pods into a waste box. I find this method to be more efficient than putting the beans into a bowl and leaving the pods behind. [As I learned many years ago when I worked at a fast food restaurant, it is faster to take the bun to the burger than to take the burger to the bun (!).] After you shuck a few hundred bean pods, you will quickly come to your own conclusion on how to be efficient. Once you are down to just beans and some pod trash, you can winnow out most of the trash in the wind, pouring the beans from box to colander and vice versa. Be careful! It is easy to lose several hours of work with just one slipup. After you have only beans in the colander or bowl, you can then sort them for cracks and off types, as well as sort out any stray varieties that ended up in your box of pods. I find it quite soothing to stand in my living room and look out the window while I shuck beans.

Edamame Soybeans

This year, 2012, was the first year I was successful in growing edamame soybeans for seed. (I still had no luck with field soybeans for drying.) The two varieties were Tankuro and Envy. I would like to be able to grow field soybeans too, especially since 90% of US-grown soybeans are genetically modified, but soybeans like hot weather, which we do not have. This is another problem I am attempting to solve.

Favas

Favas are a wonderful crop because they are easy to grow, easy to harvest, and put a lot of nitrogen into the soil when used as a green manure/cover crop. The downside is double-shelling the fresh beans. However, this is another task that can be done while listening to the radio, watching TV, or just drinking beer and chatting.

The small-seeded favas, like Banner, can be planted in the fall and will survive temperatures in the low 20's Fahrenheit. The large-seeded favas, like Windsor and Agua Dulce, do better planted in the spring. However, I am working on adapting some Windsors to fall planting this year. If we get the mild winter I am expecting they might survive and provide an intermediate stage which can be tested again in colder winters.

Favas form a significant part of my rotation plan. The first year is some kind of grain. The next year is either favas or soybeans, with the soybeans not as hardy as favas. Then the third through sixth years are root crops, fruiting crops, pea/bean crops, and leafy green crops (including cabbages and other brassicas). The reason favas are favored over crops like a rye/vetch mix is because they are easy to whack down and till in with a walk-behind tiller. Commercial mixes are formulated for tractors and if you let them go too long you have to get a tractor or do a lot of hand work. With favas, you just till them in during the flowering phase with a walk-behind tiller or whack them down with a scythe or sickle. A rye/vetch mix, on the other hand, quickly becomes a dense mat that is low to the ground. Good for tractor-scale operations; not good for the human scale.

Fennel

Fennel is an interesting crop. It has a pleasing anise flavor and is good for both bulbs and seeds. I have good years and bad years with fennel and my favorite fennel dish is scalloped with potatoes and milk. Fennel is a perennial that hangs on over wet, cold winters here in the Pacific Northwest. In Italy it is more of a winter than a summer plant.

Garlic

Garlic is another one of those necessary ingredients in the good life. I grow a couple of commercial varieties like Music and Chopaka, but my main crop is a hardneck and a softneck I got locally years ago and which both grow and store well. I plant my garlic in late October and cover it with hay. This provides the garlic with some protection over winter but also obviates the need to till between rows. I just have to weed it a couple of times. As with my onions, I punch holes in the soil with a *dibble* (made from a shovel or hoe handle and tapered to a point at one end) in a double row six inches apart each way. Since I cover my garlic, I can plant the double rows two feet apart, which is the narrowest width for me to walk and weed between rows. (Some people may be able to get by with 18 inches between rows.) Most of my garden is on 3-foot centers because of my tiller width, but compacting rows to 2-foot centers gives me 50% more planting room in that part of the garden. This brings up another point.

Row width is something all gardeners should think about from several angles. On the one hand, a narrower width would seem to be a no-brainer, especially in small gardens. On the other hand, more crops crammed into a small space means more fertilizer is required and you have to be more careful where you walk and kneel. There will also be greater water requirements and a question of companion planting. Some plants do better with other plants and some plants are antagonistic to each other. For example, beans are antagonistic to alliums (onions, garlic, leeks) and the beans will suffer rather than the alliums. As with so many things in life, it is a matter of interactive variables and tradeoffs. Row width is another one of those tradeoff questions.

Green, Purple and Wax Beans

If you manage your harvesting and do multiple plantings, you can have fresh green, purple and wax beans for 10-12 weeks during the summer and fall. For green beans, I favor Romanos, Fortex, Jade, Provider and Strike, although Blue Lake is the old standby. The Romanos and Fortex are pole beans, but there is a bush variety called Roma II which I now plant every year. It is the bean I prefer for our own home canning and freezing. The Jade beans are exquisite both in appearance and taste and hang on longer in the fall than other green beans. Purple beans are hardier than green beans and usually my first fresh bean crop. I like Royal Burgundy best. My wax bean favorites are Rocdor and Golden Rocky.

Most of my fresh beans are bush varieties because of the extra labor involved in setting up poles or wire for pole beans. However, I hit on a good solution this summer (2012) which worked well. I made circular cages out of 6-foot sections of old woven wire fencing that are 4 feet high. I cut some of the cages in half and put them on top of other cages so they are now 6-foot high and about 2 feet in diameter. A steel fence post is set into the ground and the cage is put over the post and attached with fence clips or wire. The post prevents the cage from being blown over in the wind. As the beans grow, they climb up the cage and curiously enough, they mostly stay outside the cage, where there is more sun. For the few beans inside the cage, you can just reach your hands inside. If the wire panels are too narrow for your hands, just squeeze them together. This system worked well and a person can pick many more pounds of pole beans in an hour than kneeling on the ground picking bush varieties. In addition to easier picking, pole beans significantly outyield bush varieties because they grow up instead of out. If a person measured yield by cubic feet instead square feet, the bush variety might have a greater yield, but that is not how we measure. Even so, it is still easier to pick pole beans.

I used to freeze all my green beans, but now we have a pressure canner so I do canned beans too. One of my worries for the coming years is having the power go out for more than a day at a time. When and if this happens, all our freezer food will go to waste. We usually have <u>two</u> freezers full of food in the winter so I am trending more towards canning, drying and pickling. Pickled green beans is a good option too.

<u>Kale</u>

I never had kale until eight years ago, when we moved onto our present farm. Now I cannot conceive of cold weather without it. Kale hangs on all winter and provides tasty nutrition. It is the basis of *colcannon* (mashed potatoes and kale with butter) and makes a wonderful topping over pasta. Just sauté onions in oil until they are translucent and then add your chopped kale. If you are using a cast-iron pan that holds heat, you can just cover the pan and turn off the heat. If not using a heavy heat-holding pan, just keep the heat on low for a minute to wilt the kale. Then just eat as is or toss over pasta. Kale is truly an international green and supposedly the ancestor of all *brassicas* – cabbage, broccoli, cauliflower, collards, Brussels sprouts, kohlrabi, etc.

My favorite kale variety is Dwarf Scotch Curled, although the White Russian, Red Russian, and Lacinato (Tuscan) varieties are also quite good. After years of letting kale go to seed and keeping my own seed, I have volunteer kale all over my garden. I just keep it where it is convenient and I even dig up volunteer plants to put into rows, just as I do with chard This can be done anytime, even in late fall.

Kohlrabi

Kohlrabi is a rather bizarre-looking vegetable, but it is great for snacking. As noted above, it was probably descended from kale and does well in cool weather. I plant it in the fall for winter use. It can be used in soups, but I prefer it raw. The two main varieties are Early White Vienna and Early Purple Vienna. The white varieties have a finer texture.

Leeks

Leeks have been called "the king of vegetables." We like them in soups and steamed with butter. To prepare them, I top them where the leaves split, leaving a long stem with both white and green parts. I cook the white part of the stem, keeping the leftover green stem for soup stock. Just throw the stems in a bag and freeze. When you want stock, just boil for a couple hours and strain out the fiber for tasty vegetarian soup stock.

Some leeks do better than others here. I am currently testing Giant Musselburgh, but Lancelot, King Richard, and Lincoln have proven to be the best for me. I also save my own seed and I have some generic leeks from several years ago. I am quite fond of *vichyssoise*, or leek and potato soup with cream. Remember this: "If you have a leek and something else, you have soup." We generally eat our leeks during the winter and spring. Their robust taste is quite satisfying.

<u>Lettuce and Salad Mix</u>

There is no money in lettuce by the head or by the bunch, at least for small-scale farmers. That is why salad mix is so popular. Lettuce cut when small also allows several cuttings, as long as you do not cut into the crown (usually about 1 inch from the ground). I get 4-5 cuttings from a lettuce bed before it gets bitter and I do succession plantings every two weeks until deep summer, when the lettuce gets bitter because of the heat. (I do one or two more plantings in early September for winter use.) A head of beautiful bibb lettuce that sells for $1.00 can easily yield $4.00 worth of cuttings over a two-month period, plus you can mix different types and colors together for a very pleasing salad mix. Some people even mix different greens together into *mesclun*, a Provençal word for mixture. In Washington state, salad mixes are subject to a very bizarre law. If you grow multiple varieties of salad or other greens and mix them together, you must have a food-processing license, which first requires a food handler's permit. However, if you grow the salad mix varieties together in one bed, you do not. Pretty nuts, eh? This is an example of why many people hate regulations. It only takes one stupid law like this one to sour many people on government in general. Ah, but I digress. Back to lettuce.

Different lettuces have different tastes and textures. There are hundreds of varieties and some of the best "gardener's porn" are the catalogs with pictures of each kind of lettuce. There are bibb varieties like Buttercrunch, Romaine varieties like Parris Island Cos, salad bowl varieties like Red Salad Bowl and many others. I like to mix 10-14 varieties together.

<u>Oats</u>

In Samuel Johnson's *Dictionary of the English Language* (1755) the entry for Oats reads, "A grain, which in England is generally given to horses, but in Scotland supports the people." Of course, the Scot's rejoinder to this is, "That's why England has such good horses and Scotland has such fine men."[7] A similar anecdote from my own life updates the importance of oats. Back in 1971, when I and a bunch of other "dirty hippies" bought land and moved up to northern Minnesota to build cabins, grow our own food, etc., the following exchange took place.

Local townie: "Them dirty hippies even eat oatmeal."

Local logger: "Hey, wait a minute. I eat oatmeal every morning."

The rest of the conversation is lost to memory (I heard it secondhand anyway), but the importance of oats as a grain cannot be overstated. Not only does it have a pleasing taste, but it is very good at lowering cholesterol and blood pressure. It also helps in lowering blood sugar level, which helps to mitigate Type II diabetes. I find that I desire oats more during the winter than in the summer, but eating for the seasons is part of a healthy lifestyle anyway. I especially like oatmeal in apple crisp.

I have grown several kinds of oats and am currently growing hulless oats. These oats do not have the tough outer husk, or *chaff*, of regular oats. Getting this tough husk off is beyond my current capability with my electric chipper/shredder, so rather than get a new piece of equipment that could cost a lot of money, I am trying to grow enough hulless oats for our use. The problem with hulless oats is not growing them, but keeping birds away. The further away from human traffic areas, the more attractive these oats are to the birds. Birds know an easy meal when they see one. Finally, oats should be part of your grain rotation, not only for their health value, but because they grow in conditions too cold and wet for spring wheat.

Onions and Shallots

Onion soup made with fresh onions is a revelation – and you cannot get them at your local supermarket. Onions are another of the necessities in life and they are easy to grow from sets. Sets are "starter" onions you buy in bulk. I order some through a seed company and also buy some at the local farm store. The sets are actually last year's crop which were pulled prematurely and stored over winter, which is why they sometimes bolt (they are in their second year of growth). They also have a tendency to be flat on the top and bottom when they mature in your garden – why I do not know.

Shallots are multiplier onions. That is, they multiply into several bulbs in a head, like garlic, rather than growing bigger as a single bulb, like onions. They used to be classified as their own species but that is no longer the case. Shallots are milder than onions but have their own subtleties that are appreciated by skillful cooks. I like to make eggs in butter with a shallot added for a mild oniony note. Raw oysters also pair well with diced shallots in a mild vinegar. Shallots are usually grown from bulbs planted in the fall, but you can also plant them in early spring, like garlic. They just grow bigger if they have more time in the ground. You can also start shallots from seed. I have found both shallots and onions grow better in raised beds than in rows, the main advantage being better control of weeds. All the alliums need to be weeded regularly.

Parsley

Parsley is not just a garnish. It hangs around all winter and provides a nice finish on winter meals when raw greens are in short supply. There are various kinds of parsley and even some varieties of root parsley. Parsley is a plant that needs little attention. I plant it in a corner of a raised bed and forget about it. It survives and thrives like a weed and I just break some leaves and stems off when I need them for cooking.

Parsnips

Parsnips are a winter root vegetable with more sweetness than you might realize. We even make a dish of puréed parsnips with cream that we serve over penne pasta. Not only is this quite a sweet dish in the midst of the winter blahs, but the alliteration of "puréed parsnip penne pasta" will appeal to the *literati* at your table. If you are lamentably lacking in literati at your own table, try this dish and they are bound to turn up.

Parsnips are difficult to grow because they take so long to germinate and are not hardy as seedlings. They also need plenty of moisture until they are well-established. I grow some every year, but I do not have as much success as I would like. Parsnips get sweeter after a freeze, as the plants put out more sugar as a natural "antifreeze." This is also why overwintered mustards are not as sharp as in the summer, and why beets and carrots become much sweeter in the winter.

Pears

Back when I was a migrant worker, I dreaded pear season. We were always up on 14-foot ladders, the picking bag was heavier since pears are denser than apples, and we always had gummy pesticide residue all the way up to our elbows by the end of the day. This was because of the extensive use of *stop-drop* (napthaleneacetic acid or NAA). European pears (e.g. Bartlett, D'Anjou and Comice) loosen up their stems before they are ripe and then ripen from the inside out. If you leave them on the tree until ripe, they become mushy. The loosening of the stem is facilitated by the hormone auxin and the NAA acts as a synthetic auxin that does not soften up the stems. The main function of stop-drop was to keep the pears on the tree until the pickers could get to them. The downside was that it hastened the ripening process a little.

Since the home gardener/orchardist does not have the same logistical problems as large growers, stop-drop is not an issue, but you still have to deal with the characteristics of European pears and the need to get them off the tree before they are ripe. The best procedure is to test your pears daily by lifting a pear gently. When one or more pears snap off easily, it is time to pick the tree. Then store in a cool place for two weeks to ripen up.

Asian pears (e.g. Kosui, Shinseiki and Chojuro) are left on the tree until ripe, but not dead ripe. This is actually more difficult than picking European pears. Sometimes I get it just right, sometimes not. Asian pears are an excellent dessert with white wine and blue-veined cheese.

Pruning pear trees is a little different than apple trees because they want to grow straight up and require more vigorous pruning. You must make cuts to spread the tree out, but spreaders in young trees also help. When I was a pruner, we started with pears between Thanksgiving and Christmas. After pears were done we moved on to apples. By doing the pears first, we made our mistakes on trees that can come back faster.

Peppers

Peppers are difficult to ripen up here in the northwest corner of the Pacific Northwest. I rarely get ripe peppers and so concentrate on varieties that are useful in their green stages. Bell peppers and Anaheim chili peppers fit the bill, of course, but I also grow Czech Black and Jalapeño hot peppers. Both of them have some heat (Jalapeños more than the Czech Blacks) and are excellent pickled in white wine vinegar. To pickle peppers, I just cover them with salt overnight and then pick them out of the salt and pack them in sterile, wide-mouth pint jars. Then I pour in white wine vinegar right out of the jug (i.e. at room temperature) and cover with the jar lids. After two weeks in storage, they are ready to eat.

Vinegar pickling can be used to preserve other vegetables as well and I have experimented with celery and cauliflower. The celery was a bit sharp, but the cauliflower took the vinegar well. Pickled green beans are a well-known pickled vegetable, but they are usually blanched and the pickling solution is boiling when added to the jars. The pickled peppers, celery and cauliflower I make are *tres* simple because the vinegar is just added cold.

Plums

We have two varieties of plums on the farm – Green Gage and Italian Prunes. The prunes are far superior in yield, but Green Gage plums have such a unique taste they are well worth growing. There are several plum varieties and native plums in many areas of the country. The prunes are delicious fresh, but also superb dried. We have an electric dryer and during the last two weeks in September, I dry as many prunes as I can.

A word about drying fruit. In order to store dried fruit you need to get it down to around 16% moisture, or six pounds of fresh fruit to make one pound of dried fruit. However, when your prunes and peaches and such are this dry, they are tough to chew. My compromise is to dry my prunes down to where they are mostly dry but still soft, about 25-30% moisture. Then I bag them in quart bags and freeze them. When we want prunes we just take a bag out of the freezer and leave it in the cupboard. The house is cool enough and the prunes do not last long enough to get moldy. I do this with other fruits too. It makes for nicer chewing in January.

Potatoes and Fingerlings

Potatoes are my main crop and my favorite vegetable. I eat potatoes almost every day. They are extremely nutritious and a good source of B complex vitamins, as well as Vitamin C.[8] This year (2012), I had thirty varieties and I started eating fresh spuds in June, as I do each year. In addition to white, yellow and red-skinned potatoes, I grow three blue-fleshed varieties and three red-fleshed varieties, which are reputedly high in *anthocyanins*. Anthocyanins are flavonoids that act as powerful antioxidants, although their presence in the field and in the laboratory may be considerably higher than in the cooked food.[9] Anthocyanins are attracting some interest in foods like blueberries and cranberries, so it is to my advantage to preserve a few red and blue-fleshed potato varieties which also contain anthocyanins. I also grow blue and red-skinned potato varieties with white or yellow flesh, but the anthocyanin content is likely lower than in the varieties with pigmented flesh.

I usually grow some potatoes under mulch as an experiment, but my main crop is planted in bare soil. I hill up my rows either with a rake or using a hiller attachment on my walk-behind tiller. My mulch experiments are based on Ruth Stout's methodology.

Ruth Stout was a much-beloved figure in the 1960's and 1970's and wrote articles and books on her "no work" method. Ruth was born in 1884 and led an adventurous life. She owned a tea shop in Greenwich Village and went with other Quakers on a trip to Russia in the 1920's to assist with famine relief. She and her husband moved to "Poverty Hollow" (their farm) in Redding, Connecticut in 1930 and she started gardening. Ruth championed hay and straw mulch as a permanent covering in her garden and was able to maintain quite a garden well into in her 80's. Her garden was covered year-round and when she wanted to plant, she just pulled back the mulch. She had no need of separate compost piles as her layers of organic mulch were constantly breaking down and enriching the soil.[1] Her books are quite well-written and a joy to read.

I started using mulch in the 1970's and had good success with it in Minnesota. However, when I came to western Washington, I stopped using it for two important reasons, the slugs and the energy footprint. *Slugs* are a massive problem here on the west side of the Cascades and visitors from other regions are always amazed at the size and the number of our native shell-less gastropods. I have used beer to attract them but it quickly becomes a major expense, even buying the cheapest sludge.

Picking slugs into a quart yogurt container is the best method and "touchless" besides. You just brush them into the container with the lid and then close the lid when you have it full. Then you toss the container into the trash. [If you are squeamish about suffocating them, you can drown them, but this is more work and has a decidedly slimey aspect.] Picking slugs is best done at dawn and dusk. Another solution is to use Sluggo, which is now approved by the Organic Materials Review Institute (OMRI). This is an iron phosphate compound which the slugs do not like, so I spread a barrier around valuable crops like tomatoes and strawberries. I then try to pick the slugs out of my other crops. I do not mind a minimal amount of slug damage. I also till during dry periods in winter to expose slug eggs to the cold.

Another downside of using mulch is the energy cost. As I noted earlier, a 50-pound hay bale has about 7800 kilocalories of embedded energy and if you are buying the hay, it can be quite expensive for the amount needed. For example, one 50-pound bale will put down a good cover between two 50-foot rows on 3-foot centers, so 7800 kilocalories is spread over 150 square feet, or 52 kilocalories per square foot. Overall, my energy expenditure for gasoline and human labor per year is about 10 kilocalories per square foot, so using hay for mulch is 5 times as energy expensive. If I have to buy the hay at $4 a bale, the cost to put a bale down between two 50-foot rows is only 2.7 cents per square foot, but there is a considerable amount of labor involved in getting the hay into the barn, getting the hay to the field, and spreading it out by pitchfork. The most efficient energy use of hay is sheet mulching of spoiled hay that is free and does not have to be stored (which also requires electricity and an elevator to get it up into the haymow). Now I just do experiments to test varieties under varying conditions. For example, French fingerlings did quite well under hay mulch in 2012, but Red Thumb fingerlings did not.

Which brings me to the main reason I grow thirty varieties of potatoes – *diversity*. As our climate degrades and weather patterns grow ever more volatile, not only do we need staple foods well-adapted to our climate, we also need variation within the crops we grow. Some varieties grew well in 2010, but poorly in 2011 under the same type of cultivation and management. My best variety in 2010 was Nicola, in 2011 it was Bintje, and in 2012 the best variety was Yukon Gold. For fingerlings (a specialty potato that is smaller in size and cylindrical in shape), the best yielders were La Ratte in 2010, French in 2011, and Red Thumb in 2012. All of these high yielders were grown in bare soil, not under mulch.

Potatoes can be stored in the field in mild winters, just like beets or carrots. I have had good luck leaving them until February 1st and digging them at that time is not really such a chore. Just put on your rain pants and wear gloves so your hands do not get numb. Varieties proven to be good for field storage are Inca Gold, Satina and German Butterball. An added benefit to leaving some of your potatoes in the field is that you often get volunteers. Here's a tip for planting. Separate your varieties by color or shape (standard vs. fingerling) when you plant so you know what you are getting next year when your volunteers come up.

Pumpkins

Pumpkins are another wonderful volunteer crop. I like to leave a few pumpkins out in the field to break down and feed the soil. These pumpkins invariably put up some plants. I even toss pumpkins that mold in storage into specific locations in the garden. That is because each pumpkin represents the top of the plant food chain and is like a bag of fertilizer. Think of this the next time you see pumpkins for 29 cents a pound in November. If your homemade fertilizer is 50 cents a pound (like mine), it would be wise to buy as many truckloads of pumpkins at the cheaper price as you can and just throw them out into the field to rot. You can easily control any volunteers by cultivation if they are undesirable. The pumpkin meat and seeds will attract birds and rodents, and they will likely poop on the ground as they eat for even more fertility. Pumpkin seeds are also a valuable protein source for vegans. Pumpkins are easy to grow and you can plant them in with your corn to save space. You gain even more space by adding pole beans to your corn and pumpkins.

Purple Orach

Orach is sometimes called mountain spinach because it can take extreme weather, like in the mountains. Orach is another important volunteer as it comes up before spinach and lasts through the heat of summer. I grow the purple variety, but green off-types come up too. Some people eat it raw, but I prefer it cooked. It is a colorful compliment on pizza. Once you plant it in your garden you should have it every year.

Radicchio

Radicchio is a bitter salad green that just grows on you. I even like it quartered and grilled. I usually plant some in the fall and it provides a nice tangy note to winter salads. This is another vegetable that takes well to a raised bed and this will also help it survive winter temperatures. Indigo is a good variety.

Radishes

Radishes are easy to grow and easy to eat. My particular favorite is Champion, which will actually outcompete weeds if planted in well-tilled soil. Some people also grow the large daikon varieties and there are even varieties grown for snacking with beer. This past year I planted some Round Black Spanish in the fall and they lasted until January. It was quite a treat to have radishes as an appetizer for New Year's.

Raspberries

When we bought our farm, there were already some raspberries along a fence and in a clump nearby. I put up some posts and wire to train the unfenced bushes, but the fence provides a nice structure for most of our raspberry crop. Raspberries are ubiquitous here in the northwest corner and it does not take much to prune them or wire them up for maximum production. The main problem is picking the berries regularly, but they freeze well and are great in January.

Rhubarb

I put down a row of rhubarb in our first year on the farm and the plants have been solid ever since. I like to put hay mulch over the plants in the winter, and it improves their yield. We have also discovered sweet cicely can be used to sweeten rhubarb, which saves on sugar. Most people like strawberry/rhubarb pie but pie made from just rhubarb is good too.

Rutabagas and Turnips

Rutabagas are quite good in vegetable beef soup in the winter. They have a mix of sweetness and crunchy texture that blends well with potatoes and carrots. I also like them raw and hold off planting until fall because they get worms easily. The same goes for turnips, which are also not worthwhile to spring plant unless you specifically want turnip greens. Both turnips and rutabagas will hold on in mild winters until March.

Salsify

Salsify is another root crop that holds all winter, but it is little known. It is sometimes called oyster plant because the roasted roots have a taste similar to oysters. I like salsify quite a bit in the winter and we usually just peel it, roast it, and eat it with salt. The roots are generally small and thin, so it takes a bit of work to process, but the taste is well worth it.

Shell, Snap and Snow Peas

I never had snap peas until I started growing them, but they quickly became my favorite. They really are like candy without the cavities. The "snap" in snap peas comes from the thicker shells that hold more water. You can sauté them like snow peas or let them mature and pick them as shell peas if you want to grow just one kind of pea. My favorite snap pea variety is Sugar Ann, which is the earliest and does not require trellising. Sugar Snap is the old standby, but you really should trellis them or they are difficult to pick. Here is a trick when picking your peas. Go down the row and lay them over to one side. Then as you harvest, pick the up side and then lay the vines over and pick the other side. This will also mark where you stopped in the row.

Peas do not need nitrogen because they are legumes and the nitrogen-fixing bacteria on their roots gather nitrogen from the air. They need some phosphorus and potassium, but I find they gather enough residual P and K from the crop planted the year before – saving on fertilizer and another reason for crop rotation. As you may remember, my rotation is *grain-favas-root-fruit-pea-leaf*, which puts down a legume one out of eveery three years. The pea rotation can be beans or favas, just as the fava rotation can be peas or beans.

My favorite shell pea is Little Marvel, which we grew in our home garden in the 1950's. Little Marvels do not need to be trellised either. If you want a pole pea for ease of picking, I have had good luck with Tall Telephone. I also like Alaska shell peas, but I plant them for pea shoots. Pea shoots are young pea vines cut at the height of two or three inches and they are great in salads. As for snow peas, I have not found a solid variety yet, even though I try new varieties every year. If I had to make a recommendation, it would be Oregon Sugar Pod II.

Sorrel

Sorrel is a bitter green with a curiously refreshing taste. In the summer, I often eat a leaf or two when I am thirsty. It makes a hardy winter soup which is beloved by the French and the Poles. Sorrel is a perennial so you can just plant a short row of it and it will last for years. It also grows wild, but the domestic variety has a finer taste.

Spelt

Spelt is a subspecies of hexaploid wheat and is classified as *Triticum aestivum spelta*. It seems to have two distinct origins, one in SW Asia and one in Europe several millennia ago. Rumor has it that spelt was the go-to grain in medieval Europe when the wheat failed, and it also is reputed to require less nutrients than wheat. Information on spelt is sorely lacking and my experiments with it have yielded inconclusive results. However, it does test out higher in protein than wheat (17% for spelt versus 13-15% for wheat).[11] The problem with spelt is the tight *glume* (chaff) that does not shatter easily. Modern wheats have been bred for reduced chaff but spelt preserves the "old style." Some people have a problem getting this tight glume off and if you buy commercial spelt seed to plant, you should expect to get it with the glume intact. However, my electric chipper/shredder removes nearly all the chaff, so I have no trouble with it.

Even though it is higher in protein, spelt has less gluten than wheat. *Gluten* is the protein that provides elasticity to your bread dough when you add water and heat. It is a complex interaction, which is why bread making is an art. Straight spelt loaves come out like dense, chewy bricks, albeit higher in protein. It depends what you are looking for in your bread. I like to replace up to one-third the wheat in my bread mix for spelt bread. I do the same when making barley bread. Spelt bread has a very pleasing nutty flavor and provides variety in your baking.

Spelt is usually planted as a winter wheat, but experiments in Canada indicate it will yield well when spring-planted.[12] The main caveat is the seed needs plentiful soil moisture to break down the tight glume, so it should be planted earlier than wheat. The old saying is "plant your barley in the mud and your wheat in the dust." The spelt should be planted along with the barley. Like barley, spelt could be planted both fall and spring and you would double your chances of getting a good crop. I have not yet tried a spring planting of spelt.

Spinach

Spinach is usually the first spring green and it does not last long into the summer heat. It can be cut young like salad mix, and you will get several cuttings before it gets too fibrous. There are quite a few hybrid spinach varieties on the market, but I find the best for my area to be Bloomsdale Long Standing, an open-pollinated savoy (wrinkled) variety. For a smooth-leaved variety, you can try Olympia or Space, which is slightly savoyed. Both are hybrids.

Strawberries

I put down some everbearing strawberries years ago in the back corner of my garden, which I had designated as my perennial area. However, I tended to forget about them and got few strawberries, so I moved them to an area with higher foot traffic and put them into raised beds. This was a marked improvement and we now have plentiful strawberries for eating and freezing. As far as taste goes, there is really no comparison between commercial and home-grown strawberries. Here in Whatcom County we have lots of strawberry growers but their berries never come close to the sweetness of ours.

Strawberries are especially favored by slugs and leaving them on the plant until they peak in flavor is a real battle in slug-prone areas (like the Pacific Northwest!). Here again is where more care from the gardener gives you plentiful returns. [Remember my supposition that agriculture became popular because you could get more food by putting in more labor?] Picking the slugs at dawn and dusk is best, but using Sluggo also helps. If you use a raised bed, you can just keep the grass or soil weed free right next to the wood sides and then just put Sluggo down on the perimeter.

Summer and Winter Squash

My favorite winter squash has been Buttercup as long as I can remember. Buttercup has dry orange flesh with a somewhat sweet potato-like taste. I even have my own variant, which I call Flame Buttercup. This was a chance mutation I noticed almost twenty years ago in my home garden and probably comes from a cross with Turban and Kabocha. The squash is dark green and blocky in shape but with a pattern of orange-yellow "flames" licking up the sides. It is quite a beautiful squash and has a wonderful taste. However, I grow other squashes too.

Every year I grow some Butternut winter squash, but it is always an iffy proposition because they take so long to mature. I like Butternut best in soup. I have also grown Boston Marrow winter squashes and they can grow to over thirty pounds in weight. Another old variety is Hubbard, and they are an excellent squash too. All of these squashes are *Cucurbita maxima*, except Butternut, which is *Cucurbita moschata*. Other winter squashes that are popular are Acorn and Delicata, which are both *Cucurbita pepo*.

Squashes are *outbreeders*, which mean they require other plants for pollination. This opens up a wide window for cross-pollination, so you have to keep different varieties well apart to keep your seed pure. For example, if you want to grow both Buttercup and Hubbard (both *C. maxima*) you must keep them well apart – usually a quarter-mile at least. However, you can put *C. pepo* (Delicata), *C. maxima* (Buttercup) and *C. moschata* (Butternut) in close proximity as they will not cross-pollinate. What I do is grow only one *maxima* – Buttercup – and one *moschata* – Butternut. Then I keep my two *pepo* species (pie pumpkins and Delicatas) well apart.

All summer squashes are *Cucurbita pepo*, so saving seed can be a space problem, which is why I do not save summer squash seed. That means I can plant Bennings Green Tint (white scallop), Sunburst (yellow scallop), Golden (yellow zucchini), and Raven (black zucchini) together. I do have to separate them from the Delicatas and pumpkins, though. The easiest way to solve this problem is to only save seeds from *maxima* and *moschata*. I struggle with isolation distances for my *pepo* varieties every year.

Sunchokes

Sunchokes are a member of the sunflower family and have a smaller but similarly bright yellow, appealing flower. They are my default staple root crop and because of their importance I discussed them in Chapter 9. They store well in the ground and last all winter covered with dirt and inside a barrel in the barn. They are still called *Jerusalem artichokes* by some, but this is really a misnomer. Sunchokes are native to North America and were described by Samuel Champlain in 1605. He thought they tasted like artichokes and their name became *girasole articocco* in Italian (sun-following artichoke).[13] The English later changed the "girasole" to Jerusalem, probably through the same kind of etymological whims that changed "head" to "bread" to "loaf" in Cockney rhyming slang. ("Use yer loaf" means "Use your head.")

As I mentioned earlier, sunchokes store their carbohydrates as *inulin* rather than starch, which means they can be a good root vegetable for diabetics. However, since the inulin is indigestible, there can be some gastric distress if a person has never had them before, or is used to a low fiber/white flour diet. Cooking a small amount at first and gradually increasing their dietary use will minimize digestion difficulties. I sometimes eat sunchokes raw, but I usually cook them like potatoes. You can plant them in the spring, but they are usually planted in the fall. I grow them in a new place every year, so I now have sunchokes in several places. They are essentially edible perennial weeds with a decorative flower.

Tomatillos

Tomatillos are quite interesting, as they have a sharp flavor that is quite good in salsa. If you want them milder, you have to let them get quite ripe. Tomatillos grow well up here on the western side of the Cascades and I always have volunteers. I like the Purple, Verde Puebla and Zuni varieties. As might be assumed by the variety names, tomatillos are native to Mexico, so you would expect them to do well in arid climates. The fact they do well in a maritime climate is quite interesting from a biological standpoint.

Tomatoes

Much has been written about tomatoes and everyone seems to like them. Up here in the northwest corner of the Pacific Northwest, it can be difficult to get your tomatoes to ripen properly. There is also a blight problem and I have had some blight four out of the last five years. The late blight that hits tomatoes is the same *Phytophthera infestans* that devastated potatoes in Ireland in 1845, but early blight is a different fungus and not so devastating. That is why I am always worried about late blight and try to keep my tomatoes out of my irrigation areas. I use soaker hoses to get water to tomatoes instead of overhead sprinklers. This helps a little bit, but after August 1st, I start to worry. Most small-scale growers up here use hoop houses, which help a lot, but the downside to hoop houses is a significant loss of flavor. As mentioned earlier, my supposition is that plants need wind and other stressors to develop their flavor profiles.

I have my own variety of tomato - a large pink beefsteak tomato I call Commie Pinko. I also like to grow Oregon Spring (very early) and a cherry tomato called Sun Gold. The Oregon Spring variety was developed specifically for our maritime climate by James Baggett at Oregon State University. He also developed Siletz and Legend, which also do well up here. The Sun Golds are a hybrid that is probably the most popular cherry tomato now. Its flavor is really quite outstanding but since it is a hybrid, I am experimenting with a new open-pollinated variety called Honeydrop. I hope to be able to rely on Honeydrop if I cannot get Sun Gold seed. For sauce tomatoes, I like Roma and Saucy Paste.

Many people make a big differentiation between indeterminate and determinate varieties. *Indeterminate* tomatoes spread all over the place and need to be staked or trellised. The *determinate* varieties are bushier and supposedly do not need staking, but that is not really true. Determinates are supposed to ripen all at once and indeterminates will continue to ripen until they are killed by frost, but again, this difference is not as distinct as the seed catalogs report.

Triticale

Triticale is a cross between wheat and rye. It combines the golden color, flavor, and yield of wheat with the cold-hardiness of rye. It is likely wheat/rye crosses have been around as long as wheat and rye have been grown (~10,000 years), but modern triticale was developed as part of the Green Revolution. The process is similar to the development of polyploid wheat (more than two sets of chromosomes). A cross is initially sterile because it has an odd number of chromosomes, but when the chromosomes spontaneously double, the seed embryos are viable. For example, durum wheat (*Triticum turgidum*), with a chromosome number of $2n = 28$, AABB, can be crossed with rye (*Secale cereale*), $2n = 14$, RR to produce $n = 21$, ABR. When this is done in a controlled laboratory environment using the chemical *colchicine* for doubling, the result is triticale (*Triticosecale*), with a chromosome number of $2n = 42$, AABBRR. This is a hexaploid (6 sets of 7 chromosomes), just like common wheat. Once this process is complete, the seed will be viable.

The triticale I grow was sold as a cover crop seed so it is another mystery variety. However, it grows over six feet tall and could be Pika, which has that characteristic. I am also experimenting with a variety called

San Juan. I like triticale because of its cold-hardiness and resistance to lodging (stalks tipping over in the wind), as well as its hearty taste. It has relatively little gluten however, so it does not rise well. The solution is to use only one-fourth to one-third triticale flour per loaf, like barley or spelt. You will get a flatter loaf but with great taste.

There is an important caution involved in growing triticale, just as in growing rye. Both rye and triticale can harbor a fungus called *ergot* (still possible in barley and wheat but much less likely). Ergot is a potent hallucinogenic toxin that infects the plant in cold wet conditions and is visible as a bluish-brown growth on some seeds. It is likely the rise of witches in the Middle Ages came from peasants eating rye contaminated with ergot. Since these people did not know what was happening to them, they really thought they were possessed by the Devil. Of course the Church was happy to torture and kill them.

Ergot is easy to identify in the field and those harvesting with a scythe or sickle can just separate out the infected stalks as they see them. It is preferable to burn these stalks, as the fungus lies dormant in the soil and can carryover year to year. On a historical note, Albert Hofmann invented LSD (d-lysergic acid diethylamide) in 1938 based on his research on ergot alkaloids and their use in medicine to halt postpartum bleeding.[14]

Wheat

In Chapter Three I went through the development of wheat and its importance to the development of human societies. Wheat is a *polyploid* (more than two complete sets of chromosomes), as are many of our domestic crops like oats, potatoes, bananas, peanuts, barley, plums, apples, sugarcane, coffee and cotton. Polyploidy acts to preserve hybrid vigor (heterosis), preserve diversity and may even have a role in shielding organisms from accumulations of deleterious recessive mutations. Flowering plants exhibit a much greater degree of polyploidy than higher vertebrates like ourselves (humans are *diploids* with a chromosome number $2n = 46$, or 23 homologous chromosome pairs). This is likely because of complications in mitosis and meiosis, abnormal numbers of chromosomes being more likely the more sets of chromosomes there are. It is even conjectured 10% of spontaneous abortions in humans are due to the formation of polyploid zygotes.[15]

Wheat represents to me the complement of the plant world to the human organism. It is a polyploid and we are diploid. It grows in one place and we move about. It has built-in diversity which we simulate (and amplify!) through *culture*. It feeds us and we provide it the opportunity to spread over much of the known world. As I write this paragraph, it is just after Thanksgiving, a day when turkey is the king of the table. However, even with a bounty of harvest goods all around, what do I crave most at Thanksgiving? You guessed it – stuffing. What is it about bread that makes it good year-round and present at every meal? There seems to be a deep affinity between humans and wheat. I like it and if I was unable to eat it, I would feel quite deprived.

I grow both spring wheat and winter wheat. I grew some emmer wheat this year and I am trying to get some of my spring wheat to grow as winter wheat. This is a good year (2012) to try this as we are expecting a drier, warmer winter than usual. In other words, I can ratchet down the cold tolerance of some crops in stages with a mild winter this year. (I am also attempting this with Windsor favas, as I mentioned earlier.)

Acclimatizing a crop has more than one parameter. For example, one of my varieties is a hard white winter wheat recently developed at a local agricultural research station. I noticed it is not acclimatizing as well to our changing climate as some of my heirloom wheats. My working hypothesis is that it was developed not only for machine harvesting, but for the mainstream practice of harvesting before fully mature and finishing off drying in storage. My best wheats so far are Red Fife (an heirloom from 1842), Glenn (a new wheat released in 2005) and a hard red winter wheat I bought as a cover crop but that has done surprisingly well.[16] I now call the latter wheat F.A. Red, after my farm (F.A. Farm), named in part for what is most basic in developing real food – Full Attention. (Our motto: "Food With Full Attention – Fresh Absolutely!")

12 THE FINAL CHAPTER

It is likely we are entering the final chapter of industrial civilization. Without fossil fuels, industrial agriculture cannot survive and the earth cannot support 7-8 billion people. We have a slim chance if we all work together and share the wealth, but this is unlikely to happen, simply because of the wasteful, profligate lifestyles of the American populace. The problem is not really overall population numbers, but too many Americans. It is time to lay the blame at the door of the people who consume the most energy. Since World War II, the greatest threat to civilization has been the energy wasted in the United States of America. In order for Americans to have too much, whole populations are in danger of starving and one billion people go hungry every day. This is neither just nor sane. But how did we get to this unenviable crisis? Let us recap.

Culture is what makes us human. Over the last 2 million years our adaptation of culture has allowed us to spread all over the planet. We depend on culture as a filter and buffer between ourselves and the physical environment. Most of us gather the resources we need from the cultural environment rather than the physical environment. Culture has worked quite well, but over the last 150 years we have been steadily replacing culture with cheap oil energy. This replacement process increased in speed and impact after World War II. Now the oil is not so cheap and the buffer of plentiful energy we depend on is thinning. Soon we will once again have to deal directly with the physical environment. The laws of physics will once again have a direct impact on our lives. In order to forestall this, we need to go back to using cultural means to solve problems instead of just throwing more energy at them.

Unfortunately, evolution does not work backwards and culture is part of our species' evolution, so it is unlikely we can just go back to a simpler time. In addition, there are far too many of us on the planet. We have overshot the carrying capacity of the earth several times over. This has only been possible because of the large quantities of cheap oil energy we use to grow food and make products necessary for our lives. Nearly all of our products are essentially made of petroleum and we eat petroleum energy ever day. Without this petroleum energy, the earth cannot support as many humans. We will have to deal once again with physical limits and large-scale dieoff is inevitable – UNLESS we adopt alternative means of feeding ourselves.

The key to solving our present problems is not to do more of the same that got us here. We need real alternatives. Even though we cannot retrace our steps to pre-industrial times, we can use cultural innovation to create new solutions. First we have to recognize that civilization depends on slaves. Since the industrial revolution and especially in the age of cheap oil, we have merely substituted fossil fuel energy slaves for human slaves. Without cheap oil, we would have to go back to institutionalized slavery to hold onto civilization. Even if this were not morally reprehensible, it is unlikely institutionalized slavery could work on a large scale like it did in the past. People are just too knowledgeable now and they are not going to go for it. Even though the prison-industrial complex is working hard to reinstitute slavery, it is very inefficient. Slavery needs an institutionalized cultural background to work.

Since a return to slavery will not work, we have to look for another solution. Even though we will not be able to enslave human energy to replace our petroleum energy slaves, this does not mean we cannot use human energy to good effect. In fact the human organism is the *most efficient engine* we have. Bipedalism is very efficient because of the pendulum action of walking. We have opposable thumbs which allow us do detail work efficiently. We can make all kinds of tools and use them with very little energy compared to fossil fuels. We also have large brains so we can solve problems as we work. The human body is so efficient we can grow food by manual labor at about the same energy expenditure as we use all day long just doing our daily tasks. However, this means we actually have to put our hands into the soil on a daily basis. In short, we can use our efficient human engine without enslaving people.

Another benefit to using the human engine is the *positive feedback loop* of using an engine to grow its own fuel. With an internal combustion engine at 20% efficiency, we waste four times more energy as heat and gasses than the energy that actually produces work. However, the human engine stands this relationship on its head. Not only can we generate more energy than we consume, we can use some of the energy we consume to grow more food. A little knowledge of the laws of thermodynamics goes a long way here.

The solution of working <u>with</u> the laws of physics instead of trying to subvert them works to our advantage. By growing our own food, we learn to work with nature, modify our behavior to adapt to seasonal conditions, and slow down. This allows us to be content with simple pleasures instead of over-hyped, over-caffeinated consumerism that just leaves us depleted and wanting more of the sugar rush that is killing us in the first place. What we find when we adapt to the natural world is that we return to a state of grace. Strangely enough, we soon find the laws of physics are on our side. At that point we have become flexible and attuned.

Become flexible by growing food.
Start the paradigm shift with your hands.

BIBLIOGRAPHY

Alexander, R. McN., "Bipedal animals, and their differences from humans," in *Journal of Anatomy* 2004 May; 204(5): 321–330. Available online at: http://www.ncbi.nlm.nih.gov/pmc/articles/PMC1571302/

Braidwood, Robert J., Symposium: Did Man Once Live by Beer Alone? *American Anthropologist* Volume 55, Issue 4, pages 515-26, October 1953. Available online at: http://onlinelibrary.wiley.com/doi/10.1525/aa.1953.55.4.02a00050/pdf

Bridgham, Jamie T., Eric A. Ortlund & Joseph W. Thornton, "An Epistatic Ratchet Constrains the Direction of Glucorticoid Receptor Evolution, *Nature* **461**, 515-519 (24 September 2009).

Brown, Lester R., *Plan B 4.0: Mobilizing to Save Civilization* (2009), New York: Norton.

Brown, Lester R., *World on the Edge: How to Prevent Environmental and Economic Collapse* (2011), New York:Norton.

Campbell, Neil A., Lawrence G. Mitchell and Jane B. Reece (1994), *Biology:Concepts & Connections,* Redwood City, CA:Benjamin Cummings.

Catton, Jr., William R. (1980) *Overshoot: The Ecological Basis of Revolutionary Change,* Urbana:University of Illinois Press.

Cochran, Gerry and Henry Harpending (2009), *The 10,000 Year Explosion:How Civilization Accelerated Human Evolution,* New York:Basic Books.

Cochrane, Willard W. (1993), *The Development of American Agriculture:A Historical Analysis, 2nd ed.,* Minneapolis:University of Minnesota Press.

Cohen, Joel E. (1995) *How Many People Can the Earth Support?*, New York:Norton.

Coleman, Eliot, *The New Organic Grower, 2nd Edition* (1995), White River Junction, VT:Chelsea Green Publishing.

Cook, Earl F. (1971) "The Flow of Energy in an Industrial Society," *Scientific American,* Volume 225 Issue 3.

Diamond, Jared (1999:268-9), *Guns, Germs, and Steel:The Fates of Human Societies,* New York:Norton.

Ehsanzadeh, Parviz, *Agronomic and Growth Characteristics of Spring Spelt Compared to Common Wheat* (1998), Doctoral thesis, Department of Plant Sciences, University of Saskatchewan, Saskatoon. Available online at: http://library.usask.ca/theses/available/etd-10212004-001220/

Erdkamp, Paul (2005) *The Grain Market in the Roman Empire:A Social, Political and Economic Study,* Cambridge University Press.

Fancher, Raymond E. (1985) *The Intelligence Men: Makers of the IQ Controversy,* New York:Norton.

Georgescu-Roegen, Nicholas (1971) *The Entropy Law and the Economic Process,* Cambridge:Harvard University Press.

Gould, Stephen Jay (1981:265) *The Mismeasure of Man,* New York:Norton.

Hargrove, James L. (2007) "Does the history of food energy units suggest a solution to 'Calorie confusion'?" *Nutrition Journal* 2007, 6:44, Published 17 December 2007. Open access article at: http://www.ncbi.nlm.nih.gov/pmc/articles/PMC2238749/

Harlan, J. R. and D. Zohary, "Distribution of Wild Wheats and Barley," *Science* 1966 Sep 2;153(3740):1074-80. in Wenke, J., *Patterns in Prehistory: Humankind's First Three Million Years, 3rd ed.,* (1960:260-61), New York: Oxford University Press.

Harris, Marvin (1968) *The Rise of Anthropological Theory:A History of Theories of Culture,* New York:Crowell.

Haviland, William A. (2003) *Anthropology, 10th ed.* Belmont,CA:Wadsworth/Thomsen Learning.

Heilbronner, Robert L. (1999, 1953), *The Worldly Philosophers:The Lives, Times, and Ideas of the Great Economic Thinkers, Revised 2nd ed.,* New York:Touchstone.

Heinberg, Richard (2007) *Peak Everything: Waking Up to the Century of Declines,* Gabriola Island:New Society Publishers.

Heller, Martin C., and Gregory A. Keoleian (2000) *Life Cycle-Based Sustainability Indicators for Assessment of the U.S. Food System*, Ann Arbor, MI:Center for Sustainable Systems, University of Michigan.

Howard, Sir Albert, An Agricultural Testament (1943, 1940), New York:Oxford University Press. Available online at http://www.zetatalk3.com/docs/Agriculture/An_Agricultural_Testament_1943.pdf

Jurmain, Robert, Lynn Kilgore, Wenda Trevathan and Harry Nelson (2003) *Introduction to Physical Anthropology*, 9th ed., Belmont,CA:Wadsworth/Thomsen Learning.

Klein, Naomi, *No Logo* (2000), New York:Picador.

Kottak, Conrad Phillip (2002), *Anthropology: The Exploration of Human Diversity*, 9th ed., Boston:McGraw Hill.

Kroeber, A. L. and Clyde Kluckhohn (1963) *Culture: A Critical Review of Concepts and Definitions*, New York:Vintage Books.

Kroeber, Alfred L. (1917) "The Superorganic," *American Anthropologist* Volume 19, Issue 2, April-June

Kroeber, Alfred L. (1925) *Handbook of the Indians of California*, Bulletin 78, Bureau of American Ethnology, Washington.

Kroeber, Theodora (1970) *Alfred Kroeber: A Personal Configuration*, Berkeley:University of California Press.

Kümmel, Reiner, *The Second Law of Economics: Energy, Entropy and the Origins of Wealth* (2011), New York:Springer.

Lindemann, W.C. and C.R. Glover, *Nitrogen Fixation by Legumes, Guide A-129* (2003), New Mexico State University Cooperative Extension Service. Available online: http://aces.nmsu.edu/pubs/_a/a-129.pdf

Milkovitch, Matt, "Prison Labor Works for Colorado Growers," *Fruit Growers News*, Issue 37: January 2012. Available online at: http://fruitgrowersnews.com/index.php/magazine/article/prison-labor-works-for-colorado-growers/

Morris, Ian (2010), *Why the West Rules – For Now:The Patterns of History, and What They Reveal About the Future*, New York:Farrar, Straus and Giroux.

Morris, Ian (2010:190), *Social Development*, downloadable e-book of additional material for *Why the West Rules – For Now* (2010). Available online at http://www.ianmorris.org/docs/social-development.pdf

Murphy, David J. and Charles A. S. Hall (2010) "Year in Review – EROI or Energy Return on (Energy) Invested," *Ann. N.Y. Acad. Sci.* 1185. Available online at http://onlinelibrary.wiley.com/doi/10.1111/j.1749-6632.2009.05282.x/abstract

Murphy, Pat, *Plan C: Community Survival Strategies for Peak Oil and Climate Change* (2008), Gabriola Island:New Society.

Pimentel, David and Marcia Pimentel, *Food, Energy and Society*, London:Edward Arnold (1979).

Pimentel, David, Alison Marklein, Megan A. Toth, Marissa N. Karpoff, Gillian S. Paul, Robert McCormack, Joanna Kyriazis and Tim Krueger, "Food Versus Biofuels: Environmental and Economic Costs, *Human Ecology*, Vol. 37, No. 1, February 2009.

Rodale, J.I., Robert Rodale, Jerome Olds, M.C. Goldman, Maurice Franz and Jerry Minnich, *The Encyclopedia of Organic Gardening* (1973, originally 1969), Emmaus:Rodale Press.

Rodale, J.I., Robert Rodale, Jerome Olds, M.C. Goldman, Maurice Franz and Jerry Minnich, *How to Grow Fruits and Vegetables by the Organic Method* (1971, originally 1961), Emmaus:Rodale Press.

Sahlins, M. (1968:85-89). "Notes on the Original Affluent Society" in *Man the Hunter*, R.B. Lee and I. DeVore, Editors, New York: Aldine Publishing.

Salamini, Francesco, Hakan Özkan, Andrea Brandolini, Ralf Schäfer-Pregl, and William Martin (June 2002), "Genetics and Geography of Wild Cereal Domestication in the Near East," *Nature Reviews Genetics* 3:429-441.

Sankey, Paul, David T. Clark and Silvio Micheloto, (2010:51). *The End of the Oil Age. 2011 and beyond: A reality check*. Deutsche Bank: Global Markets Research. Online: http://bioage.typepad.com/files/1223fm-05.pdf

Service, Elman R. (1963, 1958), *Profiles in Ethnology:*A Revision of *A Profile of Primitive Culture*, New York:Harper & Row.

Solomon, Steve, *Gardening When It Counts* (2005), Gabriola Island, BC:New Society Publishers.

Spengler, Oswald (1991, 1918) *The Decline of the West, Abridged ed.,* (translated by Charles Francis Atkinson), New York:Oxford University Press.

Stanford, Craig B., "The Social Behavior of Chimpanzees and Bonobos," *Current Anthropology* Volume 39, Number 4, August-October 1998, pp. 399-420.

Steward, Julian H. (1972) *Theory of Culture Change: The Methodology of Multilinear Evolution*, Urbana:University of Illinois Press.

Stout, Ruth & Richard Clemence, *The Ruth Stout No-Work Garden Book* (1973). Emmaus, PA: Rodale Press. See also: http://en.wikipedia.org/wiki/Ruth_Stout

Tainter, Joseph A. (1988) *The Collapse of Complex Societies,* New York:Cambridge University Press.

Tennyson, Alfred Lord, *In Memoriam H. H. H.* (1850), Canto 56.

Thoreau, Henry David (1854:38) Walden, or Life in the Woods. Online at: http://azeitao.files.wordpress.com/2007/05/walden.pdf

World Agriculture:Towards 2030/2050, Interim Report of the Global Perspective Studies Unit, Food and Agricultural Organization of the United Nations, Rome, June 2006.

END NOTES

These end notes meant to be helpful starting points for further research, as well as references. It is important to understand the context as well as the person quoted and referenced. All website references were accurate at the time of writing, but if they are no longer accurate, a simple web search should suffice for more information.

Preface

[1] Thoreaus's cabin cost: Thoreau, Henry David (1854:38) Walden, or Life in the Woods. Online at: http://azeitao.files.wordpress.com/2007/05/walden.pdf

Introduction

[1] EROI of oil production: Murphy, David J. and Charles A. S. Hall (2010:102-118) "Year in Review – EROI or Energy Return on (Energy) Invested," *Ann. N.Y. Acad. Sci.* 1185. Available online at http://onlinelibrary.wiley.com/doi/10.1111/j.1749-6632.2009.05282.x/abstract

Chapter 1: Culture

[1] *Homo habilis* and related early hominids: Haviland, William A. (2003:170-91) *Anthropology, 10th ed.* Belmont,CA:Wadsworth/Thomsen Learning.

[2] Definitions of culture: Kroeber, A. L. and Clyde Kluckhohn (1963) *Culture: A Critical Review of Concepts and Definitions,* New York:Vintage Books.

[3] Culture as the superorganic: Kroeber, Alfred L. (1917:163-213) "The Superorganic," *American Anthropologist* Volume 19, Issue 2, April-June 1917.

[4] Primate cultural behavior: Jurmain, Robert, Lynn Kilgore, Wenda Trevathan and Harry Nelson (2003:170-173) *Introduction to Physical Anthropology, 9th ed.,* Belmont,CA:Wadsworth/Thomsen Learning.

[5] Quantifying cultural elements: Steward, Julian H. (1972:102, 1955) *Theory of Culture Change: The Methodology of Multilinear Evolution,* Urbana:University of Illinois Press.

[6] Reification and *Spearman's g*: Gould, Stephen Jay (1981:265) *The Mismeasure of Man*, New York:Norton.

[7] Binet's reservations: Fancher, Raymond E. (1985:77) *The Intelligence Men: Makers of the IQ Controversy,* New York:Norton.

[8] Herbert Spencer: http://en.wikipedia.org/wiki/Herbert_Spencer

[9] Kroeber's mid-life crisis: Kroeber, Theodora (1970:101-19) *Alfred Kroeber: A Personal Configuration,* Berkeley:University of California Press.

[10] Kroeber's magnum opus: Kroeber, Alfred L. (1925) *Handbook of the Indians of California*, Bulletin 78, Bureau of American Ethnology, Washington.

[11] Spengler, Oswald (1991, 1918) *The Decline of the West, Abridged ed.,* (translated by Charles Francis Atkinson), New York:Oxford University Press.

[12] Harris, Marvin (1968) *The Rise of Anthropological Theory:A History of Theories of Culture,* New York:Crowell.

Chapter 2: Energy

[1] Calorie requirements for horses: http://www.dayvillesupply.com/hay-and-horse-feed/calorie-needs.html

[2] Laws of thermodynamics: http://en.wikipedia.org/wiki/Laws_of_thermodynamics

[3] Efficiency of gas automobile engines: http://www.fueleconomy.gov/feg/atv.shtml

[4] Energy flow of humans: Cook, Earl F. (1971:135-142) "The Flow of Energy in an Industrial Society," *Scientific American,* Volume 225 Issue 3.

[5] Body size in early hominids: Jurmain, Robert, Lynn Kilgore, Wenda Trevathan and Harry Nelson (2003:268) *Introduction to Physical Anthropology, 9th ed.,* Belmont,CA:Wadsworth/Thomsen Learning.

[6] SI units: http://physics.nist.gov/cuu/Units/units.html

[7] Horsepower: http://en.wikipedia.org/wiki/Horsepower

[8] History of the calorie: Hargrove, James L. (2007) "Does the history of food energy units suggest a solution to 'Calorie confusion'?" *Nutrition Journal* 2007, 6:44, Published 17 December 2007. Open access article at http://www.ncbi.nlm.nih.gov/pmc/articles/PMC2238749/

[9] Energy conversion: http://www.unitconversion.org/unit_converter/energy-ex.html

[10] Carbon equivalents in Sweden: http://www.nytimes.com/2009/10/23/world/europe/23degrees.html?pagewanted=all

[11] Energy content of gasoline: http://www.convertunits.com/from/joules/to/gallon+[U.S.]+of+automotive+gasoline

[12] Energy content of diesel: http://www.convertunits.com/from/joule/to/gallon+[U.S.]+of+diesel+oil

[13] Barrel of oil equivalent: http://en.wikipedia.org/wiki/Barrel_of_oil_equivalent

[14] Calorie content of food: http://caloriecount.about.com/

[15] The 1500 mile number: http://www.slate.com/articles/life/food/2008/09/whats_in_a_number.html

[16] Food miles: http://en.wikipedia.org/wiki/Food_miles

[17] Diesel engine efficiency: http://www.fueleconomy.gov/feg/di_diesels.shtml

[18] Solar radiation: http://eesc.columbia.edu/courses/ees/climate/lectures/radiation/index.html

[19] Earth's energy budget: http://en.wikipedia.org/wiki/Earth's_energy_budget

Chapter 3: Organization of Human Societies

[1] Organization of human societies and primitive as a pejorative: Service, Elman R. (1963:xv, emphasis in the original), *Profiles in Ethnology:* A Revision of *A Profile of Primitive Culture,* New York:Harper & Row.

[2] Types of human societies: Diamond, Jared (1999:268-9), *Guns, Germs, and*

Steel:The Fates of Human Societies, New York:Norton.

[3] Types of human societies: Haviland, William A. (2003:621) *Anthropology, 10th ed.* Belmont,CA:Wadsworth/Thomsen Learning.

[4] First English definition of culture: Kroeber, A. L. and Clyde Kluckhohn (1963:11) *Culture: A Critical Review of Concepts and Definitions,* New York:Vintage Books.

[5] Negative effects of farming on human physiology: Cochran, Gerry and Henry Harpending (2009:76ff), *The 10,000 Year Explosion:How Civilization Accelerated Human Evolution,* New York:Basic Books.

[6] The original affluent society: Sahlins, M. (1968:85-89). "Notes on the Original Affluent Society" in *Man the Hunter,* R.B. Lee and I. DeVore, Editors, New York: Aldine Publishing.

[7] Band, tribes, chiefdoms and states: Service, Elman R. (1963:xx-xxvii, 1958), *Profiles in Ethnology:*A Revision of *A Profile of Primitive Culture,* New York:Harper & Row.

[8] *Ibid.*

[9] *Ibid.*

[10] *Ibid.*

[11] Complexity; conflict and intergration theories: Tainter, Joseph A. (1988:29-38) *The Collapse of Complex Societies,* New York:Cambridge University Press.

[12] *Ibid.*

[13] *Ibid.*

[14] Nature "red in tooth and claw": Tennyson, Alfred Lord, *In Memoriam A. H. H.* (1850), Canto 56.

[15] Marginal return: Tainter, Joseph A. (1988:92-94) *The Collapse of Complex Societies,* New York:Cambridge University Press.

[16] Inflection points: http://en.wikipedia.org/wiki/Inflection_point

[17] Reasons for the Roman collapse: Tainter, Joseph A. (1988:148-52) *The Collapse of Complex Societies,* New York:Cambridge University Press.

[18] EROI of oil production: http://www.theoildrum.com/node/3810 and http://www.energybulletin.net/stories/2011-10-28/two-more-ethical-challenges-canadas-oil-sands

[19] EROI of oil production: Murphy, David J. and Charles A. S. Hall (2010:102-118) "Year in Review – EROI or Energy Return on (Energy) Invested," *Ann. N.Y. Acad. Sci.* 1185. Available online at http://onlinelibrary.wiley.com/doi/10.1111/j.1749-6632.2009.05282.x/abstract

[20] Problems ahead: Cook, Earl F. (1971) "The Flow of Energy in an Industrial Society," *Scientific American,* Volume 225 Issue 3.

[21] Social development: Morris, Ian (2010), *Why the West Rules – For Now:The Patterns of History, and What They Reveal About the Future,* New York:Farrar, Straus and Giroux.

[22] United Nations Human Development Index: http://hdr.undp.org/en/

[23] Effect of the Industrial Revolution: Morris, Ian (2010:190), *Social Development,* downloadable e-book of additional material for *Why the West Rules – For Now* (2010). Available online at http://www.ianmorris.org/docs/social-development.pdf

[24] Sloth, fear and greed: Morris, Ian (2010:26), *Why the West Rules – For Now:The Patterns of History, and What They Reveal About the Future,* New York:Farrar, Straus and Giroux.

[25] Controlling error: Morris, Ian (2010:640ff), *Why the West Rules – For Now:The Patterns of History, and What They Reveal About the Future,* New York:Farrar, Straus and Giroux.

[26] The most parsimonious measure: Morris, Ian (2010:626), *Why the West Rules – For Now:The Patterns of History, and What They Reveal About the Future,* New York:Farrar, Straus and Giroux.

[27] Polyploids: Campbell, Neil A., Lawrence G. Mitchell and Jane B. Reece (1994:284-85), *Biology:Concepts & Connections,* Redwood City, CA:Benjamin Cummings.

[28] Evolution of wheat: Salamini, Francesco, Hakan Özkan, Andrea Brandolini, Ralf Schäfer-Pregl, and William Martin (June 2002), "Genetics and Geography of Wild Cereal Domestication in the Near East," *Nature Reviews Genetics* 3:429-441.

[29] *Ibid.*

[30] *Ibid.*

[31] Foraging cereals prior to the Younger Dryas: Morris, Ian (2010:85ff), *Why the West Rules – For Now:The Patterns of History, and What They Reveal About the Future,* New York:Farrar, Straus and Giroux.

[32] Wild grain foraging and high EROI: *Ibid.*

[33] Wheat experiments in 1966: Harlan, J. R. and D. Zohary, "Distribution of Wild Wheats and Barley," *Science* 1966 Sep 2;153(3740):1074-80. in Wenke, J., *Patterns in Prehistory: Humankind's First Three Million Years, 3rd ed.,* (1960:260-61), New York: Oxford University Press.

[34] Roman wheat yield: Erdkamp, Paul (2005:43) *The Grain Market in the Roman Empire:A Social, Political and Economic Study,* Cambridge University Press.

[35] 7-10 kilocalories of fossil fuels needed to produce 1 kilocalorie of food: Heller, Martin C., and Gregory A. Keoleian (2000:42) *Life Cycle-Based Sustainability Indicators for Assessment of the U.S. Food System,* Ann Arbor, MI:Center for Sustainable Systems, University of Michigan.

Chapter 4: Civilization and Slaves

[1] Energy capture table, hard ceiling: Morris, Ian (2010:34, 106), *Social Development,* downloadable e-book of additional material for *Why the West Rules – For Now* (2010). Available http://www.ianmorris.org/docs/social-development.pdf.
For a simplified energy capture table see also: Morris, Ian (2010:628), *Why the West Rules – For Now:The Patterns of History, and What They Reveal About the Future,* New York:Farrar, Straus and Giroux.

[2] Timing of Roman collapse: Tainter, Joseph A. (1988:188), *The Collapse of Complex Societies,* New York:Cambridge University Press.

[3] Slavery in chiefdoms and states: Haviland, William A. (2003:621) *Anthropology, 10th ed.* Belmont,CA:Wadsworth/Thomsen Learning.

[4] Slavery in Rome: http://en.wikipedia.org/wiki/Slavery_in_ancient_Rome

[5] Mit'a in the Incan Empire: http://en.wikipedia.org/wiki/Mita_(Inca)

[6] Corvée: http://en.wikipedia.org/wiki/Corv%C3%A9e

[7] Manorialism: http://en.wikipedia.org/wiki/Manorialism

[8] Energy capture in 1400 CE: Cook, Earl F. (1971) "The Flow of Energy in an Industrial Society," *Scientific American,* Volume 225 Issue 3.

[9] Serfdom and feudalism: http://en.wikipedia.org/wiki/Serfdom

[10] Bondage and caste in India: Kottak, Conrad Phillip (2002:554-5), *Anthropology: The Exploration of Human Diversity, 9th ed.,* Boston:McGraw Hill.

[11] Energy flow of humans: Cook, Earl F. (1971:135-142) "The Flow of Energy in an Industrial Society," *Scientific American,* Volume 225 Issue 3.

[12] Roman gold: http://en.wikipedia.org/wiki/Roman_metallurgy#cite_note-10

[13] Overshoot: Catton, Jr., William R. (1980:272, 278) *Overshoot: The Ecological Basis of Revolutionary Change,* Urbana:University of Illinois Press.

[14] Differing definitions of carrying capacity: Cohen, Joel E. (1995) *How Many People Can the Earth Support?,* New York:Norton.

[15] The one-handed economist: http://www.economist.com/node/2208841

[16] Energy flow of humans: Cook, Earl F. (1971:135-142) "The Flow of Energy in an Industrial Society," *Scientific American,* Volume 225 Issue 3.

[17] US energy consumption http://en.wikipedia.org/wiki/Energy_in_the_United_States

[18] China and India: http://www.worldpopulationbalance.org/population_energy

[19] Everything nature gives us is gratis: Georgescu-Roegen, Nicholas (1971:2) *The Entropy Law and the Economic Process,* Cambridge:Harvard University Press. See also: http://www.marxists.org/archive/marx/works/1867-c1/ch24.htm

Chapter 5: Cheap Energy & Peak Oil

[1] The steam engine: http://en.wikipedia.org/wiki/Watt_steam_engine

[2] Energy capture table: Morris, Ian (2010:628), *Why the West Rules – For Now:The Patterns of History, and What They Reveal About the Future,* New York:Farrar, Straus and Giroux.

[3] Second Industrial Revolution:

http://en.wikipedia.org/wiki/Second_Industrial_Revolution

[4] Colonel Drake and the first commercial oil well:
http://en.wikipedia.org/wiki/History_of_the_petroleum_industry_in_the_Unite
d_States

[5] Reconstruction after the Civil War:
http://en.wikipedia.org/wiki/Reconstruction_Era_of_the_United_States

[6] Energy flow of humans in 1875: Cook, Earl F. (1971:135-142) "The Flow of
Energy in an Industrial Society," *Scientific American,* Volume 225 Issue 3.

[7] US agricultural advance: Cochrane, Willard W. (1993:67-69), *The
Development of American Agriculture:A Historical Analysis, 2nd ed.,*
Minneapolis:University of Minnesota Press.

[8] The Homestead Act and speculation: *Ibid.,* pp. 80-84.

[9] *Ibid.*

[10] Crop specialization in the US: *Ibid.,* pp. 91-94.

[11] Recessions:
http://en.wikipedia.org/wiki/List_of_recessions_in_the_United_States

[12] Manufacturing:
http://en.wikipedia.org/wiki/American_system_of_manufacturing

[13] 19th century immigration: Cochrane, Willard W. (1993:264-5), *The
Development of American Agriculture:A Historical Analysis, 2nd ed.,*
Minneapolis:University of Minnesota Press.

[14] US Steel: Heilbronner, Robert L. (1999, 1953:237), *The Worldly
Philosophers:The Lives, Times, and Ideas of the Great Economic Thinkers,
Revised 2nd ed.,* New York:Touchstone.

[15] Energy densities: http://en.wikipedia.org/wiki/Energy_density

[16] Diesel locomotives: http://en.wikipedia.org/wiki/Diesel_locomotive

[17] US oil production to 1970:
http://www.eia.gov/dnav/pet/hist/LeafHandler.ashx?n=PET&s=MCRFPUS1&f
=A

[18] Partial list of products made from oil: http://www.ranken-
energy.com/Products%20from%20Petroleum.htm

[19] The Hubbert curve: http://en.wikipedia.org/wiki/Hubbert_peak_theory

[20] Oil price as percentage of GDP: Sankey, Paul, David T. Clark and Silvio Micheloto, (2010:51). *The End of the Oil Age. 2011 and beyond: A reality check*. Deutsche Bank: Global Markets Research. Online: http://bioage.typepad.com/files/1223fm-05.pdf

[21] Worldwide electricity from coal: http://en.wikipedia.org/wiki/Coal

[22] EROI of oil production: Murphy, David J. and Charles A. S. Hall (2010:107-109) "Year in Review – EROI or Energy Return on (Energy) Invested," *Ann. N.Y. Acad. Sci.* 1185. Available online at http://onlinelibrary.wiley.com/doi/10.1111/j.1749-6632.2009.05282.x/abstract See also: http://europe.theoildrum.com/node/4712

[23] EROI of oil production: Murphy, David J. and Charles A. S. Hall (2010:109) "Year in Review – EROI or Energy Return on (Energy) Invested," *Ann. N.Y. Acad. Sci.* 1185. Available online at http://onlinelibrary.wiley.com/doi/10.1111/j.1749-6632.2009.05282.x/abstract

[24] Methane is a potent greenhouse gas: http://www.epa.gov/methane/

[25] Little hope to reduce greenhouse gases with natural gas: https://www2.ucar.edu/atmosnews/news/5292/switching-coal-natural-gas-would-do-little-global-climate-study-indicates

[26] Natural gas in short supply: http://www.postcarbon.org/article/827909-top-11-faqs

[27] Industry perspective: http://www.naturalgas.org/overview/resources.asp

[28] Peak everything: Heinberg, Richard (2007) *Peak Everything: Waking Up to the Century of Declines,* Gabriola Island:New Society Publishers.

[29] The "perfect storm": http://www.guardian.co.uk/science/2009/mar/18/perfect-storm-john-beddington-energy-food-climate and to read the actual speech http://www.govnet.co.uk/news/govnet/professor-sir-john-beddingtons-speech-at-sduk-09

[30] Porritt's timeline: http://www.guardian.co.uk/environment/2009/mar/23/jonathon-porritt-recession-climate-crisis

[31] FAO Report: *World Agriculture:Towards 2030/2050,* Interim Report of the

Global Perspective Studies Unit, Food and Agricultural Organization of the United Nations, Rome, June 2006.

[32] UN Secretary-General's recommendations: http://www.dailymail.co.uk/news/article-2095506/UN-chief-Ban-Ki-moon-calls-global-economic-sustainability-changes-report-reveals-need-50-food-2030.html

[33] Rice: http://irri.org/about-rice/rice-facts/rice-basics

[34] Changes to rice: http://www.scribd.com/doc/34620921/Rice-Today-Vol-6-No-3

[35] *Ibid.*

[36] More hungry people now: http://www.nytimes.com/2009/09/20/weekinreview/20martin.html?_r=0

Chapter 6: Political & Financial Failure

[1] The Growth Model: http://en.wikipedia.org/wiki/Neoclassical_growth_model

[2] A rising tide: http://en.wikipedia.org/wiki/A_rising_tide_lifts_all_boats

[3] Trickle-down theory: http://en.wikipedia.org/wiki/Trickle-down_economics

[4] Everything nature gives us is gratis: Georgescu-Roegen, Nicholas (1971:2) *The Entropy Law and the Economic Process,* Cambridge:Harvard University Press. See also: http://www.marxists.org/archive/marx/works/1867-c1/ch24.htm

[5] Capital without energy: Kümmel, Reiner, *The Second Law of Economics: Energy, Entropy and the Origins of Wealth* (2011:195), New York:Springer.

[6] An example of the search for irreversibility of evolution: Bridgham, Jamie T., Eric A. Ortlund & Joseph W. Thornton, "An Epistatic Ratchet Constrains the Direction of Glucorticoid Receptor Evolution, *Nature* **461**, 515-519 (24 September 2009).

[7] Prison labor: Milkovitch, Matt, "Prison Labor Works for Colorado Growers," *Fruit Growers News,* Issue 37: January 2012. Available online at: http://fruitgrowersnews.com/index.php/magazine/article/prison-labor-works-for-colorado-growers/

[8] Daily prisoner costs: http://www.creditloan.com/infographics/how-much-does-it-cost-to-keep-a-criminal/

[9] List of Roman emperors:
http://en.wikipedia.org/wiki/List_of_Roman_emperors

Chapter 7: Realism

[1] Plan B: Brown, Lester R., *Plan B 4.0: Mobilizing to Save Civilization* (2009), New York: Norton.

[2] Brown's latest book: Brown, Lester R., *World on the Edge: How to Prevent Environmental and Economic Collapse* (2011), New York:Norton.

[3] Summary of Plan B 4.0: http://www.scribd.com/doc/22548869/A-Summary-of-Plan-B-4-0-Mobilizing-to-Save-Civilization

[4] *Ibid.*

[5] Personal consumption as 70% of GDP:
http://useconomy.about.com/od/grossdomesticproduct/f/GDP_Components.htm

[6] Plan C: Murphy, Pat, *Plan C: Community Survival Strategies for Peak Oil and Climate Change* (2008), Gabriola Island:New Society.

[7] Community solutions: http://www.communitysolution.org/solutions.html

[8] Fission-fusion in bonobos and chimps: Stanford, Craig B., "The Social Behavior of Chimpanzees and Bonobos," *Current Anthropology* Volume 39, Number 4, August-October 1998, pp. 399-420.

[9] 48% of the world lives on less than $2.00/day:
http://www.prb.org/pdf09/09wpds_eng.pdf

[10] Nearly 1 billion suffer from hunger:
http://www.un.org/en/globalissues/briefingpapers/food/vitalstats.shtml

[11] 8 billion people by 2025: http://www.prb.org/pdf09/09wpds_eng.pdf

[12] BOE measures: http://www.worldpopulationbalance.org/population_energy

[13] Energy flow of humans: Cook, Earl F. (1971:135-142) "The Flow of Energy in an Industrial Society," *Scientific American,* Volume 225 Issue 3.

[14] BOE measures: http://www.worldpopulationbalance.org/population_energy

[15] *Ibid.*

Chapter 8: Water & Food Security

[1] Long Kesh hunger strike: http://www.irishhungerstrike.com/

[2] Food and water: http://adventure.howstuffworks.com/survival/wilderness/live-without-food-and-water2.htm

[3] Urea: http://en.wikipedia.org/wiki/Urea

[4] Toilet flow rates: http://www.toiletabcs.com/toilet-water-conservation.html

[5] Food waste: http://www.epa.gov/osw/conserve/materials/organics/food/fd-basic.htm See also: http://www.foodproductiondaily.com/Supply-Chain/Half-of-US-food-goes-to-waste

[6] ERS report: http://www.ers.usda.gov/Publications/FoodReview/Jan1997/Jan97a.pdf

[7] Clifford Hardin: http://www.nytimes.com/2010/04/06/us/06hardin.html?_r=1

[8] Rochdale principles: http://www.hampdenparkcoop.com/about/history

[9] Minnesota food co-ops: http://www.mnhs.org/library/findaids/00561.xml

[10] History of Whole Foods: http://www.forbes.com/2010/10/20/forbes-india-john-mackey-whole-foods-organic-capitalism.html See also: http://www.guardian.co.uk/lifeandstyle/2006/jan/29/foodanddrink.organics

[11] Changes in American agriculture 1933-1970: Cochrane, Willard W. (1993:129-132), *The Development of American Agriculture:A Historical Analysis, 2nd ed.,* Minneapolis:University of Minnesota Press.

[12] *Ibid.*

[13] Farms in the 1950's: http://www.livinghistoryfarm.org/farminginthe50s/life_11.html

[14] Farm sizes today: http://www.ers.usda.gov/StateFacts/us.htm#FC

[15] Howard, Sir Albert, An Agricultural Testament (1943, 1940), New York:Oxford University Press. Available online at http://www.zetatalk3.com/docs/Agriculture/An_Agricultural_Testament_1943.

pdf

[16] History of organic methods: J.I. Rodale, Robert Rodale, Jerome Olds, M.C. Goldman, Maurice Franz and Jerry Minnich, *The Encyclopedia of Organic Gardening* (1973:802-04, originally 1969), Emmaus:Rodale Press.

Organic methods: J.I. Rodale, Robert Rodale, Jerome Olds, M.C. Goldman, Maurice Franz and Jerry Minnich, *How to Grow Fruits and Vegetables by the Organic Method* (1971, originally 1961), Emmaus:Rodale Press.

[17] Get big or get out: http://agrecon.mcgill.ca//ecoagr/doc/berry.htm

[18] Organic certification: http://en.wikipedia.org/wiki/Organic_certification

NOP Final Rule in Federal Register: http://www.ams.usda.gov/AMSv1.0/getfile?dDocName=STELPRDC5087165

[19] Dan Glickman: http://www.usda.gov/news/releases/2000/12/0426.htm

[20] Branding: Klein, Naomi, *No Logo* (2000:3-8), New York:Picador.

[21] Aminopyralid: http://en.wikipedia.org/wiki/Aminopyralid

Killer compost: https://www.motherearthnews.com/organic-gardening/killer-compost-zmgz11zrog.aspx

Possible solutions: http://www.motherearthnews.com/modern-homesteading/dear-mother-june-july-2011-zm0z11zhun.aspx?page=2

[22] Fear of losing certification: http://www.jgpress.com/archives/_free/002373.html

[23] Sinclair, Upton, *The Jungle* (1906). Available online at: http://www2.hn.psu.edu/faculty/jmanis/u-sinclair/TheJungle.pdf

Chapter 9: Accounting for Sustainability

[1] Potato farms in the Yakima Valley: http://www.fredoldfieldcenter.net/murals.shtml

[2] Ozette potatoes: http://potatogenome.berkeley.edu/nsf5/potato_biology/history.php

[3] US potato yields 1930-2005: http://potatoassociation.org/documents/A_ProductionHandbook_Final_000.pdf

[4] US apple yield in 2009: http://www.usapple.org/aboutus

Chapter 10: Farming as if Energy Mattered

[1] Metabolic rates of bipedal animals: Alexander, R. McN., "Bipedal animals, and their differences from humans," in *Journal of Anatomy* 2004 May; 204(5): 321–330. Available online at: http://www.ncbi.nlm.nih.gov/pmc/articles/PMC1571302/

[2] *Ibid.*

[3] Corn production kilocalories per hectare: Pimentel, David, Alison Marklein, Megan A. Toth, Marissa N. Karpoff, Gillian S. Paul, Robert McCormack, Joanna Kyriazis and Tim Krueger, "Food Versus Biofuels: Environmental and Economic Costs, *Human Ecology*, Vol. 37, No. 1, February 2009.

[4] Solomon's book: Solomon, Steve, *Gardening When It Counts* (2005), Gabriola Island, BC:New Society Publishers.

Coleman's book: Coleman, Eliot, *The New Organic Grower, 2nd Edition* (1995), White River Junction, VT:Chelsea Green Publishing.

[5] Embedded energy in hay bales: Pimentel, David and Marcia Pimentel, *Food, Energy and Society*, London:Edward Arnold (1979:96).

[6] Building soil: http://soilscience.info/faqs/31-about-soil/44-soil-formation

[7] Justus von Liebig: http://en.wikipedia.org/wiki/Justus_von_Liebig

[8] Law of the Minimum: http://en.wikipedia.org/wiki/Liebig's_law_of_the_minimum

[9] *Ibid.*

[10] *Ibid.*

[11] The whole is greater than the sum of its parts: http://www-history.mcs.st-and.ac.uk/Quotations/Aristotle.html

[12] Solomon's fertilizer recipe: Solomon, *Steve, Growing Vegetables West of the Cascades, 5th ed.* (2000:35), Seattle:Sasquatch Books.

See also: Solomon, Steve, *Gardening When It Counts* (2005:21), Gabriola Island, BC:New Society Publishers.

[13] Langbeinite: http://en.wikipedia.org/wiki/Langbeinite

[14] Allelopathic qualities of rye: Jannasch, Rupert, "Cover cropping with fall rye? Be careful!"
http://www.organicagcentre.ca/NewspaperArticles/na_cover_crop_rye.asp

[15] Nitrogen fixation: Lindemann, W.C. and C.R. Glover, *Nitrogen Fixation by Legumes, Guide A-129* (2003), New Mexico State University Cooperative Extension Service. Available online: http://aces.nmsu.edu/pubs/_a/a-129.pdf

[16] Methane as a greenhouse gas:
http://www.science.org.au/nova/118/118key.html

Chapter 11: Crops and Crop Varieties

[1] Discovery and excavation at Jarmo: http://en.wikipedia.org/wiki/Jarmo

Beer as the cause of cereal domestication: Braidwood, Robert J., Symposium: Did Man Once Live by Beer Alone? *American Anthropologist* Volume 55, Issue 4, pages 515-26, October 1953. Available online at:
http://onlinelibrary.wiley.com/doi/10.1525/aa.1953.55.4.02a00050/citedby

[2] Ninkasi the Sumerian beer goddess: http://en.wikipedia.org/wiki/Ninkasi

[3] Hops: http://en.wikipedia.org/wiki/Hops

[4] Etymology of buckwheat: http://en.wikipedia.org/wiki/Buckwheat

[5] Corn history timeline: http://www.ars.usda.gov/is/timeline/corn.htm

[6] Nixtamalization: http://en.wikipedia.org/wiki/Nixtamalization

[7] The Scot's Rejoinder: http://www.wholegrainscouncil.org/whole-grains-101/oats-january-grain-of-the-month

[8] Nutrition in potatoes: http://en.wikipedia.org/wiki/Potato

[9] Anthocyanins:
http://en.wikipedia.org/wiki/Anthocyanin#Potential_food_value

[10] Ruth Stout's methods: Stout, Ruth & Richard Clemence, *The Ruth Stout No-Work Garden Book* (1973). Emmaus, PA: Rodale Press. See also:
http://en.wikipedia.org/wiki/Ruth_Stout

[11] Spelt: http://en.wikipedia.org/wiki/Spelt

[12] Spring-planted spelt: Ehsanzadeh, Parviz, *Agronomic and Growth Characteristics of Spring Spelt Compared to Common Wheat* (1998), Doctoral thesis, Department of Plant Sciences, University of Saskatchewan, Saskatoon. Available online at: http://library.usask.ca/theses/available/etd-10212004-001220/

[13] Sunchokes: http://en.wikipedia.org/wiki/Jerusalem_artichoke

[14] Albert Hofmann:
http://www.rsc.org/chemistryworld/Issues/2006/January/LSD.asp

[15] Polyploidy: http://www.nature.com/scitable/topicpage/polyploidy-1552814

[16] Red Fife wheat: http://en.wikipedia.org/wiki/Red_Fife_wheat

Glenn wheat:
http://www.ext.nodak.edu/extnews/newsrelease/2005/020305/10newhar.htm

Printed in Great Britain
by Amazon